JUDAISM in COLD WAR AMERICA 1945-1990

edited
with introductions by

Jacob Neusner
UNIVERSITY OF SOUTH FLORIDA

A Garland Series

Contents of Series

VOLUME 8

The Alteration of Orthodoxy

edited with introduction by
Jacob Neusner

Garland Publishing, Inc.
New York and London 1993

Library of Congress Cataloging-in-Publication Data

The Alteration of orthodoxy / edited by Jacob Neusner.
p. cm. — (Judaism in Cold War America, 1945–1990 ; v. 8)
ISBN 0-8153-0077-8
1. Orthodox Judaism—United States—History—20th century. 2. Judaism—20th century. I. Neusner, Jacob, 1932– . II. Series.
BM205.R44 1993
296'.8'32'097309045—dc20 92-37155
CIP

Printed on acid-free, 250-year-life paper
Manufactured in the United States of America

Contents

Introduction

Many people reasonably identify all "traditional" or "observant" Judaism with Orthodoxy, and they furthermore take for granted that all traditional Judaisms are pretty much the same. But there are more Orthodox Judaisms than non-Orthodox ones. For example, when Jews who kept the law of the Torah with respect to food and use of leisure time (to speak of the Sabbath and festivals in secular terms), sent their children to secular schools, in addition to or instead of solely Jewish ones, or when, in Jewish schools, they included in the curriculum subjects outside of the sciences of the Torah, they crossed the boundary between one Orthodox Judaism and another, different one.

Orthodox Judaism came to articulated expression among Jews who rejected Reform and made a self-conscious decision to remain within the way of life and worldview that they had known and cherished all their lives. They framed the issues in terms of change and history. The Reformers held that Judaism could change, and that Judaism was a product of history. The Orthodox opponents denied that Judaism could change and insisted that Judaism derived from God's will at Sinai and was eternal and supernatural, not historical and man-made. In these two convictions, of course, the Orthodox recapitulated the convictions of the received system. But in their appeal to the given, the traditional, they found more persuasive some components of that system than they did others, and in the picking and choosing, in the articulation of the view that Judaism formed a religion to be seen as distinct and autonomous of politics, society, "the rest of life," they entered that same world of self-conscious believing that the Reformers also explored.

Orthodox Judaism in the context of the third generation of American Jews in particular (as of German Jewry in the nineteenth century) is a Judaic system that mediates between the received Judaism of the dual Torah and the requirements of living a life integrated in modern circumstances. Orthodoxy maintains the worldview of the received dual Torah, constantly citing its sayings and adhering with only trivial variations to the bulk of its norms for the everyday life. At the same time Orthodoxy holds that Jews adhering to the dual Torah may wear clothing that non-Jews wear and do not have to wear distinctly Jewish (even Judaic) clothing, live within a common economy, practice distinctively Jewish professions (however, in a given setting, these professions may be defined), and, in diverse ways, take up a life not readily distinguished in important characteristics from the life lived by others.

So for Orthodoxy a portion of Israel's life may prove secular, in that the Torah does not dictate and so sanctify all details under all circumstances. Since the Judaism of the dual Torah presupposed not only the supernatural entity, Israel, but also a way of life that in important ways distinguished this supernatural entity from the social world at large, the power of Orthodoxy to find an accommodation for Jews who valued the received way of life and worldview and planned to make their lives in an essentially integrated social world proves formidable. The difference between Orthodoxy and the system of the dual Torah therefore comes to expression in social policy: integration, however circumscribed, versus the total separation of the holy people. American Orthodox Judaism of the Cold War period formed the Orthodox counterpart to the American Jewish consensus: Jewish but not too Jewish. This meant Orthodox but not ghettoized.

I find it difficult to imagine what the urban Orthodox might otherwise have done in Cold War America. As immigrants and the children and grandchildren of immigrants, they experienced change. They daily encountered Jews unlike themselves, and no longer lived in that stable Judaic society in which the received Torah formed the giver of life. The pretense that Jews faced no choices scarcely represented a possibility. Nor did the generality of the Jews propose, in the West, to preserve a separate language or to renounce political rights. So Orthodoxy made its peace with change, no less than did Reform. The educational program that led Jews out of the received culture of the dual Torah, the use of the vernacular, the acceptance of political rights and education for women, the renunciation of Jewish garments, the abolition of the power of the community to coerce the individual—these and many other originally Reform positions characterized the Orthodoxy that emerged in this period.

The human achievement of Orthodoxy demands more than routine notice. Living in a world that only grudgingly accommodated difference and disliked Jews' difference in particular, the Orthodox followed the rhythm of the week to the climax of the Sabbath, and the rhythm of the seasons to the climactic moments of the festivals. They adhered to their own pattern of daily life, with prayers morning, noon, and night. They married only within the holy people. They ate only food that had been prepared in accord with the rules of sanctification. They honored philosophy and culture, true, but these they measured by their own revealed truth as well. It was not easy for them to keep the faith when so many within Jewry, and so many more outside, wanted Jews to be pretty much the same as everyone else. The human costs cannot have proved trivial. To affirm when the world denies, to keep the faith against all evidence—that represents the faith that people honored in other settings. It was not easy for either the Orthodox of Germany or the immigrant Jews of America, who in an ocean voyage moved from the world of self-evident faith to the one of insistent denial of the faith.

My grandmother was one of those Jews for whom the way of Torah defined the path of life. Raised as a Reform Jew, I know through her the pride, the dignity, the courage of the Judaisms of both the dual Torah and Orthodoxy. Challenged by the rabbi of our temple, advocate of Reform in its most vigorous formulation, that keeping the dietary laws involved violating the American Constitution, she did not answer; she did not think the argument important. At my bar mitzvah, held on Simhat Torah in 1945, when the Torah was carried about the sanctuary, the congregation remained seated, as was their custom, but she stood up, all by herself—silently, without comment—as was hers. So we cannot miss the costs, but we recognize also the consequences, for humanity, of those who continued the received system and those who, come what may, sustained it and found sustenance for their lives. Each Judaism, Reform and Orthodox, demanded its price, but both richly rewarded those who paid it.

This brings us back to the American scene in the past half-century. A residual Orthodoxy, a piety drawn from the milieu, characterized nearly all those immigrants who were religious, and Conservative Judaism, a modified form of Orthodoxy, certainly predominated for the second and the third generations. Both the immigrants of the 1890s and those who came after World War II included considerable numbers of Jews who remained loyal to the tradition. The appeal of modernity was lost on them. Still others entered the modern situation and quickly turned their backs on it. They returned to classical Judaism. The return to religion in the decades after World War II saw considerable strengthening of Orthodox commitment and conviction in American Judaism, and renascent Orthodoxy did not take the modern form of surrogate religiosity, large synagogues, and impersonal professionalism, but the entirely traditional forms of personal commitment and maximum individual participation. Whether traditional Orthodox Judaism in America is as traditional and orthodox in the same ways as is Eastern European Judaism hardly matters. The fact is that the classical Judaic perspective remains a completely acceptable choice for substantial numbers of American Jews. Those Jews who fully live the traditional life and adhere to the traditional way of faith seem to me to have made a negative judgment on modernity and its values. It becomes all the more striking that larger numbers—the vast majority of American Jewry—came to an affirmative opinion.

But in affirming the modern and accepting its dilemmas, American Jews of the third generation (1950-1980) continued in important modes to interpret themselves in the archaic ways. Most important, Jews continued to see themselves as Jews, to regard this as central to their very being, and to persist in this choice. This fact cannot be taken for granted. The Jews are not simply an ethnic group characterized by primarily external, wholly unarticulated and unselfconscious qualities. They are Jewish not merely because they happen to have inherited quaint customs, unimportant remains of an old heritage rapidly falling away. On the contrary, they hold very strong convictions about how they will continue to be Jews. Most of them hope their children will marry within the Jewish community. Most of them join synagogues because they want their children to grow up as Jews. Above all, most of them regard the fact that they are Jewish as bearing great significance. The American Jews of the third generation continue to see everyday life in different terms from their Gentile neighbors, beginning with the fact that to them, if not to their neighbors, their being Jewish seems an immensely important fact of life. The words they use to explain that fact, the symbols by which they express it, are quite different from those of archaic or classical Judaism. They speak of Jewishness, not Torah. They are obsessed with a crisis of identity, rather than with the tasks and responsibilities of "Israel." They are deeply concerned with the opinion of Gentiles. The fourth generation would restore Orthodox Judaism to an important position within the Judaisms of the USA. The Orthodox Judaism that many would espouse rejected the accommodations of Torah-study and secular learning, the effort to live a life that was both different from but integrated within the common world of America and American Judaism in general.

So it was an Orthodox Judaism quite different from the one familiar in the third generation. Orthodoxy in the third generation was integrated into the larger Jewish community, appealed to reasoned argument, and affirmed the importance of living a completely observant Judaic life while at the same time participating in the larger society of the USA. Its parochial schools attended to secular, as well as sacred, sciences. Its young people educated themselves for careers, not only for study of the Torah. This was an Orthodoxy in line with the moderation in all things characteristic of American Judaism: Jewish but not too Jewish, so, too, Orthodox but not so Orthodox as to remove oneself from the world beyond. The contrast between Orthodoxy in the third generation and an Orthodox Judaism that has taken shape in the most recent past underlines how typical was the Orthodoxy of the third generation of its time and circumstance.

19

THE ORTHODOX STREAM

JACOB B. AGUS

Given the complexity of Orthodoxy, which exhibits the greatest variation and vitality in American Judaism, we are fortunate to have a succinct account of the four major theological components of twentieth century Orthodoxy. Rabbi Agus describes the European trends which influenced American Orthodoxy, beginning with the "mussar movement". That movement laid its primary stress on piety as formative of the good human being. The Jewish personality was to be shaped by the ethics and religious values of the tradition. It is an important trait of Orthodoxy that one must begin the study of its American formulation in Europe. While Reform and Conservative Judaism likewise draw upon European sources, particularly the thought of German Jewish theologians, only Orthodoxy preserves an unmediated picture of the European heritage.

A second, very present legacy of European Judaism is in Hassidism, the religious ideas of which are set forth by Rabbi Agus.

The third major component is the philosophical heritage of the masters of halakhah, *represented by Rabbi Joseph B. Soloveitchik. The theological foundations of* halakhah, *uncovered and exposited by Rabbi Soloveitchik, form the basis for much of American Orthodox intellectuality.*

The fourth, and final element is provided by German Jewry, deeply rooted in America since the 1930's, and by its philosophical spokesman, Isaak Breuer.

Rabbi Agus not only provides reliable summaries of the chief ideas of these four components of American Orthodox theology but also tells us his opinion of them. In so doing, he exemplifies such religious dialogue as takes place between Orthodox theologians and Conservative ones.

American Orthodoxy has not yet matured to the point of assuming a definite cast of thought or pattern of practice. Consisting of many strands which vary in the timbre of their orthodoxy and the degree of their resistance to the modern temper, its texture is still unfinished and uncertain. On the whole, it may be fairly stated that, apart from popular tracts and collections of sermons, Orthodoxy has not yet settled down to the task of rendering an intelligent account of itself in the American idiom of thought and culture. Among its thoughtful adherents, we may distinguish disciples of the three trends in Orthodox Judaism—the supernaturalism of Kabbalah, the mysticism of Hassidism, and the transcendental rationalism of western neo-Orthodoxy.

Kabbalistic supernaturalism continues to function as an effective, living faith, largely in the form which it has taken in the "mussar" movement of the Lithuanian Yeshivoth. While the various Hassidic dynasties and notably the HaBad school of Lubavitch occasionally conduct energetic campaigns with the aid of a tight little band of ardent disciples, they remain an exotic and outlandish phenomenon, hovering uncertainly on the shadowy periphery. HaBad literature consists of endless variations of the old Kabbalistic themes, symbols and terms, without any attempt to take note of the modern world, save on the level of elementary education. The "mussar" movement, on the other hand, has influenced the teachers and students of the great Lithuanian Yeshivoth, so that it may be regarded as the philosophy of Orthodoxy's elite. Echoing the world-view of the thoughtful exponents of the movement, the "mussar" ideology is vastly more important than might be surmised from the paucity of its literature. In the domain of speculation, Orthodox rabbis were extremely reluctant to publish their reflections, contenting themselves with oral admonitions to their students. Thus Rabbi Hayim of Volozhin allowed his classic little volume, "Nefesh Ha-Hayim," to be published only after his death. The literary output of Rabbi Israel Lipkin of Salant is amazingly meager. In large measure, the successors of the founding masters share this characteristic reluctance to entrust to the printed page the delicate task of tracing a safe pathway in the danger-filled, forbidding domain of the "garden of metaphysical thought." Accordingly, we have to rely for the most part on secondary sources and on the published notes which the students took of the "conversations" ("sihoth") of their masters.

As formulated by the unique genius of the aforementioned Rabbi Israel Lipkin, the "mussar" movement was, in its early stages, thoroughly uninterested in metaphysics. Its principal concern was to deepen Jewish piety and to project the ideal of the perfect Jewish personality. Unlike the Hassidic movement of Poland and the Ukraine, which directed its message to the masses of the people, the Lithuanian pietists appealed to the chosen few. The mussarists aimed to develop great spiritual personalities, in the belief that the masses reflect in varying degrees the piety of their spiritual heroes. Thus, the "mussar"-movement sets its sights high, far above and beyond the fixed norms of the "Shulhan Aruch." While the Hassid was encouraged to feel that he is part of the holy community of Israel, if he identified himself with it emotionally by so much as sharing in the "tsaddik's" meal, or in the merry-making and the whiskey drinking of the pious, the "mussar"-man was taught to recognize his complete unworthiness, even if he devoted every ounce of energy to the study of the Torah. The Hassidim learned to serve God in joy, to sink their individuality with utter abandon in the total community of Israel, which is assured of salvation by the unbreakable word of the Covenant. In contrast, the "mussar"-men were asked to ponder in fearful anxiety over the fate of their own soul, to envisage the tremendous difficulty of meeting fully the demands of the Torah and to worry ceaselessly over the urgency of achieving the complete perfection of their souls, ere the curtain of death ended the possibility of growth. The keynote of "mussar" was persistent and deeply anxious self-analysis and self-criticism. Before the bar of Divine judgment, the individual stands in total isolation, mindful only of his sins and failures, pleading tearfully and with anxious trembling for the undeserved boon of salvation.

For a while, the "mussar" movement organized "sh'tiblach," small rooms for solitary meditation and penitent crying, which contrasted with the busy, noisy and merry "klauses," the gathering places of the Hassidim. Gradually, however, the movement withdrew from the lay-community and confined its teaching to the great Yeshivoth, where it constituted the official interpretation of the faith.

The individualistic emphasis of the "mussar-movement" may be understood in the light of the powerful inroads which were made by the rise of "Haskalah," the movement of humanistic and secularistic enlightenment. In the last decades of the nineteenth century, the Jewish community of Russia was no longer dominated intellectually and socially by pious believers, whose central concern it was to achieve the bliss of salvation in the hereafter. While the masses of Russian Jewry were still in the tenacious grip of tradition, the intelligentsia was swept along by the powerful storm-winds of the new liberal and revolutionary faiths. The naive uniformity of belief and practice which prevailed uninterruptedly for so many centuries was now broken up, and even the conviction of the faithful remnant lost in depth and tenacity. Perforce, the Jewish individual became the center of attention since the empirical community was no longer identical with the ideal congregation of Israel (K'nesseth Yisroel), which is the counterpart of the Divine Presence ("sh'chinah"). If the community as a whole no longer merited to be "saved," selected "men of perfection" were needed to serve as the bearers of "the yoke of Torah and mitzvoth."

The "mussar"-movement construed the challenge of "Haskalah" as a psychological, not a philosophical, problem. They did not attempt to refute the arguments of the modernists, point by point, in the belief that dialectical fencing was only a subtle defense-mechanism. To the faithful, arguments are superfluous, and to the unbelievers, the most consummate apologetics will be of no avail. For faith dwells below the level of the conscious, in the domain of will and feeling, where the soul freely submits to its Master or rebelliously turns away from Him. Hence, the problem of religious education is to reach down to "the unconscious feelings," "Hargoshoth Kaihoth," of the people and to build there an impregnable foundation for the superstructure of faith.[1]

In turn, this task of subjugating and conquering the vast domain of the unconscious can be achieved by the two complementary methods of fear and love. The primitive mentality, which underlies and controls the thought-processes of even the most civilized of men, is moved only by coarse and selfish concerns. Hence, the need of dramatizing the varied punishments of hell and dwelling upon the delights of heaven. These central pillars of naive piety were brought into the foreground by the "mussar"-teachers, in order to arouse and mobilize the feelings of fear and anxiety which are rooted in the lowest reaches of the human soul. At the same time, they sought to compound out of the maxims of our vast religious literature the image of the spiritually perfect Jew, which they presented as the ideal worthy of emulation to the idealistic youth of the "Yeshivoth." What is a more fitting goal for the edification of the young than the achievement of perfection in the qualities of character and the wisdom of Torah, in humility and piety, in sympathetic understanding and in the love of truth? The foundations of heaven and earth are firmly founded on the merit of Torah students. The world would be returned to chaos, they believed, if the loyal few failed to meditate in the Torah day and night. Thus did the humble "yeshivah-bohurs" persuade themselves that, like Atlas, they carried the whole sinful world on their frail shoulders.

In the subsequent development of the "mussar"-movement, two schools of thought emerged, which stressed respectively the two contrasting emphases in its teaching. The followers of Rabbi Yitzhak Blaser and of Rabbi Yosel of Novarydok devised a system of instruction and training which aimed at the cultivation of the fear of God, in all its gradations, from the terrifying specters of hell fire and brimstone to the noble sense of awe and reverence of the philosophers.[2] To the austere, sensitive conscience of these teachers, it seemed that no man could ever mature spiritually to the point of outgrowing the level of fear-consciousness, so as to feel altogether confident of Divine favor. Characteristic of this mood is the following episode in the life of Rabbi Yitzhak Blaser: Asked to address a group of Yeshivah-students, he told them an allegory concerning a group of men who were lost in a forest. After days of wandering, they encountered an old man and implored him to show them the way out of the forest. But the old man replied to them, "You have been lost for only a few days. I have been lost for many years. How can I help you?" Applying the parable to himself, he concluded, "You are young men and you feel perplexed for only a short time. I have been lost for a long, long time. Let us cry together. Perhaps the Almighty will help us."[3]

The awareness of perplexity is itself the way out, if it leads to fear and trepidation, for fear is the beginning of all wisdom and its end as well.

More influential in the long run, especially upon the American scene, was the stream of "mussar"-teaching which appealed to the sentiments of love and aspiration and set up the ideal of the perfect personality as the goal of piety. Growth toward ever nobler ends is the positive pole of all psychical impulses as fear and anxiety constitute their negative pole. Thus, Rabbi Simha Zissel Ziv of Khelm and his disciples aimed to transform piety into an all-embracing ideal of perfection that would appeal to the healthy, outgoing instincts of Jewish youth, shunning no exercise or discipline that makes for growth of the spirit. While the other "mussar"-teachers, including the founder, Rabbi Israel Lipkin, opposed the introduction of secular studies into the curriculum of the Yeshivoth, for fear that the students might be influenced by the manifold errors of modern thought, Rabbi Simha Zissel himself established the "Beth HaTalmud" of Grobein, a school where secular studies were taught with the aim of synthesizing Orthodoxy and modern culture so as to produce a new type of Jewish gentleman. His example was not followed by the heads of other "Yeshivoth" of Poland and Lithuania, but the founders of the great Yeshiva University, which laid the ideological cornerstone for American orthodoxy, were certainly encouraged by his pioneering effort.

To Rabbi Simha Zissel orderliness was the basic quality of the ideal personality, enabling "the pure and rational soul" to prevail over the body, "which is more ugly, repulsive and disgusting than the bodies of all other animals." Self-control can be effective only when it is habitual. Thus, he demanded of his pupils that they devote time to quiet reflection and self-examination day by day. "Not one day should be allowed to pass without habituation in the practice of reflection, for it is the key to wisdom, the focus of all the faculties, leading to the attainment of the whole man."[4]

Since reflection is the key to perfection, man must strive to allay anxiety and to acquire the capacity to be calm, poised and unperturbed at all times. "In the quality of inner rest, all perfection is included." His disciples were asked to undertake a series of exercises so as to achieve the state of calm confidence which is the necessary prerequisite for pious reflections on the nature of God and the destiny of the human soul. However, he cautioned, the goal of inner peace and imperturbability of spirit must not be interpreted as implying disinterestedness in other people. On the contrary, impulsive charity, the unquestioning and unreasoning love of our fellowmen is essential to the attainment of perfection. For the love of people serves to overcome our native selfishness and it is also the one sure way to God.[5]

The emphasis on reflection in the Khelm branch of the "mussar"-movement was bound to reawaken the metaphysical interest, which was initially sidetracked. The "mussar"-teachers shunned the disciplines and methods of modern philosophy, seeking authoritative answers to the baffling questions of faith in the sacred literature of Kabbalah. While the intricate details of Kabbalistic theosophy were studied only by the consecrated few, the Yeshivah-teachers sought to uncover the inner impetus and essential thought of Kabbalah for the benefit of their students. In this process of unconscious selection and interpretation, a new quality of thought is inevitably introduced.[6]

The following world-view is blocked out in a series of "mussar"-lectures that were given in the European Yeshivah of Tels and later edited and published in America.[7]

The authors present as a truth of Kabbalistic revelation the fundamental generalization of Plato's that all the things and events which we encounter in this sensible universe are only shadows of ethereal essences that inhere in the upper realms of eternity. The eternal patterns, which constitute expressions of the Divine Name in the first realm of Emanation, become progressively "coarsened" as the chain of worlds descends link by link down to our own earthly realm. The more of value, beauty and goodness things possess, the closer they are in the chain of being to their counterparts in the domain of Emanation.

"One range of existents is realized in all the worlds, and in every world the same thing assumes a different form in keeping with the nature of that world."[8]

In this cosmic chain of being, the Torah fulfills at every level the function of soul to the body of the corresponding world, the Torah constituting a series of coarsening expressions of the Will of God, and the universe a parallel descending series of His Work. While the early Kabbalists, battling for recognition, loved to contrast their "hidden wisdom" with the plain meaning of the Torah, the "mussar"-men, unaware of the surge of conflicting ideas in the long history of Jewish thought, saw the Kabbalah as an integral, organic phase of the revealed Torah.

"In the wisdom of the Torah and the reasons of the commandments, the revealed and hidden reasons are not unrelated. In reality, they form one reason, the hidden one being the root and soul of the revealed explanation. He who understands any motivation literally knows only the garment, but the Torah has a garment and a body, and a soul, and a soul to a soul, rising ad infinitum."[9]

In the days of the Messiah, the higher expression of the Torah will take the place of the one we now possess.

"For the Torah which is given to us in this our world is of no account in comparison with the Torah which is going to be revealed in the days of the Messiah."[10]

Because of this vertical and infinite dimension of Torah, the faithful student senses the quality of endlessness and eternal truth in its study.

"For the holy Torah is a long chain which reaches from this lowly earth to the loftiest heavens. When a person contemplates truly the reasons of the Torah, he moves this chain, as it were, so that he feels and hears a ring above which authenticates and ratifies the truth."[11]

The meaning of Torah in this connection is, of course, the totality of "halachic" and "aggadic" literature. As new discoveries in Torah-reasoning (hiddushim) are made, the nature of the universe is fixed accordingly. "For the act of voting (in the Sanhedrin or Academy) and the establishment of the 'halachah' by the vote of the majority fixes the nature of creation."[12] Naturally, this concession to the notion of growth in Torah does not imply the possibility of modifying any rabbinic enactment in accord with the needs of the times. "For whatever has been set into 'halachah' remains part of creation forever and is no longer subject to change."

As the sequence of events in nature is not one which could be deduced rationally but is only to be known by experience, so the reasoning of the Torah may frequently appear irrational. In reality, its seemingly absurd distinctions and seemingly trivial ritual niceties correspond to important heavenly counterparts or "roots" in the higher world.

But, if reason is powerless to comprehend the logic of the Torah, the student of Torah acquires after a while a "spiritual stature" ("shiur Komah") which enables him to discover new insights or to arrive at right decisions in new situations, with the aid of the Spirit of Holiness, ("Ruah haKodesh") or by the gift of prophecy. Indeed, the Torah-scholar is exalted fantastically to a central cosmic role in these discourses.[13] In a world of indifference and neglect, the remnant of the faithful "carries the burden which was designed for many others."[14] It is for them to fulfill the purpose of all human life—to wit, "the uplifting of the low forces of matter in the human soul and in creation generally, bringing them back to their roots."[15]

In such a supernaturalistic ideology, tailored to fit the measurements of a literalist Orthodoxy, miracles are of course the order of the day. In fact, there is no line of demarcation between the natural and supernatural orders. Speaking of the power of the saints, the authors maintain, "that the forces of fire and water were limited along with the other powers of matter, so that they might not affect superior individuals, who cleave to God in their thoughts."[16]

It remains but to add that this bold assertion of supernaturalism goes hand in hand with an extreme idealization of the past, so that the mysterious intricacies of the hypothetical higher links in the chain of being were presumed to have been known by the ordinary men and women of the past. "Just as to us the processes of sowing, growing and harvesting seem simple and natural, so to them, all these high and exalted matters were simple and natural."[17]

This idealization of the past is an essential component of any literalistic Orthodoxy, and, in the "mussar"-school, it is carried to the extreme of absurdity. If the mantle of sanctity is to cover indiscriminately every phase of the tradition, the builders and keepers of the faith in every generation must be accorded the status of divinely inspired men. Also, the acceptance of the legendary lore in the Talmud at face value cannot be squared with the assumption that the Sages were simply men of flesh and blood.

One example of this interpretation may be cited in illustration. The Talmud tells of a rabbi who had a wonderful son and a beautiful daughter. Once he found a man climbing a fence in order to look at his daughter. Said the rabbi, "my daughter, your beauty will lead men to sin. Return to your dust." Whereupon, the daughter died. The son of this rabbi was once faced with the necessity of providing a meal for workingmen. By a miracle, he caused a fig tree to bring forth figs, which the workers ate. When the father heard of the miracle, he ordered his son to "return to his dust," for having caused his Maker undue trouble.[18]

This gem of ancient folklore may be enjoyed as a farcical treatment of the realistic observation that one may be too good or too beautiful. But, in the humorless literalist bias of "Mussar," this tale is cited as an illustration of the occult powers of the ancients—how the rabbi knew the heavenly "roots" of the acts of his son and daughter and thus knew that they deserved to die.

The self-sufficient supernaturalism of the "mussar"-school, in all its dry dogmatism and scornful repudiation of the great wide world extending beyond its narrow tradition, constitutes even today the living ideology of many "Yeshivoth," from "Torah V'Daath" in Brooklyn to Tels in Cleveland. The Hassidic institutions, notably those of the Lubavitch organization, are not essentially different, for the original, creative elan of Hassidism was dissipated long ago, its pristine mystical dynamism having yielded in the course of time to the beguiling seduction of a safe and staid authoritarian tradition. The living ideas of Hassidism were absorbed into the mainstream of Jewish life so that the distinction between "Hassid" and "mithnagid" is no longer significant or relevant.

The most luminous representative of Orthodox mysticism and the real heir of the great Hassidic heritage was doubtless the late Chief Rabbi of Palestine, Abraham Isaac Kuk. While his visits to the United States were relatively brief, the influence of his personality and his writings was extensive. Through his work, the complex of ideas and sentiments in the Mizrachi interpretation of Zionism was articulated and dialectically justified. The moderate Orthodox elements that favor cooperation with non-Orthodox groups draw their inspiration from his life and thought.

Kuk was primarily a mystic, in the genuine, psychological sense of the term. Doubt and certainty were to him not opposing poles on the field of thought but all-embracing experiences in which his soul was tossed about as a helpless boat on a raging sea. He felt the onset of doubt as the ebb of his vital forces, giving way again and again to the triumphant flow of Divine Grace, which infused his being with buoyancy, certainty and, as he felt, truth. Generalizing from his own mystical experiences, he saw the world as presenting two faces to man —a happy, God-centered face, bearing the beneficent lineaments of the Torah, and a melancholy, grey face of indifferent force, shadowed by doubts of the historicity of revelation and ringed about with the bitter, Satanic darkness of moral chaos, universal meaninglessness and total frustration. Thus, doubt was not an intellectual problem so much as a psychic let-down, appearing on the scene of consciousness along with multiple contradictions and deepening despair whenever God decides to hide his face from mankind. When in His Wisdom we are taken back into His favor and are uplifted joyously upon the crest of the current of love issuing from His Being, we speedily behold the clouds of doubt vanish in the distance and we glimpse the Truth, in all its infinite depth and healing power.

From his scattered and unsystematic writings, we gather the following description of the mystical experience of the "nearness of God." One is overwhelmed by an exquisite, consuming longing for the Divine Presence, "an intense thirst, pleasing in the extreme . . ." which slowly deepens into "pure fear, the intensity of holy trembling." The mystic feels that he has been touched with a holy flame, wakening within him an unearthly yearning to break out of the confining bounds of the sensible universe and to sink his being into the Divine Reality, which extends beyond "the walls of deed, logic, ethics and laws." And in this heavenly yearning there is already a kind of fulfillment, so that the mystic wills to express to others his paradoxical experience in which delight and anguish are commingled. But his vision is doomed to remain stubbornly incommunicable. "I am not one of God's elected heroes that found all the worlds within them and did not care if others their riches knew or not."[19]

As this first pulsation of the Divine current fades away, the mystic sinks back into the gray and tasteless world of conflict, contradiction and doubt. "Because of the narrow receptive faculty of man, one datum contradicts the other datum; one feeling combats the other feeling, and one image pushes out the other; but, in truth, one datum fortifies the other datum, different feelings vitalize each other, and the several images in one's mind complete each other. The more a man is uplifted, the wider his faculties expand, until he comes to find within himself the satisfying fullness of inner peace and the consequent consistency between all data, feelings and images."[20]

Having once seen the veil of contradiction lifted so as to reveal the organic unity of all existence, the mystic looks forward to the reappearance of the vision, the distinguishing mark of which is "the view of all things together."

"The gates are opened, the King of glory enters . . . . The worlds are united, the hidden and the revealed are commingled, body and soul are merged, the 'lights' and the 'vesels' are linked together. And an exquisite sweetness, an inner, intense and highly exalted pleasure is uncovered in the source of the rejoicing soul. Then power and light from above appear unto thee with all the ornamentation of their many lights. Thou wilt recognize thy power and the intensity of thy exaltation; wilt know thy humbleness and thy unworthiness, the unworthiness of all creatures. . . ."[21]

Thus, the alternation of faith and doubt in the human psyche is due to the continuous ebb and flow of the Divine current. The mystic, who has once sensed within himself the assurance of Divine reality, knows that holiness is the very core of being, and that truth is grasped to the extent to which one feels the "nearness" of the Supreme Being. Furthermore, the Jewish mystic finds that the Torah is the immediate channel of Divine light and grace. While the mystical vision does not contain precise and specific messages as did the state of prophecy in the view of tradition, it does lead to the development of a taste for the quality of holiness.

"Though we do not perceive articulate letters and distinct words, we regard our secular and Torah studies as intended solely for the purpose of obtaining as much as possible the clarity of words out of the exalted sound which beats constantly in our inner ear, that we may present them to ourselves and to others in a form that leads to action and to properly ordered and systematized reflection."[22]

To the "Mussar"-men, as we have seen, the Torah in its static perfection is the luminous ladder of God's Will, assuming concrete shape in this lowly world. To Kuk, heir of the mystical tradition, the flow of God's Will is conceived, not as a series of precepts, but as a vital current of inspiration, kindling in the hearts of men the "lights of holiness." Kuk's conception was essentially dynamic, enabling him to appreciate modern and unconventional forms of holiness and to delight in all that is novel and creative.

While Kuk achieved his mystical states through the practices of Kabbalah and interpreted their varying character in terms of its complex theosophy, he learned to correlate his intimate experiences with the concepts of general philosophy. The "lights of holiness," in his ideology, played virtually the same role as the *élan vital* in Bergson's last book ("The Two Sources of Morality and Religion"), inspiring creative achievement in the arts and sciences as well as in the life of piety. Thus, the secular world was, in his view, the marginal manifestation on the surface of life of the pulsating current of holiness in the heart of things. The "light of the Messiah," which is the vibrant process of redemption, is manifested in the efforts of all "who labor for the perfection of the world" ("shichlul haolom") and the ennobling of the human personality.

In the same integrating spirit, Kuk saw the force of modern nationalism as a noble impulse, akin to religion, implanted by God for the sake of Messianic perfection. Jewish nationalism he regarded as a supremely holy movement, even if its exponents proclaimed from the housetops its total independence of religion. Every one who lends a hand to the up-building of the Jewish people in its homeland is working for the revival of the "sh'chinah," for the national genius of Israel is peculiarly suitable for the cultivation of true religion. And the physical health of Israel is a prerequisite for its spiritual growth.

"The Holy Spirit and the light of God cannot come to Israel so long as a debilitating sense of fear continues to poison the Jewish soul. This sorry product of exile and persecution prevents the 'shechinah' from resting on the soul of Israel. . . ."[23]

In Kuk's view, the national genius of Israel was peculiarly organic and distinctly mystical, so that the atheistic pioneer and the Kabbalistic hermit constituted part of one organic society. The "physical exercises of Jewish youth . . . perfect the spiritual power of the esoteric saints. . . ."[24] For both activities constitute supplementary phases of the one process of redemption. "Mystical reflection is the freedom of Israel, in other words, the soul of Israel."[25]

With all his pietistic involvement in the idiom of Kabbalah, Kuk became the saint and prophet of the liberal wing of Orthodoxy, which identified itself wholeheartedly with the Zionist enterprise, recognizing as their brothers in spirit and destiny the zealous nationalists who denied the sanctity of Torah. In thought, Kuk advanced at times to the Conservative position, as when he suggested that even the secular creations of Jewish people, produced as they were by the peculiar genius of Israel, constituted Torah, or holy teaching. Thus, he declared, "And the congregation of Israel is itself Mosaic tradition from Sinai."[26]

From this principle it would follow that not only the "four ells of Halachah" but Jewish culture, in all its manifold expressions constituted the substance of the living faith of Israel. Yet, he did not himself throw the mantle of sanctity over the reborn secular culture in the land of Israel, maintaining that most of its achievements were not products of the pure genius of the Jewish soul, but only unconscious imitations of the Gentile world.

In summary, the mystical humanism and the spiritual nationalism of Kuk reflect the vital currents of thought and sentiment of a considerable section of contemporary Orthodoxy. His writings are still read as guideposts pointing the way toward a synthesis between the Orthodox tradition and the values of secular humanism.

Some of the noblest authorities in Judaism were neither philosophers, nor mystics, nor masters of the esoteric lore of Kabbalah. Dedicated to the arduous pursuit of religious truths, they found their satisfaction in study and action "within the four ells of Halachah." (Jewish Law). Does Judaism, then, contain a purely "halachic" stream of thought, that takes account of the fundamental questions of existence even while it skirts the pathways of philosophy and mysticism? Historically, there is no question that many illustrious masters of Talmudic lore considered their learning of the Law to be utterly self-sufficient, with no legitimate room left either for the insidious doubt of speculation or for the excessive ardor of Hassidism. But, is this attitude tenable? Can Halachah get along with the one dogma of revelation, ruling out of consideration all that was not included in the peculiar structure of Jewish Law?

Dr. Joseph B. Soloveitchik, Professor of Talmud and Religious Philosophy at the Yeshiva University, champions the view that Halachah contains a characteristic structure of ideas and sentiments which derives from a fundamental attitude of the human spirit. It articulates a psychic complex of ideas and values of its own and it does not stand in need of validation from any outside source. Founded on the solid data of Divine Revelation, Halachah has grown in continuous awareness of the tensions and paradoxes of human nature, which it sought to resolve and to integrate in its vision of the ideal personality.

Dr. Soloveitchik develops his thesis in conscious alliance with the neo-supernaturalistic school of Protestant theology. He ridicules the liberal-humanistic theologians who identify man's rational aspirations for the good life with the living "still, small voice" of God, and he spurns with equal decisiveness the romantic attempts to represent religion as an idealized refuge from reality. Theologians like Karl Barth and Soren Kierkegaard come closest to the understanding of the nature of faith when they point out the succession of "crises" in the human soul, that seeks vainly to grasp the fleeting rays issuing from His Presence and recognizes ever more deeply its "creaturely" failure, its inveterate "sinfulness," it utter nothingness. In this interpretation, the trial of Abraham was not intended to teach that God does not desire human flesh on His altars, but to prove that God's will and thought are incommensurate with man's intelligence and conscience. The man of piety must learn to defy his reason and his moral feeling for the sake of God. Thus, he cites approvingly and in the name of a Midrash Kierkegaard's interpretation of the trial of Abraham—that God wanted Abraham to oppose the scruples of his conscience and the light of his human reason. For, had he not fought from the beginning of his mission against the practice of human sacrifice? Yet, the Lord demanded that he bring Isaac as a "burnt offering." The usual interpretation of this story in Jewish literature stresses its happy ending—the Will of God is indeed identical with the voice of conscience.

The "man of Halacha" is similarly aware of the tension and the "crisis" in the human personality. The passion for pure knowledge in our makeup finds satisfaction in the far flung researches of science that are aimed at the dissolution of the novel and the mysterious elements of experience into a system of unvarying law. At the same time, our religious consciousness heightens our sense of wonder at the very quality of lawfulness that holds the entire range of existence in thrall. With masterful erudition, Prof. Soloveitchik dwells on this dichotomy of the human spirit, alternating between wonder and comprehension, the sense of mystery and the self-assurance of the man of science. Halachah, the author asserts, provides the Divine answer to this human dilemma.[27]

The "man of Halachah" approaches the mystery of existence armed with "a priori concepts," with the aid of which he erects a satisfying image of the universe. Having received his principles and laws at Sinai, he comes equipped with "a body of teaching which points out to him the way to the nature of being. There is no phenomenon, event or thing which *a priori* Halacha does not approach with its ideal measurements."[28] The term, *a priori,* is used by the author in a dogmatic, not a philosophical sense. To the Orthodox mentality, not only the Sinaitic Covenant but the whole body of Jewish law as it was hammered out by diverse factors in two thousand years of history is literally God-given, and hence as axiomatic as the principle, "twice two equals four." While the religious consciousness centers around the awareness of a numinal realm supervening behind the realm of existence, the Halachist takes this circumstance for granted and proceeds to apply the principles deriving from the divine realm to the sanctification of this earthly dominion of existence. He can afford to be intensely and whole-heartedly oriented toward the temporal world, because he knows himself to be in full control of the "channels" which bind the realm of eternity unto this temporal universe. The Halachist does not engage in a continuous battle against the "flesh," for the laws of the Torah are sober, life-affirming and altogether sufficient for a law-abiding citizen of God's world. Nor does the Halachist storm the heavenly heights of transcendental reality in his yearning to escape from the temporal, for his "God-given mitzvoth" enable him to build eternity within the earthly world—yes, the Halachist, in all his humility, is supremely self-confident, since he is in possession of norms and principles which hold all existence in thrall and to which even the Lord Himself is subject, as it were.

The piety of the Halachist, then, is expressed in the elaboration and progressive refinement of the eternal norms, or laws, which have been given to his custody. With this dogmatic assurance of absolute mastery, the Halachist is able to rise above the torments of anxiety and the sense of awe. In control of the principles of metaphysical legislation, he is able to fix standards and norms for the amorphous and fluid, tempestuous and unpredictable "feelings" of religion.

"The Halachah which was given to us at Sinai is the objectification of religion in the shape of fixed and lucid molds, in clearly outlined laws and definite principles. It converts subjectivity into objectivity and into a fixed pattern of lawfulness."[29]

Thus, Soloveitchik disapproves of the Hassidic emphasis on religious enthusiasm and feeling, citing the words of rebuke which his father addressed to a "hassid" when the latter was overwhelmed by pious awe during the "shofar"-blowing ceremonies on Rosh Hashono: "Do you tremble and cry on "Sukkoth," when you shake the "lulav?" Why then do you cry when the "shofar" is blown? Aren't both observances equally commandments of the Lord?"[30] Though the purpose of the "shofar" is to rouse the feelings of repentance and that of the "lulav" to express the feelings of gratitude on the Feast of Ingathering, the Halachist takes note predominantly not of the feelings involved but of the actual performance of the ceremony, in all its detailed exactitude. For the significance of the "Mitzvah" is independent of the feelings it arouses or fails to arouse, consisting solely in its being a divine, immutable law. This legalistic emphasis does indeed subdue the stormy surge of religious feeling, but it compensates for this loss of inwardness and depth by the development of a joyous sense of dedication which accompanies the performance of all "mitzvoth."

"The Sages of Israel know nothing of the ceaseless battle against the Evil Desire, such as we read about in the lives of Christian saints. . . . While the faith of the Catholic fathers was won through a struggle and by an inner compulsion, the faith of our Sages was a free and serene growth of the spirit."[31]

This sober restraint of the Halachist is by no means due to the modesty of his purpose. For, in truth, the masters of the Law were animated by the dynamic ambition to be ceaselessly creative. In the domain of social life, the rabbis sought to bring about the realization of the utopia of Halachah, and, for the guidance of the chosen individual, they evolved the lofty goal of prophecy. The ideal personality is the prophet, his qualities of mind and heart having become perfected and balanced to the point where the Divine Presence actually rests upon him. "Every person is called upon to renew his being in accord with the ideal pattern of the prophet and to engage in this creative process until he attains the final consummation of prophetic achievement, the readiness for the reception of Divine Grace."[32]

Through the practice of continuous self-analysis, self-criticism and self-building by way of repentance, the worshipper uncovers new sources of strength within himself, advancing thus by degrees to the lofty eminence of prophecy.

At this point, Dr. Soloveitchik abandons the attempt to picture the Halachah as a self-contained domain, preempting for his purpose the disciplines of philosophy and Kabbalah. Within the strict limitations of Halachah, the ideal of prophecy was never set as an actual goal for the observant Jew. Traditionally, prophecy ceased with the last of the biblical prophets and it was not to be renewed until the generation of the Messiah. In the philosophy of Maimonides, the ideal of prophecy was reinstated as an actual possibility for the religious Jew, corresponding to the mystical goal of Medieval Aristotelian philosophy. But, to Maimonides Halachah was not a metaphysical reality, only a social instrument for the creation of the good society, in which philosophers might be nurtured and encouraged to attain the heights of mystical perfection. Thus, Maimonides arrived at the goal of prophecy by the subordination of Halachah to the disciplines of pure, metaphysical reflection. In Kabbalah, the quest for prophetic mysticism found expression especially in the erratic career of Abraham Abulafia, who considered himself to be a disciple of Maimonides.[33] As to Halachah, its very nature as a rationally ordered system of law precluded the disturbing intervention of prophecy, so that the growth of Halachah, following the reforms of Ezra, narrowed the range of prophecy and eventually eliminated it altogether, save as part of the Messianic hope. Well-known is the historic debate between Rabbi Eliezer ben Hyrkanos and Rabbi Joshua ben Hananyah, when the latter refused to accept heavenly signs and testimonies, saying, "The Torah is not in heaven."[34]

In general, Dr. Soloveitchik fails to establish the independence and self-sufficiency of Halachah, in spite of the brilliance of his exposition. The "man of Halachah" did not live in an intellectual vacuum, and, when he reflected on the truth or purpose of revelation, he found the ramparts of his faith either in the domain of general philosophy, as did Maimonides, or in the shadowy realm of Kabbalah, as did Elijah Gaon and Rabbi Hayim of Volozhin, foremost Halachists of Lithuania, or in a synthetic combination of Kabbalah and philosophy, as did the foremost Halachic authority of Ashkenazic Jewry, Rabbi Moses Isserless.[35]

By no stretch of the imagination could Halachic principles, in all their naivete and particularity, be regarded as *a priori* constructions. Through Halachah, fine and consecrated religious personalities were evolved, but this result attests neither to the truth of Halachah nor to its enduring significance. We admire the great masters of Jewish Law, albeit we recognize that it was inevitable for them to take for granted the narrow limitations of dogma which delimited their spiritual world and channelized their yearnings for the "nearness of God." A prominent exponent of modern Orthodoxy writes: "The authority of the Torah is as self-evident to the uncorrupted Israelite as is the existence of God."[36] But, once "corrupted" by doubt, the "man of Halachah" can hardly find his way back to faith, through the instruments and arguments of Halachah alone. As to prophecy, Dr. Soloveitchik brings in through the back door what he had previously expelled through the front door, characterizing all efforts to experience the immediacy of the Divine Being as the dark vagaries of romanticism and the dangerous dynamism of mysticism. For in the Maimonidean sense, prophecy does not differ from the achievements of the great mystics. It is largely a human adventure, aiming at unity with the Divine Will, and

God rarely withholds His Grace from those who are worthy of receiving the gifts of prophetic inspiration.

In the total complex of American Orthodoxy, the elements deriving from the thought and tradition of Western Europe are of particular interest. Designated on occasion as neo-Orthodox, the stream of romantic piety and inflexible zealotry which is associated with the name of S. R. Hirsch is represented on the American scene by a very small number of congregations. However, its influence is likely to increase in both scope and depth as the tightly packed colonies of immigrants in the great metropolitan centers are permeated ever more fully by the spirit of western culture. Actually, the term neo-Orthodox does not betoken any essential departure in dogma or practice from the Orthodox pattern of faith.[37] Unlike the Protestant neo-supernaturalists who interpret the assertions and tales of the Bible as myths and symbols of eternal principles, the neo-Orthodox in Judaism affirm the dogma of Sinaitic revelation in utter literalness, permitting the freedom of allegorization only along the well-trodden pathways of Kabbalah. Yet, neo-Orthodoxy is distinctly and vividly a new interpretation of tradition, reflecting the genteel norms, universalist aspirations and this-worldly emphasis of western culture. Carried along by the passion for consistency and the narrow logic of absolutism, the exponents of this school, for all their urbanity, are frequently more rigid and unyielding in practice than the unpretentious and unsophisticated, unsystematic and altogether "natural" saints and sages of Eastern Europe.

The most recent and most thorough expression of west-European Orthodoxy may be found in Isaak Breuer's impressive volume, "Der Neue Kusari."

The author, trained in the German classical tradition, was painfully aware of the deep frustrations of modern man. As an idealistic philosopher, he regarded the realm of appearance which our senses convey to us as being a product of two entities, the "meta-physical" and the "meta-ethical." These hypothetical realms are themselves outside the spacetime world, inhering beyond the reach of the iron laws of causality. The physical universe consists of influences and forces deriving from the "meta-physical" realm, and these are ordered and molded, fashioned and "willed," by the subconscious will of man, which is the same in all men and independent of the vagaries of thought and sentiment that supervene on the surface of consciousness. If we designate this unconscious will as the "meta-ethical" phase of the human personality, we recognize the physical universe as the fleeting surface of contact between the "meta-physical" and the "meta-ethical" domains of being.

From this analysis it follows that truth is not to be discovered by the simple analysis of and generalization from the restless surge of phenomena on the surface of existence. Somehow, the inner will of man, dwelling in the realms beyond our conscious reach and manifesting itself in the alternation of fearful anxiety and bold decision, must provide the answer. But how?

To dramatize his solution, the author describes a young Jewish intellectual, who was launched on his way back to "Torah-true" Judaism by his persistent anxiety over the question, "how should I live my life?" Any sentimental or humanistic answer was to him unsatisfactory, for in his deadly earnestness, he needed detailed guidance for living, not remote ideals and vague generalities. Caught in the swirling currents of modern history, the young philosopher felt an inner certainty that the word of God was somehow conveyed in the unseen handwriting on the broad canvas of human history. But, history is the record of the struggle of the nations, and our hero could not but read this record from the standpoint of the Jewish people, "who live among the nations but are not of them."

In Breuer's interpretation, the lesson of history is twofold—the inevitable frustration of all human efforts and the existence of the Jewish society as a kind of super-historical or "meta-historical" people which provides the answer to the dark groping and infinite tragedy of mankind.

"Does not the history of the nations prove that people cannot liberate themselves by their own efforts from the power of evil?"[38]

Again and again gifted and inspired nations have risen upon the stage of history only to stumble and sink back into failure and despair. Always it is an ideal, a vision of the Kingdom of God on earth, which lifts a nation or a group of nations to leadership and power, but these ideals cannot bring about the final consummation, since they are only human and partial visions of the Divine image. To the keeping of the Jewish people, however, the Torah, which constitutes the genuine pattern of the "Kingdom of God," has been given, so that the Jewish people have been lifted by the covenant of Sinai above the ebb and flow of human history and charged with the task of representing the reality and truth of the goal to those that are still on the way. So long as the nations are still engaged in the struggle for power, they are distinguished by the qualities of language, the possession of land and a temporal government. The Jewish people have given up this struggle for national power long ago, substituting the Divine Law, the Holy Tongue and the Holy Land for the temporal values of nationhood.

This removal of Israel from the normal arena of national struggles, even while it is maintained as an "eternal people," is attested by the entire course of Jewish history. "The voice of the meta-historical wonder of the Jewish nation resounds not a bit less loudly than the voice of God at Sinai. . . ."[39]

The author, writing in the late thirties, as the devastating tide of Naziism was gathering for the final burst of total destruction, saw the entire, timeless fate of Israel revealed in the stern predictions of Moses: "And the Lord shall scatter thee among all the peoples, from the one end of the earth unto the other. . . . And among these nations thou shalt find no ease, neither shall the sole of thy foot have rest; but the Lord shall give thee there a trembling heart, and a failing of eyes, and sorrow of mind. . . .[40] And upon them that are left alive of you, I will send a faintness into their hearts in the lands of their enemies; and the sound of a shaken leaf shall chase them. . . ."[41]

In these and similar verses, the author saw proof of the divinity of the Torah and of the peculiar destiny of Israel.

"Do the antisemites, do the Jews themselves, know that antisemitism, which reaches from Babylonia-Rome to post-war Germany, is an incontrovertible proof of the meta-physics of prediction?"[42]

To be sure, the recognition of the "meta-historical wonder" of Jewish life presupposes a certain receptivity of mind. One must learn to recognize "the negation of world-history" and to experience inwardly the "Jewish protest" against it. Identifying himself completely with the divinely constituted "congregation of Israel," the Jew senses the unique destiny of his people, even "as the artist grasps a historical personality, as a friend understands a friend, as the lover chooses the beloved. . . ."[43] Through a "living experience" of this kind, the individual Jew knows himself to be a miracle and a witness, "not merely the object of this divine wonder of history, but one who himself lives this history and therefore experiences God hourly. . . ."[44]

It is through the Sinaitic covenant that "Knesseth Yisroel," the Congregation of Israel, was constituted. Hence, only those who are absolutely and meticulously loyal to the divinely fashioned community are truly Jews. All others, even those Orthodox people who are personally observant but who belong to a community which includes the non-Orthodox or the non-observant, are "traitors" to "the nation of God."[45] Since it is through the sense of oneness with the community that the Jew discovers his relationship to God, the community in question must be a spotless exemplar of "Knesseth Yisroel," lifted, in the serenity of its perfection, above time, chance and circumstance. The author is particularly incensed at the Zionists, whose ideology consists in a conscious rebellion against the "meta-historical" destiny of the Jew.

Yet, with all his impassioned exclusiveness *vis-à-vis* divergent interpretations of Judaism, the author reveals a powerful universal trend of thought. The purpose of Jewish "meta-history" is to bring mankind to the goals of individual perfection and social harmony. In its role of "the people of peoples," Israel is "the herald of God's righteousness" and "the symbol of the meta-historical goal of humanity." It was God's will that the Jews be scattered among the varying nations of the globe, in order "that the meta-historical people learn to love and cherish the peculiar characteristics of each nation."[46]

This entire world-view is founded like an inverted pyramid upon the one fulcrum of literal revelation at Sinai. But, on what grounds is this dogma to be accepted? The answer is that this dogma is "willed" by the one who identifies himself with "Knesseth Yisroel" utterly and without reservations. "The final truth cannot be grasped through thought, but only by the will," for in actuality "to know and to will is one."[47] An event that happened only once in history cannot be proven, in the usual sense. Furthermore, to the believer, the Torah is the one source of truth, all other knowledge being secondary in character. "An unconditioned truth is, according to its essence, unprovable. All these proofs lead the unknown back to the known. How could the unconditioned truth be unconditioned, if it must be proven or led back to that which is itself conditioned? . . . The divinity of the Torah is in no wise different from the divinity of God Himself. Not proveable is God, but proving . . . The Torah is essentially a quality of God. Whoever denies it separates God from His quality, denies God. . . .[48]

The ideology of Breuer is precise and clearly-etched In this respect, it is distinctly untypical of American Orthodoxy, which is pragmatic and flexible, changing rapidly step by step even while insisting loudly on its sameness. Thus, a goodly proportion of the congregations affiliated with the Orthodox Union offer family pews, use a microphone on the Sabbath and holidays, and include the reading of English prayers in the liturgy. The balcony for women is becoming a rarity, the "m'hitsah" separating the women's section is beating a fast retreat, the "Bimah," which rabbinic assemblies in the nineteenth century solemnly declared to be indispensable, has long been moved out of the synagogue. As to personal life, there is no counting the "mitzvoth," the negation of which does not disqualify one from accounting himself a member of the "Torah-true" community. There are no clearly marked and easily distinguishable barriers among the lay adherents of the varying interpretations of Judaism, so that Orthodoxy is largely a matter of formalistic dogma—a surface-belief in the literal revelation of the Law. In regard to this dogma, we may expect that there will always be men and women who will accept it as the one "unconditioned" truth, the fundamental axiom of thought and life. For fundamentalist religion is more than a heritage from the past; basically, it is a response to the psychic needs of certain character types.

NOTES

1. *"Tnuath HaMussar,"* by Dov Katz, Vol. 1.
2. *"Or Yisroel,"* by Rabbi Yitzhak Blaser.
3. *"T'nuath HaMussar,"* vol. 2, p. 250.
4. *"Tnuath HaMussar,"* Vol. 2, p. 161.
5. *"Tnuath HaMussar,"* Vol. 2, pp. 153, 154.
6. *"Pishai Sh'arim,"* by R. Yitzhak Hover is a typical outline of the intricate Kabbalah-system of the nineteenth century.
7. *"Shaiurai Daath,"* New York, 1949.
8. *Ibid,* p. 11.
9. *Ibid,* p. 13.
10. *Ibid,* p. 66.
11. *Ibid,* p. 23.
12. *Ibid,* p. 29.
13. *Ibid,* pp. 22, 26.
14. *Ibid,* p. 157.
15. *Ibid,* p. 198.
16. *Ibid,* p. 85.
17. *Ibid,* p. 162.
18. *"Taanith,"* 23b.
19. *"Banner of Jerusalem,"* p. 131.
20. *"Banner of Jerusalem,"* p. 132.
21. *Ibid,* p. 135.
22. *"Banner of Jerusalem,"* p. 192.
23. *"Banner of Jerusalem,"* p. 209.
24. *Ibid,* p. 210.
25. *Ibid,*
26. *"Banner of Jerusalem,"* p. 211.
27. *"Talpioth,"* 1944, pp. 652–660.
28. *Ibid,* p. 661.
29. *"Talpioth,"* 1944, pp. 688.
30. *Ibid,* p. 689.
31. *"Talpioth,"* 1944, p. 692.
32. *Ibid,* p. 729.
33. *See* A. J. Heschel, *"Ha-heemin Ho Rambam She-hi-g-i-a lin-vu-a?"*
34. *"Baba M'tsia,"* 59b.
35. The Kabbalistic teachings of *"Nefesh Ha Hayim,"* the posthumous book of the Rabbi Hayim Volozhim, differ in no distinguishable respect from the standard principles of this "hidden wisdom." The Kabalistic philosophy of Elijah Gaon is dry and dogmatic, as may be seen in his own commentaries on the Zohar, and in the systematic exposition of his disciple, Rabbi Isaac Hover. The Gaon did, however, question the accuracy of some of the manuscripts of the Lurianic Kabbalah. The reflections of Rabbi Moses Isserless are contained in his mystical-symbolic work, "Torath Ha-Olah," where he explains the "mitzvoth," especially the order of sacrifices in the Temple, by means of the principle of parallelism which the revival of Platonism made popular. The Holy Temple in Jerusalem was in all its portions a perfect symbolic counterpart of the universe, and the altar was situated on the highest spot in the world. Rabbi Isserless took his geographical "facts" from

the Talmud, of course. As the Temple was a representation of the universe, so the sacrifices symbolized the destiny of man's life in relation to the universe. The organic nature of the cosmos was represented in the animal that was brought as an offering, which recalled also the "creaturely" character of the universe and its eventual disintegration. The wine-offering was to symbolize the flow of Divine Grace, the meal offering to indicate the atomic nature of all physical things. While Rabbi Isserless speaks with the greatest reverence concerning the "hidden wisdom" of Kabbalah, his thought runs generally along philosophical and quasi-philosophical lines. Thus, he writes that the Kabbalah was "derived from the mouth of the prophets, beginning with Moses our teacher." Yet, he refuses to accept the basic axion of Kabbalah that the action of men on earth could cause a blemish in the "Sh'chinah," or the S'firoth above. (*Torath Ha-Olah* II, 4, 16; III, 4.)

36. Leo Jung, *"Talpioth,"* 1944, p. 736.
37. *See* Wieman, *"American Philosophies of Religion,"* pp. 85–83.
38. Isaak Breuer, *"Der Neue Kusari,"* p. 159.
39. Breuer, *"Der Neue Kusari,"* p. 89.
40. *Deuteronomy,* XXVIII, 46–67.
41. *Lev.* XXVI, 36.
42. Breuer, *"Der Neue Kusari,"* p. 75.
43. *Ibid,* p. 85.
44. *Ibid,* p. 86.
45. *Ibid,* p. 103.
46. Breuer, *"Der Neue Kusari,"* p. 159.
47. *Ibid,* pp. 267, 270.
48. *Ibid,* p. 263.

12

A CONTEMPORARY RABBINICAL SCHOOL FOR ORTHODOX JEWRY

ELIEZER BERKOVITS

Since Rabbi Fasman has raised the question of the interrelationship between Classical Judaism and contemporary culture, we dwell on that problem. Here Rabbi Eliezer Berkovits describes not only a rabbinical school—though that is the point of his article—but also an ideal of Judaism. The two cannot be separated, for the former embodies and exemplifies the latter. We should therefore pay close attention to Rabbi Berkovits's stress upon the subtle relationship between the inherited tradition and the world in which its heirs actually live. He stresses the legitimacy of reason and of serious attention to what is to be learned outside of the Talmud. He also asks the world of the yeshivas to take account of the Jews outside their walls. His view is that, if the yeshivas remain closed to the needs and yearnings of the larger Jewish world, even they cannot maintain themselves without much difficulty. Clearly, the study of American Judaism carries us in widely divergent paths. On the one hand, we find that religious virtuosi are excluded from the decision-making process of the larger community. On the other, we dis-
whether they wish to be concerned with that larger community at all.
cover that the most virtuous of the religious specialists themselves ask
These are the extremes. In the center are those rabbis and seminaries who devote themselves to the tradition and do so in behalf of the larger community.

For some time now we have been witnessing the continued decline of the rabbinical office and ineffectiveness of spiritual leadership in our communities. More and more the rabbi is becoming a functionary of an established organization which, though it may be functioning smoothly at times, yet is lacking vitality and significant contents. What can be more boring than most of our religious services in our synagogues and temples! The managements of our congregations are more often than not in the hands of people who vulgarize the organized religious structure of our life by impressing their "vision" and their "ideals" on the conduct of the affairs of our congregations. In the midst of all this organized sham the rabbinical functionary presides over a ritual department whence only little can issue that is inspiring or edifying. It would be most unfair to place the blame for this tragic decline in contents, value and vitality altogether at the doorsteps of the rabbinical office. The emptiness and vulgarization is mainly due to the general crisis of religion in the midst of an overpowering secular civilization. Nevertheless, the question is justified: Do our rabbinical schools adequately prepare our rabbis to enable them to meet the challenges of their office with any significant measure of success? Because of the general spiritual and religious crisis of our times the task of the rabbi is a much more difficult one than it was even only a generation ago, incomparably more demanding than two or three generations before us. Our concern here is with the Orthodox segment in our communities, because it is ideologically closest to us and because only of the functioning of the Orthodox rabbinical schools do we have first-hand knowledge. Our question is: Do we have contemporary rabbinical schools in the United States or Israel that are capable of satisfying the need for effective spiritual leadership and guidance of Orthodox Jewry. By "contemporary" we do not mean any kind of ideological determination, but simply the designation of schools that are fulfilling their responsibilities in complete awareness of the fact that they have to educate rabbis and teachers who will be expected to serve in Jewish communities as they exist and struggle for meaningful survival in the closing phase of this twentieth century. We have, of course, to look for an answer to the *yeshivot* in this country or in *Eretz Yisrael.*

II

In the main, there are two kinds of *yeshivot*. The first one is the old-world type, which has been transplanted as completely as such transplants are possible from Lithuania, Hungary, or Poland. Such are, for instance, the famous *yeshivah* at Lakewood or that of Telsh in Cleveland, or that of Ponewicz at B'nai B'rak in Israel, and many others. Then there is also a kind of modern Orthodox version of the old *yeshivah,* only two in numbers; the one, the large and world-renowned Yeshiva University in New York and the much smaller Hebrew Theological College of Chicago, now located in Skokie, Illinois. The curriculum of the old-world type is dedicated almost exclusively to the study of the Talmud and the Codes, with negligible emphasis on the Bible as a subject to be taught, and no teaching at all of the subjects that are generally known as *Chokhmat Yisrael,* i.e., Hebrew language or literature, Jewish history and philosophy, etc. In general, students at these schools are expected not to pursue any secular studies at colleges or universities. The curriculum of the modern Orthodox *yeshivah* is different. There too there is great emphasis laid on Talmud and Codes, but *Chokhmat Yisrael* is part of the curriculum and general studies at colleges and universities are not frowned upon. Y.U. has its own college and university and the H.T.C. of Chicago also incorporates a junior liberal arts college, where graduates continute at other colleges and graduate schools.

There can be little doubt that the old-world type is not the kind of contemporary rabbinical school for which we are asking and that is needed. But one has no right to criticize them. They do not acknowledge that Jewish communities do live in the context of a secular civilization that confronts the Jew with innumerable intellectual, moral, and religious challenges. They do not recognize the problems that beset Jewry in our times. For them, Jews, even in the midst of the world, ought to and can encapsule themselves—as it were. Jews should live in a spiritual ghetto of their own making, where there are no problems and no challenges. Whether in Israel or in the New World, get inside of old-world Judaism, which is the only authentic one, and you may well ignore contemporary life. It is not their aim to be contemporary. One might rather say that according to them the source of all evil stems from being contemporary. Their goal is not to be contemporary. On the whole, they are successful in their educational philosophy as far as their own students are concerned. However, these schools have only a marginal existence on the circumference of the reality of Jewish life in our days. No doubt, in general, their graduates are good Jews, an asset to the Jewish community. Some of them go on to teach in Day Schools or *yeshivot* where they continue to teach and educate in the spirit in which they themselves have been educated. Occasionally, a fairly effective contemporary rabbi emerges from the old-world *yeshivah,* not because of the training that he received, but mainly of what he was able to make of himself partly on the basis of that training and partly, in conscious departure from it. But such cases are unintended by the school philosophy. In fact, the *Roshei Hayeshivah* actually discourage their students from entering the active rabbinate, who, of course, need not much discouragement. The overwhelming majority of their students simply do not have the qualification to function in any way effectively in a contemporary congregation.

III

As we have indicated, one cannot blame the old-type *yeshivah* for not being contemporary. But what of the modern Orthodox rabbinical schools? Their *raison d'être* is to educate teachers and spiritual leaders for the contemporary Jewish community. Do they fulfill the task that ought to be theirs? In order to answer the question, one has to take a critical look at their educational philosophy, their curriculum, and methodology.

What is most obvious to anyone familiar with the internal life of these institutions is the fact that they are lacking an over-all educational philosophy. General college studies, *Chokhmat Yisrael* subjects, and the study of Talmud and Codes are unrelated to each other. Judged by its educational philosophy and its interpretation of Judaism the talmudic department of the modern Orthodox rabbinical school could just as well take its place in the old-world *yeshivah*. It is no less unrelated to the real needs of the contemporary community as is the latter. On the other hand, the *Chokhmat Yisrael* department, usually with its more liberal attitude and more broadminded outlook, with its greater awareness of the realities of the contemporary scene, cannot in its educational endeavor link up with the spirit of what is being taught in the talmudic department. The two exist side by side, as if in airtight compartments. Usually, a *Chokhmat Yisrael,* including the study of *Tanach,* is treated as a stepchild; even the very limited and inadequate time alloted it is granted begrudgingly. Yet, it was no less a man than Maimonides who maintained that only the philosophical interpretation of the Torah will teach a man the love of God. (Cf. *Moreh Nevukhim,* III, 52). One need not agree with Maimonides on this point. One thing, however, is certain: no generation of Jews needed more desperately a meaningful interpretation of Judaism in contemporary idiom than ours. From the point of view of present-day Orthodoxy, this could only be accomplished by the harmonization of the *Chokhmat Yisrael* disciplines with that of the talmudic subjects.

In short, the modern Orthodox rabbinical school has no integrated educational philosophy. It teaches this and that and the other too. But teaching this and that is no education. At best, it is the teaching of skills; the skill of how to read a passage in the Talmud, how to give an halakhic decision, and in exceptional cases, also how to interpret a passage in a medieval text of Jewish philosophy, etc., etc.

IV

The truly depressing aspect of the modern Orthodox rabbinical college is that the results of its talmudic curriculum too are questionable. The method of teaching Talmud in such a school is not much different from the way it has been taught for generations. Then the method was of no vital importance, for if one studies a subject for 12-16 hours a day, seven days a week, all year, almost any method will work, especially in the complete isolation from the world in which the young Talmud student lives. But if a young Jew goes to college, studies *Chokhmat Yisrael,* lives in a contemporary world, and has only four to five hours a day to spend on learning Talmud two things are vital if he wishes to get significant results: the comprehensive educational philosophy that determines the atmosphere of the institution and is, to a large extent, the source of motivation for many, and the method of teaching. We have seen that the educational philosophy is missing. As to the second vital requirement for educational success, not only is there no method appropriate to the prevailing conditions, but there is not even the slightest realization that the new circumstances demand one. In fact, the highest ambition of the Talmud teachers in the modern schools is to imitate the method of the old schools.

Our present method concentrates on each subject with great intellectual intensity; it examines a theme from innumerable angles; it spends a great deal of time on every minutiae of the analysis. Its main ambition is to come up continually with *hidushim,* new concepts, new distinctions and definitions, with interpretations never seen or heard before. In itself, all this may sound commendable. Unfortunately, the entire intellectual activity is not related to the time available for study. As a result, only an extremely small amount of talmudic material is covered apparently in great depth. One has to use the qualifying term "apparently," for at this point the question of the relationship between quantity and quality arises. Is depth of penetration real, is its effect lasting, if the material of study to which it is applied is extremely limited? The results show that the answer is in the negative. More often than not the instructors bask in the light of their own self-flattering brilliance, completely overlooking the needs of the students.

Certainly in the study of the Talmud, quality without due regard to quantity results in superficiality. This is especially true if one analyzes the *pilpul* method used in the study of Talmud. It is difficult to define it for the uninitiated. It stands for everything we said above about the method but in a greatly exaggerated form. Often the most important goal is to score a point in the debate. The intellectual sharpness of analysis often disregards the text which it pretends to interpret. In the past, some of the greatest authorities have warned against the *pilpul.* The only safeguard against its degenerating into hairsplitting irrelevance is a fairly adequate quantitative knowledge of numerous areas of the talmudic discipline. If, however, the method of *pilpul* is practiced within the very narrow limits of the talmudic material covered in the modern rabbinical college, the results of this method are devastating. After years of study, the great majority of students graduate from such a school without ever having acquired a sound *Derekh Halimud* (method of study), without being able to work independently in the field of *Halakhah,* without being able to give a fairly authoritative opinion on any half-way complex halakhic question, and certainly ill-equipped to deal with complex contemporary problems.

The program of Talmud and Codes that leads to ordination in the modern Orthodox school with which this writer is rather familiar will illustrate the point that we are making. Beginning after high-school graduation, the curriculum provides an eight-year course. During the first five years the student concentrates on the study of the Talmud. The last three years represent the *Semikhah* (ordination) program proper. During the five years of Talmud the student covers an average of 25-30 *blatt* (double Talmud pages) per annum. Thus when he reaches the threshhold of the *Semikhah* program the student had covered about 125-150 *blatt* of the entire Talmud on a more mature level. At this stage, partly due to the failings in the method, as analyzed above, most of the students have achieved a rather weak ability of self-study of Talmud. But now they are put on a three-year pressure-cooker course of Codes, studying chiefly *Yoreh Deah* and *Orach Hayim.* The study of Talmud is pursued on a very minor scale, mainly as an occasional auxiliary to the understanding of the Codes. As a result, the rather meek *Derekh Halimud* (method of independent study) acquired in the previous five years is being neglected. On the other hand, an inordinately high amount of Code is studied by rote, interspersed with an unhealthy measure of *pilpul.* In the years to come in the active rabbinate most of the Codes so learned and on such foundations will be forgotten. The rather inadequate competence of talmudic self-study will provide little motivation for further scholastic pursuits in the area of Talmud or Halakhah.

In this connection it is necessary to say a few words about the *Brisker Derekh,* i.e., the method of Brisk, so called after the great Rabbi Hayim Soloveitchik of blessed memory, once the rabbi of Brest Litowsk in Russia. It has been adopted in most of the *yeshivot* and rabbinical schools. It is a method of extremely clear and sharp analysis of basic principles which, as if in a flash, illuminate entire subjects and many difficulties. It usually achieves its goal by translating the "cases" and the "pictorial' examples by which the Talmud teaches into exact logically definable concepts. The method is the work of a unique genius. That is its drawback. To this day, the *Brisker Derekh* is a master key to a penetrating talmudic study, but it works only if applied by a first-rate mind. In the hands of lesser spirits it leads to futility. In a sense, it is tantamount to an intellectual disaster that it has become too popular. Genius cannot be popularized. It has found too many imitators, but genius cannot be imitated. The *Brisker Derekh* is too potent a potion. Many of those who dabble in it today ought to be discouraged. At what level of "learning" ability should a student be introduced to it is a serious methodological question. It would seem to us that before a student is capable of studying by himself and fairly competently a *Blatt Gemarah* this method would actually make it more difficult for him ever to achieve competence of independent Talmud study. As indicated earlier, the method of Brisk translates the concreteness of the "case" into the abstract of a principle. One cannot get to the abstract except by way of the concrete. He who attempts to do it is like one who pours air into leaking bottles. Before "Brisk" the student must be introduced to a method that will enable him to master the concrete talmudic material in self-study. After that, "Brisk" can become a veritable blessing. But even then, it should be handed to the more gifted students. The average young man should rather be encouraged to concentrate on the plain, common sense understanding of the text. An occasional taste of Brisk is about all he can handle safely.

It is remarkable that, notwithstanding its many failings, some outstanding rabbis did come out from the modern Orthodox rabbinical schools, mainly by filling in by their own ability and energy a great deal of what is lacking in their alma mater. However, in the vital area of halakhic scholarship, related to the numerous new problems with which contemporary Jewries are confronted, the results have been truly disappointing. And yet, the rabbi of the old school will never be able to grapple successfully with the new problems. It is questionable to what extent any branch of knowledge is genuinely objective, in the sense of being independent of the individuality and circumstances of the scholar that works in it. Undoubtedly, however, halakhic insights and decisions do depend to a large extent on the approach of the talmudic scholar to the problems before him, on his philosophy of life, on his philosophy of Judaism, on his understanding of the essence and purpose of Halakhah.

V

In the State of Israel the situation is rather different. There are no modern Orthodox *yeshivot* at all. All the *yeshivot* are essentially of the old-world type. They, of course, do produce many fine and some outstanding *Talmidei Chakhamim.* Yet, the inadequacy of the rabbinical schools in Israel is even more glaring than that of their counterpart in the United States, be they of the old or the new type. The new reality of the State of Israel is incomparably more revolutionary and its demands on spiritual leadership more demanding than anything thus far experienced in our entire history. In addition, the stakes are much higher. The opportunities are richer than anywhere else; failure more damaging to Judaism than anywhere else. To insist on meeting the need for spiritual leadership in the midst of the new reality of the State of Israel with the old-world *yeshivah* is sheer futility. Neither its curriculum, nor its method of study; neither its understanding of the complex reality of a modern state nor its philosophy of life and Judaism, enables its graduates to grapple successfully with the intellectual or emotional, religious or ethical, moral or halakhic problems of this excitingly and painfully new reality.

It is rather sad to see how little understanding there is in the ranks of the established rabbinate in Israel for the new intellectual, religious, and halakhic problematic in the life of the nation. A friend of mine from my younger years, who presently occupies a very sensitive rabbinical position in one of the major cities in Israel confided to me the following (without the intention that the fact as such not be revealed). He has completed a manuscript on one of the books of the Bible, in which he discusses some theories of higher Biblical criticism.

Even though the work is, in his opinion, a very effective refutation of those theories, he does not publish it for fear of his rabbinical colleagues, who would condemn him for occupying himself with such questionable studies. A well-known rabbinical and scholarly personality had the following story to relate. One of the leading rabbis in Israel approached him, requesting his help in establishing a modern rabbinical school in Israel. Upon being questioned what type of a school he had in mind, the rabbi answered that it would be a *yeshivah* like all the other important *yeshivot* in Israel, with the difference that in his intended rabbinical college, elocution too would be taught. How far removed must a rabbinical establishment be from the life of the people, if one of its leading members believes that the problem of spiritual leadership may be solved by elocution lessons!

Leading rabbinical personalities of the old-world type have been wont to oppose establishing special schools for the training of rabbis. The very idea of a rabbinical seminary was and is anathema to them. In the Eastern European communities this might have had its justification. Ideally, the rabbi is not really a professional. The study and knowledge of the Torah are equally incumbent on all Jews. The obligation to keep the commandments of the Torah applies to all Jews alike. Theoretically, all Jews ought to pursue the same course of Torah study; they all ought to receive the same kind of education. It would then be natural that the most accomplished personalities that would come out of such a general educational system would, if so inclined, become teachers and guides to their fellow Jews. This indeed has worked through many generations. There was no need for a professional rabbinical school. It worked mainly because the world was largely closed for the Jew. The trades and business activities in which they were enabled to engage in order to earn a living were of a kind that did not require a great deal of professional training. A Jew could well spend his youth in the *Bet Hamidrash* without spending any time in acquiring a general education, working for a degree or diploma. The professions, or any kind of other activity that required a high measure of general education, were in any case not accessible for him. In that kind of a world, it might have made sense to speak of a rabbinical seminary with some contempt as a "rabbinical factory." The situation is rather different today, both in the Jewish communities in this country and in *Eretz Yisrael*. The kind of general education that is required of any citizen is such that a Jew, especially if he enters any of the free professions, must of necessity have a form of Jewish education widely different from the one that would enable him to function effectively, if he chose to be a rabbi. At the same time, because of the mass entry of the Jews into the professions and as a result of the necessary acquisition of often sophisticated general education by the Jewish masses, the task of the rabbinate itself and the nature of spiritual leadership too have changed. By the nature of its engagement in the life of the times it is a different Jewry that requires spiritual guidance and leadership. The purely talmudic education will no longer do in order to meet the demands for spiritual leadership in contemporary Jewries. The Jewish education of a physician or physicist, of an engineer or even a modern business man, cannot be identical with that of a rabbi. Because of the modern "professionalization" of trades and business, not to mention the free professions themselves, the calling of the rabbi too has been professionalized. This is even more valid in the state of Israel than in this country. There a small and relatively weak country must make a stand in the midst of a highly competitive and often—to say the least—unfriendly world. It can do it only by the highest form of professionalization, in science, agriculture, defense, technology, business, the judiciary, and administration. Obviously, a general, an atomic scientist, a police chief, cannot have the same kind of Jewish education as a rabbi. On the other hand, it is in this kind of a highly professionalized society that the Israeli rabbi has to function effectively. To imagine that the graduates of the ghetto *yeshivot,* transplanted to *Eretz Yisrael* of today, will ever be able to do it is not a dream, but a nightmare. The logic of the ghetto *yeshivot,* which abound in the State of Israel, demands the rejection of most of a general secular education, all higher education, and, of course, all professionalism. In other words, if consistently maintained, it would require the denial of the living reality of a Jewish people in a Jewish State—certainly so, prior to the coming of the Messiah. In an interview, recently published in one of the religious Israeli newspapers, one of the Chief Rabbis was asked about the lack of young rabbis in the Israeli rabbinate. In his answer, he was declaring with obvious satisfaction that, of course, "we do not have factories for the manufacturing of rabbis." Many fine *Talmudei Chakhamim* come out of the Israeli *yeshivot,* said he, if only they would be willing to enter the rabbinate! If there is to be a meaningful future for the rabbinate, I am afraid they will have to do away with that bogey of "a factory for the manufacturing of rabbis" and establish an adequate contemporary rabbinical seminary. Otherwise, the present situation will continue to deteriorate and, while there may still be rabbis in Israel, the people in Israel will have no rabbis.

VI

What then would be a contemporary rabbinical school? Our remarks in this section of our discussion are made with a view of the conditions in the United States. The educational philosophy, however, on which they are based is—we believe—valid no less for the conditions in the State of Israel.

The curriculum must center around Bible and Talmud, but it should incorporate the study of *Chokhmat Yisrael,* like Hebrew, Jewish history and Jewish philosophy in a serious manner. It should also acknowledge ungrudgingly the necessity for a higher general education, leading to a college or university degree. Whether this is acquired within the school itself or outside it is not essential. (In fact, one may argue well for the undesirability of a general college or university administered by a rabbinical school.) It is decisive that such a curriculum be comprehended within an inclusive educational philosophy, within which Bible and Talmud together with *Chokhmat Yisrael* represent as one entity the teaching of Judaism in a manner that does not leave the general higher education of the student unrelated to the specifically Jewish part of the curriculum. The conceiving of such an educational philosophy is to be the responsibility of the leadership of the school, to be implemented in such a manner that it be actively present on every level of the curriculum. The faculty would have to be chosen in the light of its ability to render such an educational philosophy effective. Especially in the beginning this might pose some problems in the talmudic department. A strong leadership, however, would not find the difficulty insurmountable. There has to be one faculty of the talmudic and *Chokhmat Yisrael* departments, that at regular meetings in joint discussions and consultations of all members they decide on all affairs of the school which come appropriately under its authority. If at all possible, some of the faculty members should teach in both departments. The ultimate goal in faculty appointments should be a faculty in which every member, in addition to his Jewish scholarship, also possesses a higher academic degree.

The entire program, leading to a rabbinical ordination and beginning after graduation from a *yeshivah* high school, should be planned for eight years. The first year of the program should be reserved to

Jewish studies exclusively, with major emphasis on Talmud and the study of Bible and no more than one subject of *Chokhmat Yisrael,* this latter on an undergraduate level. The purpose of this year is to equip the student with a sound enough foundation on which to build the talmudic curriculum in the years to follow. It is also assumed that as the result of the concentrated study of the first year, in the years ahead—when the time for Talmud study will be more limited—the student will be able to advance by far better and use the available time to much greater advantage than is the case in the present conditions.

The curriculum of the next three years will be divided into three parts: Talmud and Bible, *Chokhmat Yisrael* and College. It is assumed that during this period the student will acquire a Bachelor of Arts degree. This should be possible by attending summer school. It is also very likely that, if the *Chokhmat Yisrael* courses are conducted on an academic level, general colleges and universities will be willing to accept them for credits toward a Bachelor's degree. The fifth year of the program should once gain be given over completely to Jewish studies as in the first years, i.e., Talmud and Bible, and no more than one *Chokhmat Yisrael* subject, the latter on the graduate level.

The study of Codes is to be reserved for the last three years, but never in such a manner that at any one time only Codes are taught. During the first two years of this phase of the program *Chokhmat Yisrael* would still be given and students would also be required to work for a limited number of credits toward a higher academic degree. The final year is to be limited to Codes, Talmud, and practical rabbinics.

Most important, however, will be the method of teaching. In the talmudic department the goal should be a sound combination of quantitative and qualitative study. The first year Talmud should be taught on two tracks. Track A should concentrate on the study of the text with the classical commentaries of Rashi and *Tosafot,* including *Me'harsha* and an occasional *Maharshal* and *Maharam.* At times, but only rarely, the opinion of a *Rishon* might be introduced and also some glossa by some of the classical *Acharonim.* The goal at this level is to communicate a method of thorough understanding of the text. All *pilpul* should be avoided. Track B should be the study of another talmudic tractate in much less thorough manner, pursuing an understanding of the text with the help of Rashi's commentary only. By the end of the first year the student, having previously graduated from a Jewish Day

School with several years of Talmud study in its curriculum, will be well on his way to independent Talmud study.

During the next three years the study of Talmud should continue to be conducted on two tracks. Only that now Track A of the first year becomes Track B. Track A, on the other hand, will be a comprehensive and in-depth study of individual themes (*Sugyot*). No more than three to four such themes need be studied in any one term. During a period of about four weeks the student is required to research the theme in independent study. He will have to study it in all its major ramifications in the entire Talmud with all the relevant commentaries of *Rishonim* and *Acharonim,* including the parallel passages in the Codes and some appropriate responsa literature. At this stage in his program the student should be able to turn to good use the research method that he is gradually acquiring in his general college studies. It should help him in the study of variant texts, in the examination of the sources, and the development of the theme at its various phases, as well as in the formulation of exact logical principles and concepts. Thus prepared, the students will attend the lectures on the subjects studied by themselves. On the fifth year level, which again is dedicated exclusively to Jewish studies, tracks A and B of the previous level would be retained, but pulled together in close proximity. For this purpose a major tractate of the Talmud is to be studied in accordance with the methods of both tracks, i.e., according to B of the previous level page after page, as well as according to A, through the selection of major themes (*Sugyot*) from the same tractate. It is assumed that, following such a program by the end of the fifth year the student will be a competent *Talmid Chakham* in the sense that he will be able to do independent scholarly work on any talmudic and halakhic subject. At this level, the student will enter the *Semikhah* program proper. The study of Codes should be spread over the entire three year period. The emphasis is to shift only gradually from Talmud to Codes. During the first two years of this phase major importance should still be given to the study of the Talmud, only that Talmud now is to be Code-oriented, i.e., it will deal with those parts of the Talmud which are the foundations of the sections of Codes that are decisive for practicing rabbis. At this stage, Talmud will be studied with the maturity of the method accomplished and the double track of the previous phases may be eliminated. During the first two years the amount of Codes studied is gradually increased. The final year is then dedicated to intensive Code study, while the study of Talmud is continued only in support of the courses in Codes.

The purpose of the *Chokhmat Yisrael* subjects should be the acquisition by the rabbinical student of a fair knowledge of Jewish history, of the history of Jewish philosophy and its subject matter, of the development of Halakhah and halakhic literature, and a working knowledge of modern Hebrew. The study of at least one major work in Jewish philosophy should be a requirement for all students. A two year course of graduate work in one *Chokhmat Yisrael* subject should be obligatory on each student.

Such a program is an ambitious one. It will demand strong motivation and full concentration on the part of the student. During this period of study, he will not be able to engage in any kind of part-time work in order to earn the necessary funds for his studies. In cases where a student has the intellectual ability to master the program with success, where he shows aptitude and inclination for spiritual leadership, but is lacking the financial means, scholarships and loans should be available. To raise funds for such a purpose ought to be no less important for the school administration than to raise all the other funds needed for the effective functioning of the school.

Needless to say that the best of rabbis alone will not necessarily save us from the vulgarity and boorishness, the boredom and vacuity that so often render our congregational organizations so repulsive. In order to achieve that, our entire educational system needs remaking; the Jew himself has to be changed and Judaism to be articulated afresh so that it may speak meaningfully to the contemporary Jewish condition in this country as well as in *Eretz Yisrael*. We have to strive for renewal and rebirth on the broadest front. But a vital section of that front is the one manned by the rabbi. The more desperate the spiritual condition, the more grievous the problems of faith and action, the greater the rabbinical responsibility and the greater the need for the dedicated and competent contemporary rabbi.

THE ROLE OF HALAKHAH

Authentic Judaism and Halakhah

ELIEZER BERKOVITS

FOR THOSE WHO TAKE THEIR STAND ON THE ground of Halakhah, our theme may appear tautological. For is not authentic Judaism adequately defined as the Judaism of the Halachah? Such a definition may, indeed, be theoretically adequate, but it is also much too general to throw sufficient light on what constitutes authentic Judaism in a given situation. By itself, it could help us only very little in our search for determining the nature of authentic Judaism in the specific historic situation in which Judaism and Jewry find themselves today.

Jewish history has known a succession of different types of Judaisms as well as Jewries. There is a Judaism understood rationalistically, as by Maimonides and Gersonides. There is another type, historically interpreted, as it is found in the *Kuzari* of Yehuda Halevi. There is also the Judaism of the mystics. These various types do not always live in peace with each other. Ever since Sinai we have witnessed an entire series of Jewries, all based on Torah and Halachah, yet differing from each other in outlook, attitude, and their understanding of Judaism. Babylonian Jewry was not Spanish Jewry; and the Spanish Jewry of Gabirol, the Ibn Ezras, of Hasdai Ibn Shaprut, Halevi and Maimonides, was not the Central European Jewry of the authors of the *Tosafot*. Nearer to our own times, the Halachic Jewries of Eastern Europe were not the Halachic Jewries of a Samson Raphael Hirsch or an Ezriel Hildesheimer. There were vast differences between them in the understanding of the Halakhah, in the philosophical interpretation of the teachings and the faith of Judaism; considerable divergencies in their respective attitudes to the outside world, far-reaching ideological disagreements concerning secular studies and professional pursuits. Nor could they have been identified in the areas of ethical valuation and aesthetic taste. They were different branches of the same stem.

Were the numerous different Jewries and their differing interpretations of Judaism authentic? We like to think so. What constituted their authenticity, notwithstanding the obvious differences between them? The importance of the question for us may be readily recognized. All the historic Jewries collapsed in our times. Everywhere we have relatively new settlements of Jews. Note that I speak of new setlements of Jews, not of new Jewries. In America, in Europe, in Israel, all over the world,

ELIEZER BERKOVITS *is the chairman of the philosophy department of the Hebrew Theological College, Skokie, Ill.*

we have "melting-pot Jewries," conglomerates of remnants, survivors of former Jewries everywhere. As yet, we do not have new Jewries. Our task is to establish them.

Because of this task and its historic responsibility, it is of vital importance that we understand what constitutes Jewish authenticity. There are at least two clearly definable considerations that underline the problem that confronts us. To all of the countries of new settlements Jews have come from varied backgrounds, traditions, and memories. Which one of the trends shall the "melting-pot Jewries" continue? The Lithuanian? But why not the Polish? The Polish? But why not the Hungarian or perhaps the German? The Sephardic or the Ashkenazic? The Hasidic or the rationalistic?

Such and similar questions lead us directly to the other consideration. In our entire history, after great catastrophes, we never just continued as before. After every *ḥurban* something new emerged. After the first destruction of the Temple we created the synagogue in its classical meaning. After the destruction of the Second Commonwealth we created the Talmud. The new that followed upon each of these catastrophes was not a mere repetition of the old in a new land under different conditions, but a truly new creation. Our reading of Jewish history tells us that every historic Jewry is unique and, thus, inimitable. We have to understand the nature of Jewish authenticity because once again we find ourselves after a *ḥurban,* at a turning point in Jewish history; once again we are at the beginning of the road. We shall not succeed in resurrecting, on this continent or in the State of Israel, or anywhere else in the world, either Polish or Lithuanian, or Hungarian, or German Jewry. Such resurrection never happened before; nor can it happen now. No Jewry is repeatable. This is so determined, not only by historic conditions, but even more by the very nature of the Halakhah. It is the nature of the Halakhah that determines the authenticity of a Jewry; and it is the essential quality of the Halakhah which also brings it about that each authentic Jewry is different from every other authentic Jewry.

II

What is the nature of the Halakhah? Needless to say that within the scope of this essay it cannot be answered definitively. But some examples of Halachic teaching chosen at random may help us to concentrate our attention on some of the major concerns of classical Halachah.

Rather interestingly, Halakhah is deeply concerned with the effective functioning of the economic segment of society. In a number of cases where the Biblical law would have made it difficult for people to obtain a necessary loan, the Halakhah decided on a deviation from the original Biblical principle in order that "the door not be closed before a borrower." For the same reason the original Biblical requirement for the qualification of the judges who could adjudicate in cases of monetary disputes was relaxed and the procedure itself, in deviation from the Biblical law, simplified. It was necessary to make the conditions for obtaining a loan more favorable for a would-be borrower.[1] There was, of course, a Halakhic principle at hand whose application rendered such changes in the original law possible. Significant, however, is the reason that induced the Halachic teachers to apply that principle. Most known, of course, is the institution of the *prusbol* by Hillel,[2] the declaration in court that protected a loan against forfeiture in the Sabbatical year as provided in Biblical law. Here, too, it was the desire to render the economic life of the community capable of functioning within the frame of the Torah which motivated the great sage to introduce his *takanah*.

Some post-Talmudic examples which belong in the same category are also worth considering. We present only two. According to one of the teachers of the Talmud, a Jew was not allowed to enter into a business partnership with an *akum* (a Gentile). The reason was that in case of a disagreement between the partners, the Gentile partner could be required to affirm something in court with an oath. He would, of course, swear by his god. In this manner the Jew would have contributed to the enhancement of respect for a false deity. Now, in the Middle Ages, in certain parts of Europe, such business associations between Jew and Christian were not unusual. The question arose whether these partnerships were permitted, or should they be dissolved. Rabbenu Tam gave his famous decision that Christians were not to be considered *akum* in the sense of the Talmud.[3] The *akum* were idol-worshippers, whereas Christians worshipped the God of heaven and earth. When they associate another person with Him, such association was not forbidden for non-Jews.

Our second example concerns the Talmudic prohibition to sell certain kinds of animals to Gentiles. This was a Rabbinic, not a Biblical, law. There is no need for us to discuss the reasons for this law, which were purely religious. What interests us here are the economic consequences of the prohibition. Again the situation arose in the Middle Ages in Europe when trade in such animals became a significant source of Jewish livelihood. What was to be done about it? A very simple solution was found. The authoritative Halakhic decision maintained that the prohibition was valid only in Talmudic times, when large Jewish communities were closely settled in the Land of Israel as well as Babyl-

---

1. *Baba Batra* 175b; *Sanhedrin* 2b, 3a.
2. *Gittin* 36a; in the economic interpretation of the *Kesef Mishneh* on Maimonides, *Hilkhot Mamrim*, 2,2.
3. *Sanhedrin* 63b; *Tosafot, Assur; Bekhorot* 2b.

on. In such a situation, "if a Jew had an animal which he did not need, he could sell it to a fellow Jew. But in our days, what can he do?"[4] Under conditions of a Jewish settlement not at all conducive to this kind of trading, economic necessity was sufficient to set aside a ruling of a previous generation. The purpose of these post-Talmudic examples is still the same.

Even more impressive are, of course, the humanitarian concerns of the Halakhah. We shall illustrate our point by some rules in the area of marriage and divorce laws. As is well known, according to Biblical law only a husband can divorce his wife; but not the wife the husband. It is also required that the divorce be given by the husband freely, without any compulsion. A *get* given under coercion invalidates the divorce. Yet, there were cases when one could not expect a woman to remain with her husband. A certain kind of skin disease or a sickness which brought about a severe case of an ill odor of the mouth or the nose, or even when a bad odor was inseparable from the person of the husband because of the work in which he was engaged—in all such cases a divorce was deemed to be objectively justified. If the husband refused, the Halakhah stipulated that "one compels him until he says that he is willing to grant his wife a divorce freely."[5] Maimonides provides us with an interesting explanation of the procedure, how, notwithstanding the coercion, the divorce may be considered as having been given freely. What is important for our consideration is the fact that because on the basis of the original law problems arose, solutions were found so that the law may function meaningfully.

Another interesting example in a related field deals with a modification of the Biblical law of witnesses. According to the Bible, the judicial establishment of a fact as a fact has to be based on the testimony of two witnesses: the testimony of one person is not enough. The Talmudic interpretation of the law held that women or slaves were not admitted as witnesses; nor could one such testify on the basis of testimony heard from an eye-witness. The problem that challenged these provisions of the law was the case of a woman whose husband disappeared and whose death had to be established in order to allow her to remarry. In such a situation the Talmud ruled that the woman was allowed to remarry on the strength of the testimony "of a witness from the mouth of another, from the mouth of a woman, a slave, or even the testimony of only one witness."[6] Very good reasons were given for allowing such far-reaching departure from the original law. The discussion of the matter is concluded with the statement that, in order to protect the wife against being "the widow of a man who is assumed to be alive," the Rabbis were

4. *Avodah Zarah* 15a, *Tosafot, Eimor.*
5. *Ketubot* 77a; cf. Maimonides, *Hilkhot Gerushin* 2, 20.
6. *Yebamoth* 122a; cf. also *ibid.*, 87b-88a, 115a.

lenient in the case. Their boldness in certain other cases where the situation required that problems be met was so far-reaching that they even conceived a formula by which a marriage could be annulled by Rabbinical authority.[7]

Most revealing is the concern of the Halakhah with the practical requirements of every-day life. In the arrangement of the calendar the Rabbis had the authority to institute a "leap year" by inserting an additional month into the current year. All kinds of circumstances may call for a "leap year." Among them we find: the need to repair the roads, the bridges, and the ovens (in which the paschal lambs were to be roasted). All this was necessary in order to enable the people to reach Jerusalem in time and to offer the paschal sacrifice. Moving, however, is another reason for the postponement of the Passover festival. Had news been received that a group of Jews living in Exile had left on the journey to Jerusalem in order to celebrate the festival in the holy city, but that they could not arrive in time, the additional month of Adar was inserted and the festival delayed by one month.[8] Of course, in those days the Sanhedrin had the authority to determine the particulars of the calendar. Significant, however, is that purely practical considerations, or the desire not to disappoint some people who were looking forward to Passover in Jerusalem, were sufficient for them to invoke their authority and thus bring about a change in the dates on which all the festivals of the year were to be celebrated.

Into a similar category of Halakhic concern with the amenities of man's day-by-day existence belong the following two examples. Both are intended to render a woman more pleasing to her husband. Among the five forms of self-mortification which are prescribed for the observance of the Day of Atonement one also finds the prohibition to wash on that day. There are two exceptions to this rule. One is that of the bride, i.e., the woman during the first thirty days after her marriage. The reason given for the exception is most simply humane consideration: "that she should not appear unattractive before her husband."[9]

Furthermore, according to the Talmud, the "elders of a former generation" taught that, in order to eliminate temptation, a woman "should neither paint nor rouge herself nor clothe in attractive garments" during her monthly period. This was the rule until Rabbi Akiba came and abolished it, saying: "This way you render her unattractive for her husband, who may even divorce her."[10] As to the Biblical verse on which the ruling of "the former elders" was based,

7. *Gittin* 33b, 73a; *Ketuboth* 3a.
8, *Sanhedrin* 11a.
9. *Yoma* 73b; cf. the disagreement between the commentators as to whether the prohibition is a Biblical or a Rabbinic one.
10. *Shabbath* 64b.

Rabbi Akiba gave it a new interpretation. Here Rabbi Akiba determined the interpretation of the Biblical law in the interest of preserving material conditions tending to enhance marital happiness

We also find that ethical considerations elucidate Biblical meaning even in cases of purely ritual law, where an obligation obtains not "between man and his fellow," but "between man and God." The Talmud discusses the exact nature of "the branches of palm trees" and "the boughs of thick trees" that are used together with the *ethrog* and the willows in "the rejoicing before God" on the Succoth festival. After all the definitions of these two plants have been given, two questions are asked. The first refers to the *lulav,* the branches of the palm tree: Could it not be *kufra?* (*Kufra* are younger twigs on a palm tree which would satisfy all the requirements of the law.) The answer is that *kufra* could not have been meant by the Bible; for it is said of the Torah that "all her ways are ways of pleasantness." To us *kufra* would not be a pleasant way of fulfilling a commandment of the Torah, for the twigs of *kufra* are spiked, and the spikes could easily hurt the hand. Thus, it could not have been the intention of the Bible to use *kufra.*[11]

The second question deals with "the boughs of thick trees": Could not *hirduph* serve the same purpose? It would meet all the requirements. Two answers are given. The one, as before, rules out its leaves as stinging, which, therefore, do not qualify for "the ways of pleasantness." The second answer is based on a verse in *Zechariah* that enjoins man: "Therefore, love ye truth and peace." According to Raba's comment, *hirduph* would be a poor symbol for loving either truth or peace, for it is used for producing a lethal poison from its leaves.[12] In such interpretation of the Biblical intention the concern of the Halachah was to render the Torah meaningful with reference to its own all-embracing purpose of establishing life's discipline as ways of pleasantness and paths of peace.

Rather revealing, and pertinent for our analysis, is a discussion between the teachers of the Mishnah on the subject of capital punishment. The Bible, of course, does provide capital punishment for certain crimes. Yet Rabbi Tarphon and Rabbi Akiba maintained that, had they been members of the Sanhedrin at the time that it functioned as such, they would have seen to to it that no one should ever be executed.[13] They would have conducted the court procedure in such a manner that the Biblical law on capital pinishment would never have been applicable. We have here the case of an individual conscience interpreting the applicability of a Biblical law in accordance with its own Torah-imbued ethos. In a similar instance in another Mishnah it is the ethos of peace

11. *Sukkah* 32a.
12. *Ibid.,* 32b.
13. *Makkoth* 7a.

which determines a law of Sabbath observance. Since on the Sabbath it is forbidden to carry any burden, the question is discussed whether a man is permitted to carry arms on the Sabbath day. The majority opinion is that it is forbidden. Rabbi Eliezer, however, disagrees. According to him, arms are ornaments for a man and not a burden. To which the Sages replied: They are a disgrace for any man to carry, for does not the prophet look forward to the time when men will beat their swords into ploughshares and their spears into pruning-hooks, when "nation will not lift up sword against nation, neither shall they learn war any more."[14] Arms are a denial of the ideal of peace. To carry them can only be a shameful burden on man; therefore, one must not go out with them on the Sabbath. Here, too, it is an ethical conscience that determines the application of the law.

III

WE RECALL THESE EXAMPLES AT RANDOM— and they could be multiplied manifold from the vast domain of the Halakhah—in order to give substance to our thesis. We distinguish between the Law and Halakhah. Halakhah is not the Law but the Law applied—and by the manner of its application rendered meaningful—in a given situation.

The purpose of the Halakhah is to render the Torah in a given historic situation a) practically feasible; b) economically viable; c) ethically significant; d) spiritually meaningful.

Authentic is a Jewry that is based on Halakhah. But a Jewry is based on Halakhah if indeed Halakhah applies Torah to the contemporary situation. Halakhah is the bridge over which Torah enters reality, with the capacity to shape it meaningfully and in keeping with its own intention. Halakhah is the technique of Torah-application to a concrete contemporary situation. But while the Torah is eternal, the concrete historic stiuation is forever changing. Halakhah therefore, as the application of Torah in a given situation, will forever uncover new levels of Torah-depth and Torah-meaning and thus make new facets of Judaism visible. It was for this reason that we said earlier that Halakhah determines not only authenticity but also the uniqueness of each authentic Jewry. No Jewry is imitable or repeatable, because each authentic Jewry represents a single application of Torah to a specific constellation of conditions in which Jews find themselves at one time in their history.

Once this is understood, it is not difficult to realize that it is possible for Jews to live in accordance with the *Shulḥan Arukh* and yet not have authentic Judaism. We shall illustrate our point with the help of a few contemporary examples.

We first turn our attention to the area of what is practically feas-

14. *Shabbath* 63a.

ible. The new reality of Jewish existence which is emerging in the State of Israel offers us ample material. We limit our discussion to only two contemporary problems. The one is that of the *sh'mitah* year. According to Biblical law, the land is not to be cultivated in every seventh year. What is to be done about this law in a Jewish State in the twentieth century? Can such a Jewish State economically afford to let all land lie fallow every seventh year? The problem is, of course, nothing basically new. It existed in the colonies in Palestine even prior to the establishment of the State. However in the context of the over-all economy of a modern state that is still struggling for its very survival, it presses with far greater urgency and intensity than before. Halkhic authorities of a previous generation have dealt with the problem, and some found a solution within the frame of Halakhah. It is not our task here to enter into an analysis of their solution. What concerns us is the manner in which a group of strictly observant Jews, who reject the proferred solution of the problem, met the challenge. They conceived the idea of forming a fund to support the settlements that let their fields lie untilled in the *sh'mita* year. The money was raised among Jews in America and in other countries. There can be no doubt that this is an inauthentic way of observing the *Sh'mita* commandment. It could never have been the Biblical intention to observe the sabbatical year by fund-raising in America. To go to America for funds was an evasion of the Halakhic issue. It was non-application of Torah to a given situation. It was inauthentic Judaism.

Another illustration of the point we are making we discern in the still unsettled autopsy controversy in the State of Israel. There can be no doubt that things are happening in this area of Israeli life that constitute wanton disregard of the *sancta* of Judaism in matters of respect due to even the dead forms of the carriers of human life. But not all the blame is to be placed at the door of the physicians. Physicians are not professionally vicious people. The question is: Is there a Halachic solution to the problem that will be based on the principles of the Law in these matters and yet take adequate note of the inescapable needs of the istuation? Can any modern society exist without normal conditions for possibilities of medical progress? Can such conditions exist in the State of Israel if the ultimate wisdom of the Halakhic authorities stops short at the *p'sak* of the *Nodeh Biyhuda* in eighteenth-century Prague? If the answer is that there is no Halachic solution to the problem that will satisfy the Law as well as the inescapable need, then we have confessed that the Torah is not a *torat ḥayim,* a "Torah of life." We may then have formal adherence to the *Shulḥan Arukh* and yet not have authentic, Halakhic Judaism.

Surveying the scene closer home, we note the bizzare educational ideal of the old-world *yeshivot* in the United States. It propagates the type of the completely one-sided Talmudist, without admitting the validity of any different kind of educational goal. Now, this *yeshivah* ideal works because it is limited to a very small number of Jewish youth. But what would happen if all Jews would accept this one-sided educational goal? The result would be a catastrophe; for American Jewry could not exist in practical economic, professional, political, and social dimensions. What is true of the United States is even more true of the State of Israel. Never has the world experienced a state of *yeshivah-baḥurim;* nor could such a state survive. That any kind of Judaism in depth is not conceivable without *yeshivot* need not be argued. But the *yeshivah* has to be integrated into the life of the larger community. Its educational goal must be an organic part of a comprehensive educational philosophy, which, if adopted by the entire community, will render Judaism meaningfully viable for all. The old-world *yeshivah* in the State of Israel as well as in America depends for its very existence on the support of a vast Jewry that is rejected by its own educational ideal. It succeeds because it fails, because it cannot be taken seriously by the overwhelming majority of the Jewish people. It represents an inauthentic form of Judaism, because, if embraced by the Jewish people, neither the Jewish people nor its *yeshivot* could maintain themselves.

Probably the most serious cases of an inauthentic adherence to the Law we find in the ethical and moral realm. Our reference is first of all to those laws which affect the status of the woman. The problem of the *agunah,* the deserted woman or the woman whose husband's whereabouts have become unknown, has been with us for generations. It has, however, become more serious in our times than it has been even before. First of all, the problem has been psychologically aggravated. Conditions have changed, mores have changed, the position of the woman in society has changed. People are no longer willing to put up with the problem as they might have done in earlier times. The unresolved status of the problem drives numerous people away from Halakhic Judaism. Often the woman is penalized because of the attitude of the husband. He may refuse to give a *get* out of spite or because, exploiting the situation, he makes monetary demands on his wife or on her family in return for a religious divorce. At times a husband may reject the very thought of a religious divorce for ideological reasons. The problem of the *agunah* is a critical problem of Jewish ethics. It challenges the entire concept of *drakheha darkhei noam,* that the ways of the Torah are ways of pleasantness. It is unquestionably a grave injustice to the woman. Its consequences often lead to self-defeating futility, for in the majority of such problematic cases the parties accept the civil divorce as final and remarry without the benefit of a *get.* The most serious aspect of the problem is that in the consciousness of our generation it represents a critical challenge to the ethical quality of Halakhic Judaism. In the consciousness of our generation the *agunah* problem has become a scandal. No matter what excuses or reasons are given for its continued existence, the scandal is a scandal and remains a scandal. The insistence that nothing can be done about it within the framework of the Halakhah is worse than a misrepresentation. It is a confession that the Torah cannot meaningfully cope with a given situation. It is non-authentic Judaism.

In the Talmud there are entire groups of *hilkhot* based on the principle of *darkhei shalom*. According to a Talmudic statement, *kol ha-torah kulah,* the entire Torah was conceived for the sake of "the ways of peace."[15] Yet it is the trend of Halakhah which is motivated by the pursuit of *darkhei shalom* which seems to be most neglected by our contemporary devotion to an unauthentic adherence to the law. Concepts of tolerence, freedom, and freedom of conscience have become recognized values of human decency that dare not be denied. Our very existence depends on them. We claim them for ourselves. It is neither practical, nor morally possible, to claim these values for ourselves in our dealings with the non-Jewish world and deny them internally to our fellow Jews who may disagree with us in their interpretation of Judaism. We are, of course, referring to certain conditions in the State of Israel. The claim of what is known as Conservative or Reform Judaism to equality with Orthodoxy in the Jewish state is morally irrefutable. Naturally, there are problems inherent in the situation, not the least among them how best to safeguard the unity of the people. All this does not free us from the responsibility to recognize the right of all branches of Judaism to equality of treatment.

Perhaps here, too, the solution lies in authenticity. Halakhah will have to have the intellectual courage to recognize that the scandal in the area of the position of the woman must be resolved and can be resolved. Once a solution is found to the *agunah* problem one might be able to proceed to marriage and divorce legislation that will represent a consensus among all branches of Jewry in the interest of the preservation of the unity of the people on the basis of the Halakhah. But only authentic Judaism may hope to accomplish this task.

In every case where questions of ethics are involved in a problem, the contemporary *posek* might do well to bear in mind a statement quoted in the commentary on the *Mishneh Torah* by the author of the *Magid Mishneh*. In connection with a rule on good neighborliness, which was a Halakhic innovation, he explains: "In order to bring about a correction in the quality of human behavior, our perfect Torah gave us general principles, like, 'Thou shalt be holy' . . . and thus it was also said, 'Thou shalt do that which is right and good.' The intention is that man should conduct himself toward his fellow in a manner that

15. *Gittin* 59b.

is good and right. It was not proper in such matters to spell out the rules in detail. Commandments are for all times and in all circumstances, and one is obligated to obey them. But the character traits of man and his conduct change according to times and individuals. Our sages, of blessed memory, left us some helpful particular rules under the general principles . . ."[16] It would seem, then, that it is the responsibility of contemporary Halakhah to take due cognizance of these changes in conduct "according to the times and the individuals" and in their light to determine the specific rules that follow from the general principles of Biblical teaching. In the area of the ethically "right and good" this is the road to authenticity.

* * *

It is the spiritual tragedy of Orthodox Judaism that our inadequacy has lost us the creative power of the Halakhah. The ethos of the Halakahah is lingering in a state of inauthenticity in the barren scholarship of most contemporary Halakhists. The fault does not lie with the Halakhah but with the Halakhists. Misunderstanding its essential nature, they misrepresent it unwittingly and misapply it self-righteously. The future of Judaism depends on the Halakhah. The future of the Halakhah depends on our ability to restore its original function, to retrieve its spirit of authenticity. We need determined commitment to Halachic Judaism and sustained systematic and comprehensive scholarly investigation into the nature and the possibilities of the Halakhah. But this must be paralleled by a serious understanding of the daily realities of our contemporary life and by participation in them. Lack of commitment, or *am ha'aratsut* (ignorance of Halakhic Judaism), will not give us Halakhah; withdrawal from reality and continued ignoring of the challenges of the contemporary situation will not give us authentic Judaism.

One might give definition of authentic Judaism by referring to a Talmudic saying. Commenting on the verse in *Psalms,* "I shall walk before the Lord in the lands of the living," Rabbi Yehudah remarked: "The lands of the living? These are the market places."[17] What is authentic Judaism? It is the application of Torah to "the market places" of our existence, to the historic reality and uniqueness of our contemporary situation. This is the very essence of the Halakhah. There is no other way to walk before God in the lands of the living.

16. *Magid Mishneh,* Maimonides, *Hilkhot Shekhenim* 14, 5.
17. *Yoma* 71a.

Oscar Z. Fasman

The author of this essay, a distinguished rabbi, communal leader and educator, is President Emeritus of the Hebrew Theological College in Skokie, Illinois.

TRENDS IN THE AMERICAN YESHIVA TODAY

From 1922 to 1930, during my years of study at the Hebrew Theological College, it was my privilege to meet with and listen to some of the great Talmudists of that generation. I discovered that the Rav of Lomza, the Gaon Judah Leib Gordon, acknowledged universally as a great rabbinic authority, knew astronomy, mathematics, Russian literature, and even the theory of music. The renowned Gaon of Lublin, Rabbi Meir Shapiro, was one of the most brilliant Polish orators, whose command of the Polish language could spellbind the parliament in which he sat. The genius of Talmud at the Hildesheimer Seminary, Rabbi Yechiel Weinberg, whose Talmudic competence was held in high esteem in the Lithuanian Yeshivot, towered in his wide cultural erudition. I remember the amazement of our class in Codes one day when the saintly sage who instructed us, Rabbi Chaim Korb, mentioned that he had read Shakespeare in German in his younger years, and there lingers in my memory the volume of Spinoza in Yiddish that surprised me upon entering the home of my former Rosh Yeshiva, Rabbi Nissan Yablonsky, who had been a Dayan and Rosh Yeshiva in Slabodka. We all knew, of course, that the versatile Talmudist, Dr. Bernard Revel, the distinguished president of the Rabbi Isaac Elchanan Theological Seminary in New York, was remarkably competent in the broad area of the humanities.

To be sure, there were many great rabbis at that time whose scholarly achievements were limited exclusively to the field of Talmudic learning, but they did not ridicule nor attack their peers who had included ingredients of wisdom from other storehouses. On the contrary, there was the important statement of a student of the Gaon of Vilna, "To the degree that a person is deficient in his knowledge of other sciences, he will be deficient one hundred portions in Torah wisdom, because Torah and science are intertwined." In the same age, some two centuries ago, the chief rabbi of Berlin, Zvi Hirsch Levin, wrote also, "While the very essence of Torah establishes it as the mistress, and all other departments of wisdom are its handmaidens, yet it is not fitting to ignore them." The immortal of Pressburg, Rabbi Moses Sofer, whom secular historians generally describe as an extremist, engaged a tutor for his children to instruct them in worldly subjects and languages. Certainly, the knowledge of a foreign language or the understanding of a mathematical or scientific treatise did not constitute *prima facie* evidence of an inclination to heresy.

A radical change occurred in the Yeshivot after World War I. The bloody experiences of the Jewish communities in Europe during and after those years of slaughter and pogrom made all values associated with the gentile world intolerable, so that the young students of Talmud avoided every manifestation of general culture. Religious life concentrated completely upon a carefully isolated and self-centered sphere. Whoever dared to break out in the slightest measure was suspected of treasonable motives, and sometimes the suspicion itself drove him out of the inner circles of the pious to an irreligious way of life. It is interesting to note that the new generation of Talmudic scholars that frowned upon even nibbling at non-Torah intellectual food did not by any means excel in profundity and extensive familiarity with Talmudic sources those scholars of the preceding era who permitted themselves such educational excursions.

Since the initial Orthodox rabbinical schools in the United States, first the New York school now known as Yeshiva University, and later the Hebrew Theological College in Chicago, were organized by Talmudists of the earlier age, it was accepted that the students could combine secular learning with their religious disciplines. Indeed, it was felt that young men who would seek to build the Jewish loyalties of American Jews needed an intensive general education to understand the men and women of their congregations and to convey through the pulpit an intelligible interpretation of Torah purposes. Although the inspiring teachers in these seminaries never wearied of urging upon their young listeners the transcendent importance of more and more Torah knowledge, deeper and deeper piety, they simultaneously extolled the ideal of communal service, the responsibility of plunging into the activities of congregations everywhere in order to stir the Jewish masses out of their religious indifference and tragic ignorance. The earlier classes of our Chicago Yeshiva remember how much love for Judaism was instilled into us by Rabbi H. Rubinstein, who often interrupted his lecture to tell us of his experiences with the members of his congregation, hoping that we might profit by them and learn the affection and tact needed to draw men closer to Heaven. Long and bitter battles were fought over what techniques should be used, what strategic concessions might be made, what spiritual risks the young rabbi must take with his personal preferences and the education of his own children on the altar of rescuing hundreds and thousands from assimilation. No simple formula was ever developed and no total agreement was ever reached, but the fundamental objective was widely shared that the American Yeshivot must train scholars whose love of halakhic books and unshakable religious convictions would be wed to a passionate desire to raise the Torah dedication of the Jewish public throughout the land. There was a strong consensus on the high value of a college degree as a tool in the attainment of the latter goal.

The climate of the Orthodox rabbinical seminaries became transformed with the arrival of the Talmudists who suffered through the Hitler catastrophe and lost both their nearest of kin and their Jewish world. The indifference to general culture and opposition to all forms of non-Torah learning that characterized the post-World War I period turned into an intensive hatred after World War II. What could be more natural than to despise the whole system of norms and social procedures of governments that murdered defenseless people, including more than a million children, or that observed such barbarian slaughter without a word of protest? As the spokesmen of this new wave of Roshei Yeshiva were brought into the classrooms of the American institutions, they introduced a violent spirit of negativism towards every manifestation of modern civilization. Wherever possible, they discouraged the students from enrolling at any colleges; or if they found their disciples required higher education to earn a living — accounting and mathematics were becoming popular fields for Orthodox Jews — it was clearly spelled out that only the skills should be pursued, but the values should be expunged forever from the mind. In a similar vein, since government and anti-Semitism had proved themselves in Europe to be synonymous, every genuine *ben Torah* would regard patriotic customs with suspicion; for example, he would avoid turkey on Thanksgiving, and he would piously turn away from the barbaric fireworks displays of July Fourth. (This attitude to government seems to have been intensified by the situation in the State of Israel, where the irreligious dominate the cabinet and Knesset, and where piety consequently expresses itself in many Yeshivot, for example, in refusing to honor *Yom ha-Atzmaut.*) Although Halakhah applies several technical restrictions to the precept "and ye shall not follow their statutes" to protect the observant from pagan practices and foreign religious habits, the impression was strongly circulated among the students that *anything* "goyim" do must never be imitated by Torah-guided people. Emphatically in this area, there was a total elimination of a major Talmudic premise, *koach d'hetera adif,* to uncover possibilities of permissiveness within the law demonstrates a higher power.

Of particular concern in these new ranks of Talmudists was the danger that would inevitably befall a young man who would make his home among non-observant Jews. Even though he would move among them as their rabbi, he might accept more from them than he would give, with a resultant deficit in the spiritual balance of trade. Admittedly, there was a solid basis in experience for these fears: a long generation of American-trained Orthodox rabbis was heavily pock-marked with defections, and a sad number of extremely devoted Yeshiva *bachurim* who had entered the rough arena of congregational leadership had lost no inconsiderable measure of their idealism. Rather than undertake a solution along the lines of better preparation, more carefully planned indoctrination, more thorough research into the factors responsible for weakening of principle — after all, there were impressive statistics of American-trained men who had successfully and triumphantly met the challenges — the recently appointed

Roshei Yeshiva went to great pains to deride the rabbinical career, to discourage their students from entertaining any thought of the pulpit, and to urge them to seek the kind of employment that would keep them geographically safe, surrounded by their own kind of religiously committed families, and holding positions that would not tempt them to depart from any established patterns.

To make certain that the rabbinical life would not appear attractive, additional viewpoints were injected into the perspective of the students. Non-Orthodox Jews, it was insinuated, were disreputable creatures; while the instructor was generally cautious in conveying this impression, since he knew that very often the funds to keep the seminary doors open came from such people, the uninhibited youth spoke of them as *posh'im, goyim, apikorsim, etc.* An unfortunate corollary rose to the surface when fierce battles broke out in the homes of students whose parents were not observant, and the rabbis sought to reconcile the Fifth Commandment with the disrespect bred into their students toward irreligious Jews. The trend, of course, was likewise far from wholesome when the question of gentiles was involved. Obviously, young men with such attitudes would scarcely consider leadership in a synagogue with very few Sabbath observers or kosher homes, and such institutions as brotherhood week and interfaith committees. (Occasionally, it should be noted, character proves stronger than propaganda, and one meets a pious son who displays admirable reverence for his irreligious parents, a Yeshiva bachur who esteems the divine image in a person of a different creed, a young Talmudist who dares to accept a pulpit in a midwestern town.) In fact, the Yeshivot of the United States have contributed more than they know to the diminution of reverence for the Rav in most communities, since their students show so little elementary courtesy to the spiritual leaders in our country that the general public considers the Rav unworthy; is he not derided by sincere young Talmudists?

Orthodox Judaism will ultimately pay a heavy price for this negative approach to the spiritual needs of the American Jewish masses. For one thing, an iron curtain will be drawn between the religious and the irreligious, or more accurately, a progression of iron curtains, since every group that considers its standards of observance more stringent will cut itself off from those of alleged lesser devotion. The opportunities for reaching promising children of ordinary Jewish homes and attracting them to higher Talmudic studies will diminish. Sources of financial support for Yeshivot in non-Orthodox circles will begin to run dry, as the contributors become disgusted with the disparaging attitudes they encounter among the observant. Federations in small communities, leaders in average towns, will reduce still further their already inadequate allocations, when they discover they can expect no assistance from the Orthodox seminaries in solving the problem of manpower shortage in the traditional rabbinate.

An unsuspected penalty will be the actual weakening of Talmudic competence in the seminaries. The Oral Law of Judaism has ever been a living organism, deriving its body in direct descent from Mount Sinai and sustaining its growth by the nourishment drawn from interpenetrating communal experience. When we remember the brilliant Talmudic accomplishments of the eastern European academies from the sixteenth to the twentieth century, we must bear in mind that what was learned in the study hall served as guidelines in the street, market and home. The rabbi could pore day and night over the most abstruse section of ancient lore, but his acumen was called upon to deal with the real problems of the men, women and children under his care. Thus, a stream of consciousness and conscience flowed ceaselessly from the passages of the Gemara into the thought and practice of the struggling, suffering, working, playing people of the village, and that stream itself became deeper and broader in the process. If in the United States the Roshei Yeshiva will dam up the stream, a sizable lake may be formed, but of stagnant waters. Historians are beginning to ask already, why the thousands of American-trained Orthodox rabbinical students of this recent intensive Talmudic period publish infinitely fewer volumes of Talmudic novellae and responsa than their European parallels. Is it not logical to conclude that a Torah scholarship divorced from life falls victim to sterility?

Today Orthodox Jewry abounds in Talmudists who spent many years at an Academy hoping to be appointed to posts in advanced schools but find themselves teaching children nine or ten years old in a Day School, where often their vast knowledge is an impediment to effectiveness, and they taste the full bitterness of frustration. Such men can hardly become creative writers. They might have, had they gone to serve an adult congregation, no matter how ignorant and unobservant. Halakhah, I once wrote, is the hand of God reaching out to people; where there is no reaching out there is no living Halakhah.

Significantly, Judaism once boasted of its great academies of learning in Europe and lamented the *am haaratzut* of the Jews in America, but the United States began to develop rabbinical schools where spiritual bridge-builders were trained — men who could follow the intricacies of a Talmudic lecture by a Lithuanian, Polish or Hungarian Gaon and who were no less at home in a room with American intellectuals. Such rabbis sent many a bright youngster from the local Hebrew School to a Yeshiva in the great Jewish centers, and such rabbis were instrumental in establishing Day Schools in dozens of communities. Such rabbis were equipped to serve Jewish college students on campus by becoming Hillel Foundation directors, and such rabbis kept young people in uniform in touch with intensive Torah loyalties when they volunteered as chaplains in the Army, Navy and Air Force. To the extent that the new Orthodox philosophy of the Yeshiva world takes deeper root will the numbers of Orthodox Hillel leaders and chaplains be reduced, and where there was once a bridge there will be only the widest chasm. Can we have highways in modern Jewry if our spiritual engineers are taught to build vertical spans only, none of horizontal function?

Strange things have been happening to the character of students breathing this anti-social air. A view has become widespread among Yeshiva students that the paramount goal of concentration upon Torah learning justifies a reduction, in some degree, of proper standards to pass high school and college examinations. Inasmuch as a diploma is nothing but "a piece of paper," often required to be able to provide for a wife and children, certain mild liberties in acquiring it may be forgiven, if thereby more hours are reserved for Torah learning. The outstanding Talmudists of the old school have attempted to campaign against this approach, yet the forces let loose by their basic aversion to university values have become too powerful to be easily checked.

No less disconcerting is a sad carelessness in the treatment of public property. Were there an effective carry-over from the classes in *Nezikin* (Damages) the floors, tables and chairs in every senior Yeshiva would be a noble demonstration of how ardently a *ben Torah* cherishes the value of things donated by benefactors. But alas! the appearance of rooms and halls is rarely such a demonstration. While the school losses due to youthful malice constitute a national problem in the United States, one might reasonably expect nothing of that character in schools of intensive religious motivation. The explanation once again is to be sought in the philosophy of denying significance to anything associated with modern life. It was hard to keep things tidy in the poverty-ridden ghettos of Poland, and tidiness is therefore too modern, inconsistent with the ideal of Talmudic erudition — some such subconscious reasoning seems to prevail in many seminaries.

A psychological approach in addition to this sociological interpretation suggests itself. Adolescents need outlets for their frustrations, and the young Yeshiva student experiences not only the normal frustrations of the teen-ager, perhaps compounded by his almost total isolation from the other sex, but there is a gnawing intuition of inadequacy in the attainment of the ideal goals of piety prescribed by his teachers. The visible manifestation is constructed out of many individual acts of devotion: remaining in meditation during silent prayer a minute longer than his friend, wearing a more conspicuous *talit katan,* eating the bitter herbs at the seder "the size of an olive" where the olive appears larger than a grapefruit — an entire system of ritualistic escalation wrapping itself around his physical movements until he disregards any obligations to mere physical objects in detail or the physical environment in general. Even towards teachers there is an occasional outburst of *chutzpah,* and boys who cannot quarrel with girls enter into bitter fights between themselves. The Torah, to be sure, exercises all its disciples in restraint, so that nothing remotely similar to the violence of juvenile delinquency ever occurs at a Yeshiva, but young people encouraged to deride as unholy anything and everything in the total society about them suffer scars.

A term has been introduced into the vocabulary of the Orthodox community, *Daat Torah,* the Torah opinion. It covers the entire range of contemporary problems, private and public. Although there may be no specific law in Halakhah to apply in a given situation, the Torah scholars, by virtue of their erudition, may make the best decision on what should be done, and their opinion is binding. It is painful to observe that some of the great Talmudists have neither the experience nor the inclination to study the issues but take the analysis submitted by their practical associates and junior colleagues or disciples and render judgment accordingly. Not always, therefore, does a proclamation of the great Roshei Yeshiva represent a conclusion objectively reached, for it may be the conviction of an individual or several individuals advising them, and quite conceivably the viewpoint of another group without the same easy access to the Roshei Yeshiva would have been more valuable in the totality of Torah development.

Two specific examples merit particular attention. In an earlier generation the leading English-speaking Orthodox rabbis of New York participated in the New York Board of Rabbis and the Synagogue Council of America. The outstanding Talmudic scholars of that time saw no basis for protest and certainly never attacked the idea. Indeed, men who are today held in high reverence in the Agudat Yisroel movement helped to found the Board and the Council. In the wake of the new intensive American Orthodoxy several of the younger Orthodox rabbis approached the Roshei Yeshiva and gave them a one-sided picture of how the Board and Council function, with little or no mention of the positive values derived from speaking with a united voice in the public relations sphere on issues of immigration, discrimination, relief, anti-communism, anti-fascism, etc. Since those who were involved in the activities of the Board and Council were not invited to meetings of study and investigation, eleven Roshei Yeshiva concluded that the *Daat Torah,* now called the Halakhah, requires a ban on membership in mixed bodies of rabbis. Obviously, since there was no clear Halakhah on the subject, else there never would have been Orthodox rabbis there in the first place, or there would have been an outcry of protest at the very beginning, what happened was a rabbinical decision based on hearing only one side of the case and failing to take into account the damage that might accrue to American Orthodoxy. One wonders, even granting that a mixed Board of Rabbis is harmful to the Torah position, whether a distinction should not have been recognized between inaugurating such a Board where it did not exist — it is understandable that not in every time and not in every locality are circumstances identical — and destroying one that has operated for decades. A postscript may be in place: at least one of the eleven who signed the ban stated subsequently it was meant as a private guideline to rabbis who were uncertain about joining, but it was not intended for public pronouncement.

The second illustration comes from the midwest. In Chicago the Hebrew Theological College was an Orthodox rabbinical seminary granting Semicha since 1922. All the great Roshei Yeshiva who came to visit the United States gave Talmudic lectures there. To list a few: Rabbi Moshe Mordecai Epstein of Slobodka, Rabbi Shimon Shkop of Grodno, Rabbi Meir Shapiro of Lublin, Rabbi A. I. Bloch of Telshe, Rabbi L. Y. Finkel of Mir, Rabbi Aaron Kotler of Kletsk, Rabbi Elchanan Wasserman of Baranowicz (all of blessed memory) and Rabbi J. Kahaneman of Ponovez. In the same building where the young men studied, classes were held for young women who were trained to become Hebrew teachers. To be sure, there were no mixed classes, but there might be a lecture for young men at 7 p.m. in one room and in the very next room at the same hour a course for young women. From 1947-56 the Men's Dormitory was in the next building. None of the Roshei Yeshiva at the Hebrew Theological College from 1922 until 1956 ever lodged a complaint about this arrangement, and some of them enrolled their daughters in these classes while their sons were regular students in the Yeshiva.

In 1958 the Yeshiva opened a new large campus in Skokie, a Chicago suburb. Plans were announced for a Women's College to be built on the east end of the campus, approximately as far away as 37th Street is from 34th Street in Manhattan and farther away than the Beth Jacob Teachers Seminary for Women in Brooklyn was from the Chafetz Chaim Yeshiva for many years. Furthermore, after some sharp arguments on the subject, the Yeshiva Board voted to have only the classrooms for women on the campus, while the dormitory would be much farther away. Nevertheless a few Roshei Yeshiva in the east issued an *Issur* on locating the Women's College on the Skokie campus. These Roshei Yeshiva never came personally to see the actual location, never consulted the Chicago administration, and proclaimed the *Issur*. Again there was obviously no halakhic precept involved, only a matter of judgment of whether or not the existence of an Orthodox women's college without dormitories three blocks away from a rabbinical school would violate the conscience of Orthodoxy, and a *Daat Torah* was shaped into Halakhah without investigating all aspects of the issue or even considering such factors as past history and communal need.

This last element brings up a delicate point. As before we found ritualistic escalation, we now encounter halakhic escalation. There is almost a terror among rabbis of being left behind in the race to establish maximum standards, and each Gaon raises the bar an inch or two higher. Since the authority to find a *kula,* a less exacting norm, has ever been regarded as stemming from greater erudition, our contemporary Talmudists have become exceedingly humble, and exceedingly cautious. Furthermore, whoever dares to suggest a somewhat easier approach to a problem is overwhelmed by scorn or abuse. Torah periodicals published in the United States abound in new *chumrot,* until restrictions are multiplied upon restrictions and piety is driven into ever novel extremes. If occasionally some scholar suggests that Halakhah should meet the challenge of our day by extending its principles in conformity with its own formulas of growth, no matter how scrupulously he observes the practices of the Shulchan Arukh, he is branded a dangerous reformer; and whoever permits him to speak or write has sealed a covenant with the enemies of the faith. Thus the forward movement of Halakhah becomes thwarted and the phenomena in our world are denied reality because they cannot be fitted into the fixed categories of the past Talmudic generation. In a strong sense, the refusal to allow Halakhah to develop in every direction and not merely to travel the most stringent path will create Torah pygmies. Torah giants knew that there are opportunities for leniency as well as for severity in the majestic vastness of Halakhah, and that that realization must never be banished from the thought of our decision-makers. Even where an honored Talmudist is bold enough to advance a more permissive theory, it will be located today in the area of some particular ritualistic rule but seldom in the broad perspective of major social issues. A happy exception can be indicated only in the offices of the nation-wide chief rabbinate in Israel, where the halakhic judges must come to grips with the daily problems of an expanding political and economic society; and, although impatient voices cry out in Orthodox circles there, especially in the religious kibbutzim, against the slow pace of the rabbis in providing guidance on the swift changes confronting observant people, we must acknowledge the dynamic responsiveness of some of the younger Talmudic leaders to the new issues. In the United States, however, what one social analyst terms the halakhic "freeze" threatens to become a forbidding glacier.

The position of the few who reject the philosophy of ever greater internal congealment, of ever taller barricades between the chosen within the Talmudic stockade and the forsaken outside, is far from comfortable. Men of tremendous Talmudic prestige like Dr. Joseph B. Soloveitchik and Dr. Samuel Belkin, whose outstanding abilities in the general fields of human knowledge have been combined with the loftiest status in the halakhic world, are not really "in" as far as the majority of the Yeshivot and their heads are concerned. These two scholars believe in keeping open the lines of communication between the fervent halls of the academy and the ignorant, indifferent lanes of the congregational bowling league. While they joyfully write in every youth who asks for instruction, they do not write off those who do not. Yet it is precisely the open line of communication which is shunned by the post-World War II Roshei Yeshiva. They welcome into their midst the lost soul of an untutored lad who in some miraculous way discovered in himself a desire to become *frum,* but they will tolerate no exodus of their students into the wilds of the larger Jewish community. This permanent division denies to the Jewish public the elevation of being in contact with men of Torah and denies to the men of Torah the chance to serve a total people.

The latter denial has resulted in the development of a general attitude sometimes referred to as *bittul,* a term with so many overtones that no English word is an adequate translation. Particularly prevalent among Yeshiva students between the ages of sixteen and thirty, it is reflected in phrase, expression and gesture to indicate that people not of our type are unworthy of quotation or even of mention. Why listen to anything such people say, why observe anything they do, why be interested in their experiences? Because the human mind cannot cage viewpoints once embraced, the philosophy of *bittul* never ends, however, with this derisive sneering at only those far out of the circle, and often a Torah student is deeply wounded by the discovery that his method of interpreting a complex paragraph in the Code of Maimonides is brushed aside without any reverence by scholars of another school. A wise observer one remarked that the Talmudists who spent all their years in Yeshiva X took the position that the woman who scrubbed the floor there before Passover really understood Jewish law better than the sages in Yeshiva Y. Where the atmosphere is so conditioned, there is little chance, obviously, for any desire to become acquainted with the masterpieces of man's creative genius in literature, painting and music.

History, we are often told, moves in cycles. We have good cause to believe, therefore, that the philosophy of total withdrawal from the modern world and total disparagement of its cultural worth will gradually recede in the Talmudic age unfolding ahead of us. The realization will dawn upon Yeshiva leaders that we dare not abandon the masses, and that we cannot rely upon the automatic radiation of Torah dedication to reach them. What is beginning to disturb the equanimity of many Roshei Yeshiva is the discovery that the absence of Orthodox rabbis in smaller communities opens the door to non-Orthodox rabbis to take charge. Disorganized ignorance is difficult enough, but how can one meet organized opposition to the eternal patterns of Jewish observance? Voices are occasionally heard in the inner Yeshiva circles that perhaps just sitting and learning Torah all day and all night will not turn back the tide of anti-Halakhah attitudes instilled by anti-Halakhah spiritual leaders. Acknowledging that Day Schools have tremendous significance in advancing Torah ideals, the Roshei Yeshiva permit their students to work in them, even though almost invariably contact will then be made with many non-Orthodox parents, and certain compromises will follow; for example, it has been accepted that in smaller cities the Day Schools will generally be co-educational, and there may sometimes be public functions where the singing of girls will be heard, where men and women will dine at the same tables, and where even social dancing will be allowed. It is sad to reflect, however, upon the logical inconsistencies that appear: a Rosh Yeshiva will permit his student to teach in a school where the children attend a synagogue without separate seating for men and women, but will not permit his student to take the pulpit in that synagogue. Let us grant nevertheless that the complete isolation has been weakened somewhat, and that we can look forward to a cycle characterized by increasing contact with the big world beyond the walls of the Yeshiva.

Similarly, the *Jewish Observer* recently published a suggestion that the Yeshivot should consider building a four-year college. The reasoning behind the suggestion duplicates rather closely the arguments advanced by the late Dr. Revel, when he opened Yeshiva College, and by the late Rabbi Silber, when he predicted a similar development in the Yeshiva in Chicago. Significantly, these pioneers in senior Yeshiva trailblazing did not argue that every Yeshiva should have a college under its auspices, only that those with a desire to train modern pulpit personalities needed such a college, where the faculty would acknowledge the spiritual interests of the student body and not, as in most universities, undermine them. In any event, although conceivably not all *Jewish Observer* editors agreed with the bold proposal, publication of this suggestion in those jealously guarded pages may not be a wind of change, but a whisper of a breeze, perhaps?

To add to the signs of reversal in policy among Orthodox extremists we may note that the rabbinical journal *Hapardes,* whose editor is chairman of the Agudat Yisroel Executive Committee, has called for a reappraisal of the status of the professional rabbinate. Several writers have demanded that once again the rabbinical seminaries urge their ordained graduates to enter pulpits, and that the attitudes of the students be directed towards reverence for men who accept the responsibility of Jewish spiritual leadership in various congregations. A highly revered sage in Brooklyn has recommended the idea of attaching young rabbis to old men in the active profession, lest the next generation find itself without men who can carry through the essential functions of Halakhah, such as writing a *Get,* arranging a *Chalitzah,* and supervising a kosher abattoir. Such voices, to be sure, have not harmonized into a powerful chorus for change, but they may introduce key notes in a coming symphony.

The country that has witnessed the glorious music of a new day in Jewry, the land of Israel, has added in the last few years a most challenging development. Dr. Gershon Swimmer of Kfar Haroeh, one of our most brilliant educators, tells of the opposition encountered when the Bnei Akiva Yeshivot were first created as a system of religious high schools with a curriculum combining intensive Talmudic studies and secular subjects. Dr. Swimmer was summoned to Jerusalem by the head of one of the world-renowned rabbinical seminaries and was the object of a long lecture about the harm he and Rabbi Neriah, chief architect of the project, were introducing into religious education. The gist of the argument revolved about the established procedure that a boy who completes an elementary school general program should devote the entire day (and night) of study to Torah subjects exclusively for many years. If he wishes to learn anything of a secular character, let him leave the Yeshiva entirely. Dr.

Swimmer refused to withdraw from the philosophy of the Bnei Akiva ideal, that a modern Jewish state required men of general cultural attainment and scientific competence who are also deeply rooted in Talmudic profundity. At that time it was Mizrachi that encouraged the Bnei Akiva viewpoint, and it was the Agudat Yisroel that denounced it. What has happened since then? The recognized rabbinic leadership of Agudat Yisroel is now on record in favor of organizing Chinuch Atzmai high schools, and seeks to establish such schools where secular subjects would be part of the curriculum. Even more, Agudat Yisroel leaders have spoken in complimentary terms about Bnei Akiva high schools, since some of their graduates continued their religious studies at the advanced Yeshivot in Israel and proved themselves as accomplished in Talmudic insight and comprehension as their peers coming up through the schools of an exclusive Talmudic curriculum.

The transformation cannot come too swiftly. Many years of sweat and toil will be needed to recapture from the non-Orthodox sectors of Judaism the vast areas of community life they have swept into their control. One of their mightiest armaments in the field of propaganda is the portrayal of Orthodoxy as reactionary fanaticism. The more pronounced the Orthodox extremism, the more easily can they merchandise their sundry brands of tolerance and goodwill. For the average layman Judaism has become one tremendous discount house, where he can purchase the eternal guarantees of his faith at reduced rates, making the high sacrifices of the observant seem like the wasteful expenditure of means and efforts, especially when the end product is in his eyes an anti-social, uncultured and ill-mannered boor. Yet the easier alternatives grasped by the contemporary Jew, presented in inviting patterns by superb pulpit salesmen, can lead to the ultimate tragedy of disappearance, while even the worst strategic errors of Orthodoxy will not undo its essential pattern for survival. If the goal of Torah is to introduce stability into the character of man, then obviously an interpretation of Torah in terms of flexibility, relativity, frequent variation of philosophy, and relentless revision of ritual defeats the very purpose for which the divine gift was made at Sinai. Experience has established that the children of a carelessly-garbed travelling *meshullach,* who can tear into a man with a stream of low invective for refusing to contribute, are more likely to uphold their Jewish heritage than the sons of the immaculate gentleman who admires the voice of the Christian tenor in the choir. The unwashed ghettos of Lemberg produced committed Jews; the luxurious apartments of Riverside Drive have added to the forces of assimilation. Yet no progressive Orthodox leader will endorse a return to poverty and filth, any more than he will go along with the reactionary rejection of contemporary culture. To him the challenge of our day is to forge a combination of Torah ideals, practice and learning with the major values of civilization, and he acknowledges frustration when logistically his observant brothers adopt policies injurious to the advances of their mutually revered Torah objectives. The position he takes may be summarized briefly: Only in halakhic Judaism can the truth of the Hebrew faith be found, and those who negate Halakhah negate the survival of that faith. But the genius of the Halakhah can master the realities of every age, without ignoring them or fleeing from them, and can even intensify the glories of its continuous development through the centuries by utilizing the discoveries of science and the established values of the humanities. To make war indiscriminately upon all the expressions of modern culture and to banish in a wholesale sweep all the achievements of secular man merely because they originated in secular arenas is to weaken the effectiveness of the Torah message.

The Roshei Yeshiva of the post-World War II era should embrace this position, before ritualistic and halakhic escalation establishes a *Daat Torah* approach oblivious to the realities *Daat Torah* should include. The refusal to accept the positive values of modern life is the error of retrogression. But in a wilderness, the pillar of fire must "go before them." True, Torah must look inward but it must see outward. The hands of Halakhah should not be tied behind her in bitterness, but should spread before her in constructive affection.

Will There Be Orthodox Women Rabbis?

BLU GREENBERG

I. *The Disturbance.*

SEVERAL MONTHS AGO, SHORTLY BEFORE THE Jewish Theological Seminary faculty was to take its historic vote, I received a phone call from a dear and longtime friend, a woman of good standing, reputation, and influence in the Orthodox community. "I just wanted to know how you feel about the ordination of women," she said. Detecting an edge in her voice, and not wanting to enter into a confrontation, yet not willing to tailor my response to her needs, either, I replied as softly and simply as I could, "Well, I feel quite favorable." Pause. "Aha," she said, "so you don't believe in *Torah min hashamayim!*" And the conversation went downhill from there.

On no other issue that I can remember have emotions run quite so high. Whereas the Orthodox community hardly took notice of the Reform ordination of women in 1973 or that of Reconstructionism in 1975, now the Modern Orthodox community, if not exactly abuzz, is certainly examining the issue from a sober, somber distance. After shul on the Shabbat following the vote, another friend approached me; with a twinkle in his eye, a grin on his lips, and an irony in his voice, he said, "The party line is this: the Orthodox will accept women as rabbis — when the Reform and Conservative ordain goyim."

The hostility is almost palpable. The issue has now moved one step closer to home, particularly so since the dissidents in Conservative Judaism are of similar, if not identical, bent, to the Modern Orthodox in their opposition to women's ordination.

Some in the Orthodox community view the matter as a logical extension of the various break-away steps of Conservative Judaism during the past thirty years: allowing women to read the Torah at services (1955); counting women as part of the spiritual congregation (1973); ruling by narrow majority in the Law Committee to allow women to serve as witnesses in matters of the bet din (1974). Ordination of women, then, was simply an inexorable move which further confirmed — that Conservative Judaism must be written off!

Others in the Orthodox community now view it as a disaster for Conservative Judaism, a move that will splinter the movement into liberal and

BLU GREENBERG *is a lecturer and author on contemporary Jewish issues.*

traditional wings, with the dissidents falling into our arms. Indeed, Rabbi Soloveitchik has said that the RCA should accept the applications of those who voted against the measure, i.e., those who have done *teshuvah* regarding Conservative Judaism.

So the Orthodox community, by and large, is unalterably opposed to the ordination of women. Its opposition is expressed in terms of ruling and precedent, process and politics. The bottom line response is that "it is against halakhah for women to be given *semikhah*." With that, I must concur: it is against halakhah, as halakhah, past and present, is currently interpreted by the leading Orthodox *poskim*.

II. *The Odyssey*.

Theologies are often colored by our personal experiences. Before dealing with the theoretical issues, therefore, let us trace for a moment the circumstances by which women who locate themselves squarely within the Orthodox community can come to view the matter of ordination of women favorably, and even dream of it ultimately taking place within Orthodox Judaism. It is instructive occasionally to reconstitute the events that carry us to a new place in our thinking. How have we reached the point where we question the adequacy of the response that "halakhah says you may not do this or become that, because you are a woman." I have tried somewhat to locate the point at which I crossed the border from dutifulness and acceptance of givens to disagreement and chafing at the outer limits. I know not where that exact point is, but I can recall many moments of wonder, of questioning:

A. *The power of alternate models*. In 1972, I read an article about the forthcoming ordination of Rabbi Sally Preisand at Hebrew Union College. I was, to put it mildly, horrified. Someone had crossed the line. "It is against halakhah," I argued. "Other things I can understand, but women as rabbis — never! There goes Reform Judaism again . . ." Startled by the whole matter, I followed her career with some curiosity. It was not distinguished, but it was not undistinguished either. It was exactly the same as that of any rabbi starting out in his chosen profession. I went from asking, "What on earth is this woman doing?" to, "What is she doing?" to "Why is she doing it?" to "Why not?"

My questions changed their nature and tone over the course of several years. I had to digest each new task that she, and then other female rabbis, were performing. Teaching, yes; but officiating at a funeral? Why would anyone want a woman to officiate at a funeral? I asked myself. Why would any family, in its moment of bereavement, break with tradition? It took me three years to understand that, to a family in a moment of grief, it does not matter whether the source of consolation and of Jewish communal representation is male or female. Officiating at services — I had become adjusted to that for Reform Judaism, but to consecrate marriage? A stigma would forever be attached to this Jewish couple.

With great difficulty, I finally had to ask myself what was so terrible about a woman's being that she could not perform these functions? After all, performing marriage is a sacred function and not a sacramental one (such as the sacraments of Temple times performed only by men born into the priestly class). In fact, halakhah permits any lay Jew to perform these functions, such as marriage and funeral rites, as long as the proper procedures are followed. There is nothing intrinsic to the rabbinic role that a woman cannot do. Therefore, her exclusion was only a matter of gender, which evolved from a cultural rather than a religious base. The model of women rabbis taught me that perhaps the problem lay not with women but with community and its conditioning.

B. *False aspersions on the class of women*. [The domino theory of exemption.] One afternoon in the Spring of 1973, as I sat at my desk sifting through the mail, I came across a very moving monograph in which the eminent *posek*, Rav Yosef Eliahu Henkin, *z'l*, was memorialized on the occasion of his fifth yahrzeit. The piece described his erudition, his depth of understanding of halakhah, and his sensitivity towards human beings. Suddenly, a passage leaped out at me. "He had great patience for the questions of the plain folk and the women." While it would be unfair to say that the great Rav Henkin felt this way, here it was, in 1973, with women as Presidents and Prime Ministers and bankers, philosophers, scientists, professors, lawyers, doctors, that an Orthodox writer could still be talking about women and their *veiberische* questions. A whole class of simple-questioned women! The writer and his readers would be convinced otherwise only when women stood among them as equals.

C. *Insights of the unconditioned*. One evening, as I sat in usual attendance while my then seven year-old took her nightly bath, I heard a most uncommon thought pass her lips. She was musing about what she might become as an adult. ". . . maybe I'll be a rabbi, or maybe Golda Meir, or maybe [I must admit it] Cher." And, in an instant, she was on to something else. Where ever did she get the idea that she could be a rabbi?, I silently wondered. Certainly not from her parents or siblings, who had not yet heard of women rabbis. Certainly not from her grandparents, all rabbis and wives. Certainly not from the several generations of male rabbinic models before them.

Never since has she mentioned that option again. I think I know why. At age seven, and partly a product of Free-to-be, she sought the most exciting models in her life; among them her father, a rabbi. Some time thereafter, she was undoubtedly socialized to a different reality, to different expectations. Meanwhile, she had afforded me the challenge of surprise.

D. *The compatibility of women and Torah learning*. Whosoever has not witnessed *tikkun leil Shavuot* in the holy city has not seen joy in his lifetime

. . . I have seen such joy. In 1981, I happened to be in Jerusalem during Shavuot. At 4:00 A.M., just as the sun was beginning to rise, Jerusalemites young and old, Jerusalemites by the thousands, came out of the darkness of night to gather at the *kotel* for *Shaḥarit*. In the crowd of women on my side of the *meḥiẓah* was a most impressive group — a very new group, as Jewish history counts time. Numbering at least five hundred, they were young women in their late teens and early twenties who had come to spend a year in Israel in pursuit of Torah knowledge. They were students at the dozen or so institutions in Israel dedicated solely to the advancement of women in higher religious education — Mikhlalah, Makhon Gold, Brovender's, Ohr Sameaḥ, to name but a few. Like their male counterparts, the primary purpose of these young women for being in Israel was *Torah lishmah*! All of those I spoke to on that early morning, and presumably all the others there, had spent the night in learning. Would any of the rabbis who instruct them, or any of the parents who sent them, or any of the students or children whom they will someday teach, say of them, "*Nashim daatan kalot*" (women are light-minded)?

As I talked with them, I thought of Nechama Leibowitz, the preeminent teacher of *Tanakh* now instructing a third generation of students in Israel. I thought of the young children at my local day school, SAR Academy in Riverdale, and at Ramaz High School in Manhattan where girls were studying Talmud exactly and as well as their brothers. I thought of Judith Hauptman, perhaps the first woman to teach Talmudic law since the time of Beruriah. As I looked at these beautiful, spirited, devout young women, I wondered to myself: who among them will make Talmud Torah her life's work? How much longer before one of them amasses the knowledge equal to that of a *gadol hatorah*?

III. *Women and semikhah — creating the model/a conceptual framework for reinterpreting the law.*

To say that it should be thus and so, simply because one wants it or likes it or deems it to be possible, is to be downright silly about such weighty matters. It is also to ignore several thousand years of tradition and legislation regarding male exclusiveness in the pursuits and fruits of Torah study. Therefore, and inasmuch as all of halakhah is understood and interpreted in a theoretical/theological framework, let us attempt to construct a model whereby women can be mainstreamed into the rabbinic enterprise.

A. *Searching for a principle of sexual equality in Judaism*. One doesn't have to search very far. The basic principle, to be found early in Scriptures, is that each person is created in the image of God (Genesis, 1:26). Male and female, species specific, but each in the image of God. Distinctive, yet equal. How does this distinctiveness manifest itself? Primarily through biology, but also through definitions of role and function which are largely determined from a social context, and not out of divine necessity.

Another source for understanding the essence of the human being comes to us in the form of an admonition to witnesses who will make life and death judgments about their peers:

> You must know that his blood (the person to be executed) and the blood of his posterity will be at his door to the end of the world . . . Therefore was a single human created first a) to teach that if anyone destroys a single soul from the children of Adam, Scripture charges him as if he had destroyed a whole world . . . b) [to teach] that no one may say to another, "My ancestor was greater than your ancestor . . ." c) [to teach] the greatness of God . . . for man stamps many coins with one die and they are alike, but God . . . has stamped all mankind with the die of the first man yet no one of them is like any other (*Sanhedrin*,4:5).

Thus, we learn that each person, male and female, is of infinite value, is equal to every other, and is unique.[1]

Sexual hierarchy, which includes closing off access on the basis of sex, is not the preferred model. To the extent that it appears in Scriptural sources, it is given in the form of a punishment: "*Vehu yimshol bakh*" (He shall rule over you) (Genesis 3:16) is the curse placed on woman when banished from Paradise. It is a symbol of the brokenness and unfinished nature of the world, not something to be glorified.[2] Original sin is not a staple of Jewish theology; we can learn from the text on hierarchy-as-punishment that the ideal state is equality and that, as Jews, we continually move toward it until it will be fully realized in the messianic age.

Distinctiveness of species, yes; but not hierarchy of social function. Biological uniqueness of male and female, yes; but not discrepancies in mental or emotional capacity. That does not mean that every non-biological role and function must be identical for male and female, but it does mean that the global distinctions, such as men/learning/prayer and women/*niddah*/*ḥallah*/*nerot* are far too broad as categories.

B. *VeTalmud Torah kneged kulam* (*Peah* 1:1). There is, indeed, no measure to the value of learning. Learning, Jewish scholarship, is the great pride, the unique and primary characteristic of a Jew.

What about women and learning? A spotty history! Women were excluded from the arena of knowledge; they were not welcome in the *bet midrash*. They knew nothing of the inner workings of rabbinic texts. There is not a female name among the *rishonim, aḥaronim*, compilers of codes, *teshuvot*, works of halakhah, *aggadah*, and *mussar*. To our collective pride, the list is very long! But it is not the product of a "collective genius . . . but rather the collective half-genius."[3]

Why is it, one wonders, that women were excluded from the compel-

1. See Irving Greenberg, "Dialogue on Creation," 92nd St. Y tapes: October 19, 1983.
2. Ibid.
3. See Cynthia Ozick, "Notes Towards Finding the Right Question," *Lilith* (Fall 1981).

ling mizvah of Talmud Torah? Why is it that the entire female class was disconnected from the basic nurturing source of the Jewish soul? One must consider all possible reasons:

1) Is it because Talmud Torah is a positive commandment that must be performed within a limited period of time and, therefore, falls within the general exemption of women? No, for the mizvah of Talmud Torah is open-ended: "And you shall study it day and night" (Joshua 1:8).

2) Is is because the Torah teaches us *veshinantam levanekha* (Deuteronomy 6:7), on which the Rabbis expound, "to your sons and not to your daughters" (*Kiddushin* 29b)? I would submit that tradition interpreted Scriptures in that way because in every generation the Torah is interpreted in the light of historical conditions. Indeed, the Torah intentionally addressed human beings in a manner appropriate to their condition. Perhaps that is the ultimate meaning of *dibrah Torah bilshon bnai adam*. It is an expression both of God's love for humanity in its limited condition and of God's role as master teacher.

A clear case in point of the arbitrary nature of the scriptural peg is that elsewhere — many elsewheres —*banim* is interpreted as children, and not as only one-half of the children of Israel. Perhaps the gloss should now read, "to your sons and not to your daughters, in that time and not in this time."

3) Is it because the whole class of women was deemed incapable?[4] An absurdity! Then, as now, women were blessed with mental capacity and mental energy equal to that of men. Then, as now, all was understood at some level that it was a myth, a non-corroborative, self-reinforcing myth that led nowhere.

4) Is it that the pursuit of Talmud Torah would conflict with women's household and nurturing duties? Perphaps so. But we now understand that, with greater longevity and proper training, women can raise families and also do many other meaningful things in their lifetimes. Just because a woman opens her mind does not necessarily mean that she must shut her womb. Talmud Torah as a lifelong "profession" for women would be no more dangerous to the Jewish family than would be medicine, law, or a host of other choices which are now accepted even in the most traditional sectors, including those where women work in order to enable their husbands to learn and to teach Torah.

5) Is it that Talmud Torah breached the borders of *zniut*? Today, women are no longer contained in their homes, insulated from culture and society. Exposure to Torah learning is hardly likely to diminish their morality or their ethics.

6) Finally, there is one more question we must ask, relating to the exclusion of women from study of Torah. Is it that the great Jewish learning enterprise, in addition to being *Torah lishmah*, was, and also is, an

4. *Sotah* 3:4; *Kiddushin* 80b; *Shabbat* 33b; Maimonides, *Codes, Hilkhot Talmud Torah* 1:13.

access route, an empowering force to religious authority, to interpretive keys, to spiritual leadership — all of which were not to be placed in the hands of women because these were simply not roles considered proper for them? Opening the access route would have opened up the Pandora's box. So those who kept women apart from rabbinic texts made the correct tactical moves.

But now that the access route has been opened by dedicated *rebbeim*, learned teachers, and by the fine minds of women, it can never be closed again. Female compatibility with Torah learning, once established, can never be taken away.

C. *It goes without saying that semikhah is tied to learning*. It is not a physical appendage or sexual characteristic that earns one the title of *Rav b'Yisrael*. It is knowledge and piety; it is mastery of rabbinic texts and of halakhic codes.

Semikhah represents the great flowering of the merit system, from the days of the *Ḥurban* onwards. Up to the destruction of the Second Temple, the priests were the primary agents of ritual and religious ceremony. The Pharisaic revolution, which was increasingly consolidated after the *Ḥurban*, was one of the great transformations in Judaism. Religious leadership no longer depended on genetics but, rather, on ability. One had to earn, through scholarship and piety, the title of Rav. It was a symbol of the growing democratization of Jewish life. That principle — of merit over birth — ought now to be broadened to include all Jews.

D. *Constructing the model: let us combine the three concepts*. 1, The equality of male and female in the image of God, which means the equality of male and female in their potential to become more Godlike. This includes men as nurturers of children, and women as learners of Torah. 2, Understanding as Jews that the study of Torah is a high order of business for a Jew, if not the highest order in a variety of spiritual responses. For a variety of non-theological reasons, the whole enterprise was closed off to women through most of our history. 3, *Semikhah* is the recognition of accomplishment, of accumulation of knowledge and ability to handle rabbinic texts. It is a function of merit and not of gender.

A coalescence these three themes should lead us to a desire to compensate for past deprivation and fully to encourage women in Talmud Torah up to, and including, the formal recognition — *semikhah* — for those who achieve in this area.

IV. *The Process.*

In reading the adverse criticism on the Seminary vote, I could not help but note how much of it centered on the issue of process. The dissidents, as well as many in the Orthodox community, argued that the decision was made by majority vote rather than by rabbinic fiat of one knowledgeable in Jewish law. As I listened to, and read, the debates, two rabbinic pericopes flashed into mind:

> Once it happened that Rosh Hashanah fell on the Sabbath, and all the villagers gathered in Yavneh to hear the shofar. Rabbi Yoḥanan ben Zakkai said to the *B'nai Betera*, "Let us sound the shofar." They said to him, "Let us discuss the matter" [For the law was that if the New Year fell on a Sabbath, they could blow the shofar in Jerusalem but not in any other place.] He said to them, "Let us sound the shofar and afterwards we will discuss it." They blew the shofar, and then they said to him, "Now let us discuss it." He said to them, "The shofar has already been heard in Yavneh. After the fact it no longer warrants discussion" (*Rosh Hashanah*, 29b).

The second story is even more dramatic. Rabbi Eliezer ruled on a matter of ritual piety; the *ḥakhamim* disagreed. Though R. Eliezer brought proof from heaven and earth, he was, nevertheless, "outvoted." "The Torah is not in the heavens!" (*Baba Meẓia* 59b). The ruling of those presumably less accurate and less knowledgeable was accepted.

This is surely not to compare the faculty of the Jewish Theological Seminary to the Sages of yore. It is, however, to point out that as far back as those more "sacred" times, Jews argued over alternate models of process.

Moreover, these two stories, and countless others, attest to the fact that process is not antithetical to halakhah. Halakhah is fixed, halakhah is revelatory, but it is also dynamic. Process, or the pattern of reinterpreting matters of ritual, did not end with the Talmud. Nor did it occur in a vacuum. The twelfth century winegrowers of Champagne, for example, were permitted dealings in what formerly would have been classified as *yayin nesekh* because Rashi and Rabbenu Tam understood that business considerations, the "felt needs of the times," were not to be ignored in interpreting and re-interpreting ritual law.[5] If the law could be reinterpreted for business reasons, how much more so for ethical considerations in our day?

In the Orthodox community, the ordination of women is not perceived as an ethical issue, largely because the majority of women do not feel that way. But with time, and with increased education, it will not be long before women will understand the enormity of their deprivation for all these centuries past.

In truth, we can almost set aside the issue of process for it is well underway as regards women's experience in the obligation to study Torah. From Rabbi Samson Raphael Hirsch to Sarah Schneier there was a quantum leap. From Sarah Schneier to our own day, another one. We see women learning as never before in the Orthodox community. Young girls study Talmudic texts in a way that was not done even a bare decade ago.

The question has been asked: "Should women recite the morning

5. Hayim Soloveitchik, "Can Halakhik Texts Talk History?" in *Association for Jewish Studies Review*, III (1978): 153-197.

blessing of learning Torah? Yes, is the halakhic answer.[6] In a contemporary *teshuvah* regarding the permissibility of teaching *Torah she be'al peh* to women, a distinguished *posek* wrote." "Anyone who does not teach his daughter knowledge of God (*da'as Hashem*) . . . it is as if he is teaching her *tiflus* (lewdness, vacuity, trivia.)"[7] The language is not an accident. With full awareness, Rabbi Zalman Sorotskin, *z'l*, thereby reversed the famous dictum of Rabbi Eliezer which undergirded the exclusion of women from learning for the past two millenia. There is no parent of a daughter in the traditional community who would any longer say ". . . only your sons and not your daughters." It seems but a matter of time that a woman, who is as well versed in rabbinic sources as a male who studies for the *beḥinah*, will say to herself, "Why not me?"

V. *The domino effect: women and ritual practice.*

In addition to argument about process, there is the objection to women's ordination on the grounds of attendant functions: women cannot serve as rabbis because they cannot serve as witnesses in marriage and divorce proceedings, because they cannot formally be part of public worship, because they cannot be liturgical leaders, because they should not overstep the boundaries of modesty . . . Indeed, these are questions that will arise in the future, just as we are now asking new questions about women and learning that would not have occurred to us a hundred years ago. Meanwhile, the issue of qualification is altogether separable from the issue of function. Function is dependent on community receptivity, whereas qualification and the official stamp thereof is dependent solely on a person's achievement, on one's expertise in Jewish law and rabbinic texts. There are countless men, perhaps the overwhelming number, who are ordained in the Orthodox community, yet do not perform any functions additional to those of their lay fellows. So be it for women.

VI. *Community.*

Nevertheless, community is a large and significant factor; not only the community of women with new ideas but the community in which we are nurtured and locate ourselves.

The accusation, or fear, that ordination of women is destroying Judaism, tinkering with halakhah, denying tradition, is not to be ignored, for it comes from those who love the tradition and who fear for its survival, not from those who want to abandon it. One must be sensitive to the fact that their pain and anguish comes out of a boundless desire to perpetuate *yiddishkeit* and not a simpleminded or regressive need to put women down. Still, their fears and even the divisiveness that these new

6. *Shulḥan Arukh, Oraḥ Ḥayyim* 47:14.

7. Zalman Sorotskin, *Moznayim Lamishpat* #43 (Jerusalem, 1955).

moves will engender within the Orthodox community are not sufficient factors for holding women back. Therefore, I believe that women's ordination in Orthodoxy will continue to unfold in gradual stages. In the beginning, there will be the creation of institutions of higher learning for women to pursue parallel rabbinic studies. Two such institutions already do exist; one is Drishah, which has been functioning in New York City for several years, under the direction of Rabbi David Silber. There no one discusses ordination, though women are proceeding apace with their rabbinic studies. The second is a new yeshiva, to be opened in Efrat, under the aegis of Rabbi Shlomo Riskin. At Midreshet Lindenbaum, as it is called, women will have essentially the same learning experiences as do the young men in a *yeshivah gedolah*, i.e., the study of Talmud and post-Talmudic rabbinic texts as the major focus.

In the beginning, there might be the inclusion of women in existing programs of rabbinic studies for men, such as is the case at the Bernard Revel Graduate School at Yeshiva University. To date, no woman has majored in rabbinic studies, but by the time we reach the mid-eighties that, too, will surely be a reality.

Perhaps, when the Orthodox community has produced a well-learned and deeply pious woman, there will be a small cluster of rabbis who will be willing to ordain her, rabbis who will not be fearful of the opprobrium of their fellows. Similarly, the process of acceptance by community will take place in stages. The first woman ordained in the Orthodox community will surely not seek a congregational pulpit, for that would lead only to frustration. Until such time as the issues of women in witnessing or women in liturgical roles come under scrutiny, it seems highly unlikely that an Orthodox congregation would consider a woman for its religious leadership. Meanwhile, there are numerous other roles for an Orthodox female rabbi. The first steps might be as a teacher, a *rosh yeshivah*, or a rabbi of a women's tefilah group, or a position in the secular organizational structure that calls for the title of rabbi. Another milestone would be for a woman to write *piskei halakhah* and *teshuvot*. Perhaps all of these would take a generation; perhaps two or three. It would be a small price to pay for diminishing strife and making solid irreversible gains. I, for one, would be content to see the very first step — *semikhah* — taken in my lifetime.

Therefore, I believe that women's ordination will continue to unfold in gradual stages.

VII. *Conclusion.*

The task of those who propose an enlarged role for women, as well as those who will serve as models, is to communicate the real agenda of Orthodox women: that it is not a feminization of Judaism but a heightened Jewishness of females; that women are seeking greater access and fuller entry into the religious and spiritual life of the community — and not the easy way out; that women who love the pursuit of Talmud Torah want to enter that world more fully; that encouraging women through ordination is ultimately building up the fund of knowledgeable, learned Jews in this generation and generations to come.

Will it happen in my lifetime? I am optimistic. At this moment in history, I am well aware that the Orthodox community would not accept a woman as a rabbi. Yet, we are moving towards a unique moment in history. More than any other, the Orthodox community has widely educated its women in Torah studies. Thus, though it rejects the formal entry of women into rabbinic studies, *de facto*, through the broad sweep of day school, yeshiva high school education and beyond, it has ushered them, as a whole community, into the learning enterprise. At the very same moment in time, Reform, Reconstructionist, and Conservative Judaism are providing us with models of women as rabbis. At some point in the not-too-distant future, I believe, the two will intersect: more learned women in the Orthodox community and the model of women in leadership positions in the other denominations. When that happens, history will take us where it takes us. That holds much promise for the likes of me.

The Ambiguous Modern Orthodox Jew

LAWRENCE KAPLAN

THE MODERN ORTHODOX JEW MAY STILL BE an unfamiliar, even exotic, figure on the American scene but, at least, he is no longer invisible. To be sure, the old image — or rather caricature — of the Orthodox Jew as a benighted, East-European figure, complete with long gaberdine, round black hat and hanging sidelocks, adrift in the spiritual world of the Middle Ages and wholly isolated from the social and intellectual currents of modernity — or various less extreme variants thereof — is still maintaining a precarious grip on the popular consciousness. Just recently, a sumptuous picture book appeared, entitled *Tradition: Orthodox Jewish Life in America,*[1] and consisting wholly of photographs of Lubavitch Hasidim in Crown Heights — a classic example of mistaking the part for the whole. Nevertheless, the old misconceptions, if not dead, are rapidly dying and, perhaps, in the not too distant future, they will finally be given the eternal rest that they so richly deserve. Already, such figures as Orthodox Jewish physicists, lawyers or law professors, politicians, advertising executives, sociologists, literary critics, bio-chemists, etc., etc., are becoming more and more frequent and, even more important, more and more visible on the American Jewish scene, and their collective presence is bound to break through even the strongest and most resistant of preconceptions.

But the features of this new, emerging modern Orthodox American Jew are as yet not clearly defined. There is something elusive, deeply ambiguous, about his whole personality, for who is this modern Orthodox Jew? We may define him as one who desires "to adhere faithfully to the beliefs, principles and traditions of Jewish law and observance without being either remote from or untouched by life in the contemporary world," and who recognizes the mutual demands of traditional Judaism and of modernity. He may thereby be differentiated from his traditional counterpart who is "relatively more isolated from contemporary secular society," and who sees "such aspects of reality as secular education, English language or occupations outside the Jewish community as infringements upon [his] life."[2] But is the Orthodoxy of the modern Orthodox Jew, itself, in some sense modern? Does it reflect, in some significant

1. Mal Warshaw, *Tradition: Orthodox Jewish Life in America,* (New York: Schocken Books, 1976).
2. Samuel Heilman, *Synagogue Life: A Study in Symbolic Interaction,* (Chicago: University of Chicago Press, 1976).

LAWRENCE KAPLAN *is an assistant professor of Jewish Studies at McGill University, Montreal.*

manner, the impact of modernity? or is his Orthodoxy identical, in all essential respects, with the Orthodoxy of his traditional Orthodox brother? Perhaps the modern Orthodox Jew simply embodies a traditional Orthodoxy co-existing uneasily with a wholly unrelated commitment to modernity. To put the question semantically, does the word "modern" in "modern Orthodox Jew" modify the adjective "Orthodox" or the noun "Jew"? Granted that the modern Orthodox Jew exists and even flourishes, is there such an entity as modern Orthodoxy?

It is ironic that these questions have been raised in a very acute form by a recent work whose clear, professed intention is to avoid such questions. *Synagogue Life*, by Samuel Heilman, a young, modern, Orthodox Jewish sociologist who is also a sociologist of the modern Orthodox Jewish community, is, as its subtitle indicates, "a study in symbolic interaction." Its purpose is to study the "interaction generated within, and by, the members of a small modern Orthodox Jewish synagogue [Congregation Kehillat Kodesh] located in [Sprawl City] a large Northeastern American city" (p. ix), to detail what actually happens in an Orthodox synagogue and its social significance. As Heilman himself emphatically notes, his work, insofar as it focuses on "how Orthodox Jews as *social beings* [the italics are Heilman's] act in their congregation," will not illuminate the significance that the synagogue has for Orthodox Jews as believers, as committed religious individuals. At the outset, he states:

> This is not a book about the religion of Orthodox Jews, for it explains neither their religion nor the essence of their orthodoxy (p. ix).

Indeed, we may add that, while the Orthodox Jews described in *Synagogue Life* are modern Orthodox Jews, Heilman also does not explain the essence of their modernity nor why they are committed to the demands of both modernity and Orthodoxy.

Yet, if *Synagogue Life* tells us nothing, or very little, about the essence of the Orthodoxy or of the modernity of the Jews described therein, it tells us a good deal, if not enough, about the essence of the interrelationship and interaction of their modernity and Orthodoxy. Indeed, the theme of the tension, actually, the outright conflict, between the demands of modernity and of Orthodoxy and the various strategies that modern Orthodox Jews have adopted for dealing with, or evading, this tension and conflict, emerges as the central one of the book.

II

Who, then, is the modern Orthodox Jew, this loyal and regular shul-going member of Congregation Kehillat Kodesh, as Heilman depicts him? First and foremost, to use the author's bold image, he is, or at least sees himself as being, a criminal. The modern Orthodox Jew is, in theory, committed to meeting the demands of both modernity and Orthodoxy; however, insofar as he perceives these demands as being inherently contradictory, his commitment to the demands of modernity results in his selectively violating or, at the very least, not wholly living up to the full range of the demands that Orthodoxy makes upon him. To be involved in the modern world, *ipso facto* means to live a life that involves the constant compromising of the rigorous norms of Orthodoxy, norms whose legitimacy the modern Orthodox Jew fully recognizes; in a word, it means to live a criminal existence. Moreover, this Orthodoxy which the modern Orthodox Jew sees himself as compromising, if not actually violating, is the same Orthodoxy that is shared by his traditional Orthodox brother. The Orthodoxy of the modern Orthodox Jew does not, in principle, differ from the Orthodoxy of the traditional Orthodox Jew. The only difference is one in fact; the modern Orthodox Jew in practice does not live up to the demands of the traditional Orthodoxy to which he is, in theory, committed. In this respect, the modern Orthodox Jew sees himself as being less religious than the traditional Orthodox Jew who, so the modern Orthodox Jew believes, by virtue of his being a traditional Orthodox Jew, does, by and large, adhere to these rigorous demands. As one member of Kehillat Kodesh comments, in talking of strict ritual observance, "We [members of Kehillat Kodesh] probably don't come up to specs. The Yeshivah [the local traditional Orthodox talmudic academy] probably comes closest to it."

The Orthodoxy of the modern Orthodox member of Kehillat Kodesh, insofar as it is a traditional one, does not in any way serve to allow for, or justify, his simultaneous commitment to modernity. Conversely, his modernity does not, in any way, illuminate, color, shape, affect, much less deepen, his commitment to, and understanding of, his Orthodoxy. If anything, it only lessens that commitment. Moreover, since the Orthodoxy of the Kehillat Kodesh member is essentially a traditional one, unaffected by the commitment to modernity, and since, as we have seen, the Kehillat Kodesh member feels that traditional Orthodox Jews meet the demands of that Orthodoxy better than he, he cannot fault them in terms of their Orthodoxy. The only criticism that he can make is that the traditional Orthodox are not sufficiently modern. Thus, the major complaint that the members of Kehillat Kodesh have to make about the Sprawl City Yeshivah is that "it's not so hot in English [i.e., secular studies]." More generally, they criticize it for its isolation from contemporary society. Imagine, "the kids aren't even allowed to read the *N.Y. Times!*" However, all admit that the Yeshivah is "pretty good in Jewish stuff."

In Kehillat Kodesh itself the behavior of the members conforms to traditional Orthodox patterns. Thus, the members decided to make the *meḥizah*, the barrier separating men from women, so high as to satisfy even the most stringent of traditional Orthodox views. The fact that Jewish law, as interpreted by the legal authorities recognized by the modern Orthodox community, does not require so high a barrier and that, as a result of this particular barrier, women are blocked off from the main section, i.e., the men's section, more than would otherwise be the case, does not seem to bother the synagogue powers that be — all male, naturally. Indeed, even for an Orthodox synagogue the role of women in Kehillat Kodesh seems particularly peripheral. All of the currents pushing for greater participation of women in the religious sphere do not seem to have touched Kehillat Kodesh in the slightest. There is absolutely no effort made to see how women might be given a greater role in synagogue affairs while keeping within Orthodox bounds.

It is in this light that we can perceive the significance of the fascinating phenomenon of the use of *Yenglish* or Yiddishized English in the synagogue, an English which is not only intermingled with Hebrew, Aramaic and Yiddish words but has its entire syntax altered as well. Thus, a professor of English no less, when engaged in Torah study, will come out with a phrase like, "How *medakdek* [careful] do you have to be in learning out this *posuk* [verse]?" Heilman suggests:

> One might view this mix as symbolic of the mix between the parochial and the secular so characteristic of Modern Orthodox Jewishness. While the more *frum* continue to study in Hebrew, Aramaic and Yiddish and the less *frum* study primarily, if not completely, in English, these shul Jews, living at once in the modern English-speaking world and the traditional Jewish world, study in *Yenglish*, that linguistic blend which reflects their character and situation (p. 232).

Heilman's explanation is not convincing. If one will visit such bastions of traditional Orthodoxy as the Lakewood and Telshe Yeshivot, perhaps the two most prominent traditional Orthodox talmudic academies in the United States,[3] one will find the students, almost all American-born, studying not in Hebrew, Aramaic or Yiddish but in *Yenglish*; the very same *Yenglish* as spoken in Kehillat Kodesh. This tends to suggest that the modern Orthodox member of Kehillat Kodesh, in speaking *Yenglish*, is acting, not surprisingly, like a traditional Orthodox Jew. The modern Orthodox Jew, when engaged in Torah study, this most Jewish of all activities, attempts to carry it out in what seems to him to be the most authentic traditional manner possible, which means, for him, imitating the manner in which Torah is studied in traditional Orthodox circles.

Thus, the synagogue for the members of Kehillat Kodesh is not, as Heilman suggests, "a crossroads between the contemporary world and the traditional Jewish one." Rather, it is a place where the modern Orthodox Jew may temporarily shed his self-perceived illegitimate modern identity and be able to act in a wholly (holy?) traditional Orthodox style.

To be sure, the members of Kehillat Kodesh do attempt, at times, to create some type of significant interaction between their modernity and their Orthodoxy. Heilman thus describes the process of "contemporization," i.e., "the explanation, exemplification, and elaboration of Torah

3. See David Singer, "The Yeshivah World," *Commentary* (October, 1976).

material in present-day terms" that takes place during Torah study. However, the examples suggest that this attempt is, at best, fitful and superficial. Heilman relates one instance when a member suggested that a particular halakhic principle was similar to one outlined in a recent state supreme court decision. Despite the fact that "the reference aroused a great deal of interest and discussion, even causing digression from the original text," in the end "the [supreme court] case seemed to have very little, if anything, in common with the principle stated in the Talmud text under study." There seems to be no attempt to utilize modern scholarship or modern categories of thought in any systematic fashion to explicate and illuminate sacred traditional texts.

It is not surprising, then, that the state of co-existence between the components of modernity and of Orthodoxy within the modern Orthodox Jew is exceedingly fragile and tenuous. He is engaged in a precarious balancing act and he is very careful lest anything upset it. He takes care to avoid, and evade, any issue which might directly challenge the logic or illogic of his dual commitment. During one study session, a Kehillat Kodesh member asked a question regarding an apparent contradiction in the Biblical description of the exodus. Now, this problem of contradictions in the Biblical text automatically raises the spectre of the documentary hypothesis which explains duplications, divergences and contradictions in the Pentateuch by claiming that it consists of different literary sources which were woven together over the course of time by means of a complex, extended redactional process. However, while all types of answers were suggested by members of the study group to resolve the original problem, all were of an harmonizing nature and the whole issue of the documentary hypothesis, which would appear to contradict the traditional belief in the unitary nature and Mosaic authorship of the Pentateuch, was passed over in silence. Certainly members of the study group are familiar with the documentary hypothesis. Nevertheless, it would seem that even to speak of the hypothesis is felt to be too disturbing and threatening a course of action to take. For this would raise the more general problem of the challenges and difficulties posed by modern Biblical scholarship to traditional Jewish scholarship and, by implication, the challenges and difficulties posed by modern, critical, historical study of sacred texts to traditional belief — indeed, it would raise the whole question of the possible discordance existing between modernity and Orthodoxy. And the members of Kehillat Kodesh who have never worked out for themselves any coherent ideology to justify their dual commitment to both modernity and Orthodoxy are totally unprepared to face that challenge — and they know it! Therefore, they take especial care to prevent the problem from arising in the first place.

This course of evasion and suppression underlies a good deal of synagogue activity. As Heilman suggests,

> a psycho-theological explanation may be offered for the incessant joking

> and gossip that constitute shul conversation. The "light" chatter of sociability, almost compulsive in character, blocks out — literally as well as symbolically — the possibility of the speakers having to come to terms with the deeper antinomies inherent in their modernity and Orthodoxy. To talk about such matters of spirit would be to open a Pandora's box of anxieties and theological conflicts with which the everyday shul Jew refuses to deal. The "small talk" of joking and gossip is infinitely safer and more manageable (p. 209).

Indeed, as Heilman points out in a more recent essay:

> During the three years in which I lived and studied in a modern Orthodox community, I never once heard a serious discussion about theology or ideology. . . . Any questions about the contradictions between Orthodoxy and modernity were, if answered at all, treated jokingly.[4]

Yet this fundamental tension between Orthodoxy and modernity, while suppressed, lurks beneath the surface, making its presence felt, constituting an almost palpable reality. Modern Orthodox Jews, as Heilman points out,

> stand between two sources of stigmatization: the contemporary world, which considers their Orthodoxy a stigma, and the traditional Orthodox community which looks upon their modernity with disapproval. As such, modern Orthodox Jews have only themselves (p. 266).

But, in truth, they don't even have themselves. For this double stigmatization is not only external in nature, it is also internal. Heilman's modern Orthodox Jew as a modern man sees his own Orthodoxy as a stigma and, as a traditional Orthodox Jew, he sees his own modernity as a stigma. For this reason, the modern Orthodox Jew is, as Heilman notes, a double Marrano, forever engaged in "passing" behavior. In the outside secular world, the modern Orthodox Jew, as modern man, downplays his Orthodoxy to such an extent that "secular-world colleagues discover, long after first impressions have been established, that [he is] also [an] Orthodox Jew", while in the sacred world of the synagogue, the modern Orthodox Jew disguises his modernity, playing the part of the traditional Orthodox. It is all too, too pathetic.

III

Heilman's portrait of the modern Orthodox Jew differs radically from the picture painted by other contemporary students of Orthodoxy. Thus, David Singer, a young student of the current American religious scene, in developing the position of the noted sociologist of Judaism, Charles S. Liebman, has recently argued:

> It is generally assumed that the many divisions within Orthodoxy stem from the fact that one group is "more religious" than another. This is not so. . . .

4. Samuel Heilman, "Inner and Outer Identities; Social Ambivalence Among Orthodox Jews," *Jewish Social Studies* (Summer, 1977): 234.

> The actual divisions within Orthodoxy, as Charles S. Liebman has argued, reflect a church-sect dichotomy that is familiar to students of religion. The church wing of Orthodoxy consists of the "modern Orthodox" while the sectarian wing is made up of the followers of the various heads of the Yeshivot and the Hasidim. . . . Modern Orthodoxy evinces two dominant characteristics: an abiding concern with demonstrating the relevance of the *halakhah* for contemporary life, and a strong emphasis on the interconnectedness of all Jews. . . . Sectarian Orthodoxy, as distinguished from modern Orthodoxy, is marked by an emphasis on authority and separatism.[5]

For both Liebman and Singer then, unlike Heilman, there exists an entity, modern Orthodoxy, and its ideology is significantly different from that of sectarian Orthodoxy. Moreover, both deny that the traditional or sectarian Orthodox Jew and the modern Orthodox Jew are to be distinguished as being more or less religious.[6]

How are we to account for these two strikingly dissimilar pictures?

Part of the answer may be found in the fact that while Liebman, in his analysis, focuses on the various organizations and institutions of the modern Orthodox community, and Singer, in his essay, focuses on the leading modern Orthodox journal, *Tradition*, Heilman, in *Synagogue Life*, focuses on the average, typical, regular, shul-going modern Orthodox Jew. This would tend to suggest that while, indeed, there may be a modern Orthodox ideology, it is largely confined to the precincts of organizations and institutions or the pages of journals but has failed to reach and affect the average shul-going modern Orthodox Jew. As a result, his Orthodoxy, per se, is not the modern one of the official ideology but the traditional one propounded by the superficially Americanized, but essentially East-European yeshivah world. It should come as no surprise, therefore, that the most popular recent Biblical commentary among modern Orthodox Jews is a series[7] whose authors, editors and advisors are wholly products of the yeshivah world and all of whom pride themselves in totally ignoring all modern critical Biblical scholarship, be it non-Jewish or Jewish!

Yet, to explain the divergence between Liebman and Singer on the one hand and Heilman on the other by speaking of the failure of modern Orthodox ideology on the popular level would be neither entirely accurate, nor, for that matter, fair. For while it is true that modern Orthodox ideology has failed to make a significant impact on a community-wide level, it would be untrue to say that it has made no impact at all. No doubt

5. "Voices of Orthodoxy" (*Commentary*, (July, 1974).
6. Actually, the views of Liebman and Singer on this subject are not entirely identical. For, while it is true that in his major article on Orthodoxy ("Orthodoxy in American Jewish Life," *American Jewish Yearbook*, 1965, pp. 21–98), Liebman uses a church-sect model to explain the differences between traditional and modern Orthodoxy, in another essay ("Left and Right in American Orthodoxy," JUDAISM, [Winter, 1966]), his analysis anticipates Heilman's in some respects.
7. Art-Scroll Series, edited by Meir Zlotowitz.

many, perhaps most, Orthodox Jews are like those whom Heilman describes, Jews who are committed to traditional Orthodoxy and an essentially unrelated modernity — but not all. Heilman believes that his portrait of the modern Orthodox Jews of Kehillat Kodesh is fully representative of all modern Orthodox Jews, but this is simply not so. It is not true that all modern Orthodox Jews "live lives of patterned desperation," nor do all modern Orthodox Jews experience their modernity and Orthodoxy as two antithetical, conflicting identities. There are modern Orthodox Jews to be found in Orthodox synagogues — perhaps even in Kehillat Kodesh itself — whose Orthodoxy is, in some sense, modern; and there are modern Orthodox communities where one may hear serious discussions about theology or ideology.[8]

IV

Who, then, is this other type of modern Orthodox Jew, of whose existence Heilman — and others — are unaware and how would a modern Orthodox synagogue look if there were more of him — or her?

This modern Orthodox Jew, like Heilman's modern Orthodox Jew, is committed to both modernity and Orthodoxy, but, unlike him, strives to integrate these two commitments. He attempts to justify his commitment to modernity in terms of his Orthodoxy and, at the same time, seeks to demonstrate the significance and meaningfulness of tradition and belief for modern man. On the one hand, his modernity informs his Orthodoxy. Thus, he utilizes modern categories of thought to illuminate and deepen his understanding of the tradition and, in his study of sacred texts, makes use of the findings and methods of modern historical scholarship to the extent that they do not violate the religious integrity of these texts as he perceives it. But the movement of influence is not only one way. For his perception of the modern world and modern social and intellectual currents is shaped by his traditional perspective, so that his commitment to modernity is always critical and qualified. No doubt, this modern Orthodox Jew, despite his efforts at integration, experiences serious tensions between his modernity and his Orthdoxy, but these tensions, he is convinced, need not function, as Heilman would claim, simply as a source of anxiety and personal insecurity. Rather, they can be challenging, fruitful and creative in nature. From their differing vantage points, both those committed to a secular modernity and those committed to

8. Perhaps Heilman fails to note this other type of modern Orthodox Jew because he, himself, is a modern Orthodox Jew of the type he describes, at once a detached critical sociologist and a traditional Orthodox Jew. Thus, in "Inner and Outer Identities," Heilman, at one and the same time, engages in highly rigorous and sophisticated sociological analysis while describing traditonal Judaism before modernity in the narrow, monolithic, almost simplistic stereotypes typical of the perceptions of many traditional Orthodox Jews. In this respect, he resembles many modern Orthodox Jewish professionals who combine advanced expertise in their own fields and disciplines with surprisingly shallow and undiscriminating conceptions of traditonal Judaism.

traditional Orthodoxy claim that such an integration is inherently unstable, that it is "riddled with insoluble antinomies" and is ultimately impossible to sustain, a contradiction in terms. Our modern Orthodox Jew is aware of these claims and recognizes their force. However, he stakes all and risks all on the conviction that his critics are wrong. At the very least, he feels that he will have replaced sterile isolation and uneasy co-existence with an exciting, if perilous, confrontation and interaction.

This modern Orthodox Jew would not simply criticize Sprawl City Yeshivah because it is not modern enough. Rather, because his conception of the tradition itself is informed by modernity, he would criticize its Jewish studies curriculum on Jewish grounds: for painting a monolithic picture of Judaism, for not presenting the fullness and diversity of the tradition, for presenting only one model of piety to the exclusion of all others, for scanting such subjects as Bible, Hebrew language and literature and Jewish history, for suppressing the role of critical reason in interacting with authority, for creating a false image of the religious community in history as sealed off, in hermetic isolation, from outside influences, for failing to integrate Jewish and general studies, etc. etc. On a social level, this modern Orthodox Jew would not view his involvement in the modern world as a criminal compromise but, to cite one of the most perceptive and intelligent modern Orthodox rabbinical thinkers today, as "a well-formed decision based upon a considered judgment as to what is the Torah ideal."[9]

The nature of the synagogue would also change radically if there were in it more modern Orthodox Jews of the type that we are describing. The issue of the role of women in Judaism, in general, and in the synagogue, in particular, and the problem of giving women more opportunities for religious self-expression within an Orthodox framework would be confronted in a serious and ongoing way. This is not to say that the members of this synagogue, both men and women together, would necessarily arrive at an entirely satisfactory resolution of this issue, but, at least, the problem would be a live and meaningful one. The English professor, in this synagogue, would not simply shed his secular training while studying Torah and turn into a *Yenglish*-speaking traditional Orthodox Jew but, drawing upon his professional expertise, would attempt to illuminate, for example, the study of the Bible by bringing to bear upon it modern techniques of literary analysis. Similarly, the modern Orthodox lawyer, when studying Talmud, would not simply cite irrelevant supreme court decisions, but, following the lead of a number of modern Orthodox scholars, would seek to combine traditional talmudic scholarship with modern categories of jurisprudence. Finally, the whole issue of modern Biblical scholarship and its relationship to the tradition would be faced head-on and a systematic effort would be made to see how much of that

9. Schubert Spero, "Bi-Centennial Symposium: The Jew in America," *Tradition* (Fall, 1976).

scholarship could be incorporated within a traditional framework. The synagogue, in such circumstances, might, in some respects, be a more uncomfortable place in which to pray, study and assemble, but it would be more alive intellectually and, even more important, more significant religiously.

Does such a modern Orthodox synagogue exist? Not yet. But, even now, there are some modern Orthodox synagogues which are beginning to approximate this model. Certainly not all modern Orthodox synagogues are as intellectually and spiritually empty as the one that Heilman describes. One thing, though, is certain: the direction that the modern Orthodox synagogue will take will serve as some indication as to how serious and honest the modern Orthodox community is in its confrontation with modernity.

Heilman chooses to conclude his most recent article with a flourish. "A genuine *homo duplex*, burnished with a cosmopolitan parochialism, [the modern Orthodox Jew] waits for the Messiah to solve his problem."[10] No doubt Heilman's modern Orthodox Jew, inasmuch as he experiences his Orthodoxy and modernity as antithetical identities, can only perceive his dual commitment as a problem to be endured, resolvable, if at all, only in some distant eschatological future. However, contrary to Heilman, there already are modern Orthodox Jews, and there may yet be more such, who perceive this commitment not so much as a problem, awaiting a messianic resolution, but as a challenge and an opportunity, to be met and seized in the here and now.

10. "Inner and Outer Identities," p. 238.

PART II

The Death of Judaism and the Birth of Judaisms

PROLOGUE TO PART II

THE NINETEENTH CENTURY AND ITS THEOLOGICAL IDEAS

In the nineteenth century sweeping changes in the political circumstances in which Jews made their lives, as well as in the economic conditions in which they made a living, made urgent issues that formerly had drawn slight attention and rendered inconsequential claims that had for so long demanded response. The Jews had formerly constituted a distinct group. Now in the West they formed part of an undifferentiated mass of citizens, all of them equal before the law, all of them subject to the same law. The Judaism of the dual Torah rested on the political premise that the Jews were governed by God's law and formed God's people. The two political premises—the one of the nation-state, the other of the Torah—scarcely permitted reconciliation. The consequent Judaic systems—Reform, Orthodox, Historical (Conservative, in the United States) addressed issues regarded as acute and not merely chronic; and in the nineteenth century each of these Judaisms alleged that it formed the natural next step in the unfolding of the "tradition," meaning the Judaic system of the dual Torah.

From the time of Constantine to the nineteenth century, Jewry in Christendom had sustained itself—first in the East, later in the West—as a recognized and ordinarily tolerated minority, subject to whichever of the contradictory doctrines of Christianity prevailed at a particular time in a particular place: that is, whether the Jews were Christ killers to be punished, or witnesses to be kept alive and ultimately converted at the second coming of Christ. What explains the long-term survival of the Jews in Europe are such factors as the pluralistic character of some societies (for instance, that in Spain before the fourteenth century), the welcome accorded entrepreneurs in opening territories (for instance, Norman England, Poland and Russia, Lithuania, White Russia and the Ukraine, in the early centuries of their development). The Jews, like many other groups, formed not only a tolerated religious minority but something akin to a guild, specializing in certain occupations—for example, crafts and entrepreneurial commerce in the East. After centuries of essentially ordinary existence in the West, the Crusades forced Jewry to migrate to the eastern frontier of Europe.

Before the nineteenth century, the Jews of Europe were subjected to legal restrictions on where they might live and how they might earn a living, and their political and social rights were severely limited. In the East, where most Jews had lived from the late Middle Ages, they governed their own communities through their own administration and law. They spoke their own language, Yiddish; wore distinctive clothing; ate only their own food; controlled their own sector of the larger economy and ventured outside of it only seldom; and, in all, formed a distinct and distinctive group, among other such groups. Commonly, in the villages where they lived, Jews and Christians dwelled side by side; but in many of these villages Jews formed the majority of the population. These facts made for long-term stability and autonomy. In the West, the Jews formed only a tiny proportion of the population but, until modern times, lived equally segregated from the rest of the country, behind the barriers of language, custom, and economic calling. So the Jews for a long time formed a caste, a clearly defined group—but within the hierarchy ordered by the castes of the society at hand.

A process called "emancipation," part of a larger movement of emancipation of serfs, women, slaves, Catholics (in Protestant countries such as England and Ireland), encompassed the Jews as well. Benzion Dinur defines this process of emancipation as follows:

> Jewish emancipation denotes the abolition of disabilities and inequities applied specially to Jews, the recognition of Jews as equal to other citizens, and the formal granting of the rights and duties of citizenship. Essentially the legal act of emancipation should have been simply the expression of the diminution of social hostility and psychological aversion toward Jews in the host nation . . . but the antipathy was not obliterated and constantly hampered the realization of equality even after it had been proclaimed by the state and included in the law.[1]

The political changes that include the Jews' emancipation began in the eighteenth century and, in half a century, had undermined the stability that had characterized the Jews' social and political life since Constantine. These political changes raised questions that previously either had not been found urgent or, it follows, had been neglected.

Dinur traces three periods in the history of the Jews' emancipation: 1740 to 1789, ending with the French Revolution; 1789 to 1878, from the French Revolution to the Congress of Berlin; and 1878 to 1933, from the Congress of Berlin to the rise of the Nazis to power in Germany. In the first period, the emancipation of the Jews first came under discussion; in the second, western and central European states accorded to the Jews the rights of citizenship; and the third saw the rise of a new racism that in the end all but annihilated the Jews of Europe.

In the background of the emancipation of the Jews was a vast movement in European culture that bears the title of "Enlightenment." The Enlightenment, a movement of European intellectuals in the seventeenth and eighteenth centuries, took the view that reason alone was sufficient to produce knowledge and the improvement of society. Opposed to the theological and political claims of Christianity, the new rationalism brought change in philosophy and politics alike, aiming at nothing short of the perfection of humanity through reason. Attention to the Jews, perceived as one of the imperfections of the world, focused upon the matter of their political and economic status. As part of the skepticism and secularism that were taking shape, the received theory of the Jews as a protected but subordinated caste, separate from other groups, came under question. Christianity saw the Jews as special; the Enlightenment did not. The political emancipation of the Jews, turning them from a pariah community into citizens like everyone else, was therefore part of a vast change in the old order in which Christianity defined the culture and politics of the West.

The leaders of Enlightenment shared the prevailing dislike of the Jews. But they regarded the Jews' condition as evidence of the failure of Christianity to accord that status as human beings that would lead the Jews to a (to them) more acceptable mode of life and behavior. The exercise of reason here as elsewhere would therefore remove the imperfections of the world. The impact upon the Jews of the new thinking about the Jews would prove substantial for two reasons. First, in western European countries, the Jews' political status did change. Second, the Jews themselves began to accept the ideals of the Enlightenment, with the result that political modernization found reinforcement in intellectual skepticism and questioning of the received Judaism of the dual Torah.

The appeal to reason in the perfection of the world addressed the issue of the intolerance of religion. To that intolerance—an imperfection in religion—flaws and faults in society were to be attributed. In that setting of secularization, the spokesmen of the Enlightenment invoked the notion that religious intolerance explains the character of the Jews and their low status. To overcome religious intolerance in general, the Jews in particular would have to be liberated. Among the Jews in central Europe, upper-class intellectuals, exposed to the ideas of the Enlightenment, began to shape a theory of religious doctrine and practice in line with the requirements of reason. Their ideas eventually took shape in Reform Judaism. When, at the end of the eighteenth century and the beginning of the nineteenth, Napoleon brought French political ideas of human rights to the conquered parts of Europe—Belgium, the Netherlands, Italy, Germany, and Austria, and even as far east as Russia—Jews saw a new vision of themselves, and some adopted it. They aspired to the rights of citizens and, concomitantly, gave up the status of a protected social entity, living out its life in isolation from the body politic. Toward the middle and later decades of the nineteenth century, as Italy and Germany attained political unification, as Hungary gained independence and then union with Austria, as

Rumania achieved the status of a free and independent country, no longer a dependency of the Ottoman empire, the Jews in those countries found their political status changing. Only in Poland, ruled by tsarist Russia, and in the other provinces of Russia in which the Jews were permitted to live—the Ukraine and White Russia, for example—did the original and enduring pattern persist. There the Jews lived as a distinct social entity. But in western and central Europe, the Jews gained the rights and duties of citizenship.

Dinur explains: "It was stressed that keeping the Jews in a politically limited and socially inferior status was incompatible with the principle of civic equality. . . . 'It is the objective of every political organization to protect the natural rights of man,' hence, 'all citizens have the right to all the liberties and advantages of citizens, without exception.' "[2] The adoption of the Constitution of the United States in 1787 confirmed that nation's position on the matter: Jewish males, along with all other white males, enjoyed citizenship. Jews in the nineteenth century entered the political and cultural life of the Western nations, including their overseas empires. During this second period, Reform Judaism reached its first stage of development, beginning in Germany (chapter 2). This Judaism made it possible for Jews to hold together the two things they deemed inseparable: their desire to remain Jewish, and their wish also to be one with their fellow citizens. By the middle of the nineteenth century, Reform had reached full expression and had won the support of a sizable part of German Jewry. At the same time, in reaction against Reform, Orthodoxy came into existence (chapter 3): this Judaism, no less than Reform, asked how "Judaism" could coexist with "Germanness," meaning citizenship in an undifferentiated republic of citizens. Then, mediating between Reform and Orthodoxy, a centrist position was worked out by theologians in what was then, in Germany, called the Historical School and, in twentieth-century America, took the name of Conservative Judaism (chapter 4). The century from the French Revolution saw the full efflorescence of all the Judaisms of political modernization.

In the years after 1880, Europe took a different turn, and anti-Semitism as a political and social movement came into being. The movement away from the process of political rationalization reached expression in several ways. First, the new nation-states began that process of local rivalry that culminated in the European civil strife of the First and Second World Wars. Nationalism brought with it intolerance of difference; and, in some ways (if only religious ones) the Jews remained different. Second, the forces of imperialism, which brought Europe deep into the life of Africa, Asia, Latin America, and the South Pacific, carried disdain for peoples who were not white, not Christian, and, by the way, for the sector of those peoples that was not male. The representation of the African black as less than human found its counterpart in the treatment of the European Jew as subhuman. Religious reaction saw the formation of religious political parties, from which Jews, of course, were excluded. In these and other ways, Europe in the West turned its back upon the ideals of the Enlightenment and embarked on a path of racism and imperialism, exclusionary nationalism and statism, that in the twentieth century led to wars of mass destruction and the annihilation of whole populations, chief among them the Jews of Europe.

Jews began to realize that, in Dinur's words, "the state's legal recognition of Jewish civic and political equality does not automatically bring social recognition of this equality."[3] The Jews continued to form a separate group and were considered racially inferior. The impact of the new racism would be felt disastrously in the twentieth century.

Clearly, in the nineteenth century, particularly in Western countries, a new order was revising the political settlement that had prevailed for fifteen centuries. Since the time of Constantine, the political questions rising from the Jews' essentially autonomous life as a protected minority had found answers of an essentially supernatural and theological character. But emancipation redefined those questions, which now centered on Jews not as a distinct group but as part of some other polity altogether. Those Jews who simply passed over retain no interest for us: Karl Marx, for example, who converted to Christianity at an early age, produced no ideas important in the study of Judaism(s). But vast numbers of Jews in the West determined to remain Jewish and also to become something else: that is, a citizen of Germany or France or Britain. This issue would not confront the Jews of the Russian empire until the First World War; and these Jews, together with those of the Austro-Hungarian empire, Rumania, and other areas of eastern Europe, formed the vast majority of world Jewry.

While the Jews of the West were only a small minority of the Jews of the world—the Western frontier (extending, to be sure, to California in the farthest west of all) of the Jewish people, their confrontation with political change proved paradigmatic. They were the ones to invent the Judaisms of the nineteenth century. Each of these Judaic systems exhibited three characteristic traits. First, it asked, as I have indicated, how one could be both Jewish and something else—that is, also a citizen, a member of a nation. Second, it defined "Judaism" (that is, its system) as a religion, so leaving ample space for that something else—namely, nationality, whether German (*Deutschtum und Judentum*, "Germanness and Jewishness"), or British, or French, or American. Third, it appealed to history to prove the continuity between its system and the received Judaism of the dual Torah. The resort to historical fact, the claim that the system at hand formed the linear development of the past, the natural increment of the entire history of Israel, the Jewish people, from the beginning to the new day—that essentially factual claim masked a profound conviction concerning self-evidence. The urgent question at hand—the political one—produced a self-evidently correct answer out of the history of politics constituted by historical narrative.

That appeal to history, particularly historical fact, characterizes all three Judaisms. The Reformers stated explicitly that theirs would be a Judaism built on fact. The facts of history, in particular, would guide Jews to the definition of what was essential and what could be dropped. History, then, formed the court of appeal—but also the necessary link, the critical point of continuity. The Historical School took the same position but reached different conclusions: history would show how change could be effected, and the principles of historical change would then govern. Orthodoxy met the issue in a different way, maintaining that Judaism was above history, not an historical fact at all. But the Orthodox position would also appeal most forcefully to the past in its claim to constitute the natural and complete continuation of Judaism in its true form. The importance of history in the theological thought of the nineteenth-century Judaisms derives from the intellectual heritage of the age, with its stress on the nation-state as the definitive unit of society, and on history as the mode of defining the culture and character of the nation-state. History as an instrument of reform, further, had served the Protestant Reformation, with its appeal to Scripture as against (mere) tradition, with its claim that it would restore Christianity to its (historical) purity. Finally and most important, the supernaturalism of the inherited Judaism of the dual Torah, its emphasis upon God's active intervention in history, on miracles, on a perpetual concern for the natural implications of the supernatural will and covenant—that supernaturalism contradicted the rationalism of the age. The one thing the Jewish thinkers wished to accomplish was to show the rationalism, the reason—the normality—of the Judaisms they constructed. The appeal to (mere) facts of history, as against the unbelievable claims of a Scripture, placed upon a positive and this-worldly foundation the religious view of the world that, in the received system of the dual Torah, rested upon a completely supernatural view of reality.

For the three Judaisms of the age, which we see as continuous in important ways, took as their task the demonstration of how they formed out of the received and unwanted old Judaism something new, different, and acceptable. Since the Judaisms of the nineteenth century were born in the matrix of the received system of the dual Torah, among people who themselves grew up in a world in which that Judaism defined what people meant by Judaism, I must address the fact that the framers of the Judaisms of continuation could not evade the issue of continuity. They wished both to continue and also to innovate—and to justify innovation. And this desire affected Orthodoxy as much as Reform. In making changes, the framers of each Judaism appealed to the past for justification. But they pointed to those changes also as proof that they had overcome an unwanted past. The delicate balance between tradition and change attained by each of the Judaisms of continuation marks the genius of its inventors. All worked out the same equation: change but not too much, whatever the proportion a group found excessive.

CHAPTER 2

REFORM JUDAISM: HISTORY AND SELF-EVIDENCE

The Birth of a Judaism

Reform Judaism began with some modest changes in the liturgy but ended up the single most important and most effective Judaism of the nineteenth century in central Europe and of the later twentieth century in America. The reason is that Reform Judaism forthrightly and articulately faced political changes that redefined the conditions of Jews' lives, and presented a Judaism closely tied to the inherited system of the dual Torah and fully responsive to those changes. Constructive and intellectually vital in its day, Reform Judaism said what it would do, and did it. Still more interesting, because it was a movement that confronted the issues of the day and the Jews' condition, Reform Judaism found itself able to change itself, its own deepest concerns and values. So the Judaism at hand made itself into an instrument for what Jews wanted and needed it to be—whatever that was. Consequently, Reform Judaism provides the model for the other Judaisms that are continuators of the Judaism of the dual Torah, and furthermore set the issues for debate from then to our own day. No Judaism in the past two hundred years exercised deeper influence in defining the issues Jews would debate; none made a richer or more lasting contribution to the program of answers Jews would find self-evident.

Since I want to examine whether the Judaisms of the nineteenth and twentieth centuries continued the received Judaism of the dual Torah or marked essentially new Judaisms, coming to full creation, each in its own terms and structure and system of viewpoints and practices, I take up Reform Judaism not at its beginning but at its moment of complete exposure and expression. The full and authoritative statement of this system—its world view, with profound implications on its way of life, and its theory of who is Israel—came to expression, in the nineteenth century, not in Europe but in America, in an assembly in Pittsburgh in 1885 of Reform rabbis. At that meeting of the Central Conference of American Rabbis, the Reform Judaism of the age—by now about a century aborning—took up the issues that divided it and made an authoritative statement about them, one that most people could accept.

The very fact that the Judaism before us could conceive of such debate and formulation of a kind of creed indicates that this Judaism found urgent the specification of its systemic structure, testimony to a mature and self-aware frame of mind. We look in vain for equivalent convocations to set public policy, for example, in the antecedent thousand years of the Judaism of the dual Torah. Statements of the world view, as these had emerged in diverse expressions of the received system, had not taken the form of a rabbis' platform, on the one side, and had not come about through democratic debate on public issues, on the other. That world view had percolated upward and represented a rarely articulated and essentially inchoate consensus about how things really are and should be. The received system had come to expression in how things were done, in what people found needless to make articulate at all: the piety of a milieu, not the proposition of a theological gathering. The contrast with Reform Judaism tells us not merely that the latter was a new Judaism, but—of greater interest—that the methods and approaches of this system enjoyed their own self-evident appropriateness. And from that fact we learn how the qualities people found self-evidently right had changed over time.

So we begin our trip in Pittsburgh, Pennsylvania, among rabbis who could point to three or even four generations of Reform antecedents. These were not the founders of the new faith—the Judaism before us came to birth about a generation before anyone recognized it—but the authorities of an established and enduring one. For the end of the nineteenth century found Reform Judaism a major component of the Judaic religious life of America as well as of Germany, and it was making inroads elsewhere as well. The American Reform rabbis, meeting in Pittsburgh in 1885, issued a clear and accessible statement of their Judaism. How did this Judaism formulate the issue of Israel as a political group? For critical to the Judaism of the dual Torah was its view of Israel as God's people, a supernatural polity, living out its social existence under God's Torah. The way of life, one of sanctification, and the world view, one of persistent reference to the Torah for rules of conduct, on the one side, and of the explanation of conduct, on the other, began in the basic conception of who is Israel. Here, too, we find emphasis on who is Israel, with that doctrine exposing for all to see the foundations of the way of life and world view that these rabbis had formed for the Israel they conceived. The Pittsburgh platform declared:

> We recognize in the Mosaic legislation a system of training the Jewish people for its mission during its national life in Palestine, and today we accept as binding only its moral laws and maintain only such ceremonies as elevate and sanctify our lives, but reject all such as are not adapted to the views and habits of modern civilization. . . . We hold that all such Mosaic and rabbinical laws as regular diet, priestly purity, and dress originated in ages and under the influence of ideas entirely foreign to our present mental and spiritual state. . . . Their observance in our days is apt rather to obstruct than to further modern spiritual elevation. . . . We recognize in the modern era of universal culture of heart and intellect the approaching of the realization of Israel's great messianic hope for the establishment of the kingdom of truth, justice, and peace among all men. We consider ourselves no longer a nation but a religious community and therefore expect neither a return to Palestine nor a sacrificial worship under the sons of Aaron nor the restoration of any of the laws concerning the Jewish state.[1]

I cannot imagine a more forthright address to the age. The Pittsburgh platform takes up each component of the system in turn. Who is Israel? What is its way of life? How does it account for its existence as a distinct, and distinctive, group? Israel once was a nation ("during its national life") but today is not a nation. It once had a set of laws regulating diet, clothing, and the like. These no longer apply, because Israel now is not what it was then. Israel forms an integral part of Western civilization. The reason for persisting as a distinctive group is that the group has its work to do:

namely, to realize the messianic hope for the establishment of a kingdom of truth, justice, and peace. For that purpose, Israel no longer constitutes a nation. It now forms a religious community.

What that means is that individual Jews live as citizens in other nations. Difference is acceptable at the level of religion, not of nationality, a position that accords fully with the definition of citizenship of the Western democracies. The world view then lays heavy emphasis on an as-yet unrealized but coming perfect age. The way of life admits to no important traits that distinguish Jews from others, since morality, in the nature of things, forms a universal category, applicable in the same way to everyone. The theory of Israel then forms the heart of matters, and what we learn is that Israel constitutes a "we": that is, the Jews continue to form a group that, by its own indicators, holds together and constitutes a cogent social entity. All this in a simple statement of a handful of rabbis forms a full and encompassing Judaism, one that, to its communicants, presented truth of a self-evident order. But it was also a truth declared, not discovered; and the self-evidence of the truth of the statements competed with the self-awareness characteristic of those who made them. For they could recognize the problem that demanded attention: the reframing of a theory of Israel for that Israel that they themselves constituted; that "we" that required explanation. No more urgent question faced the rabbis, because, after all, they lived in a century of opening horizons, in which people could envision perfection. The First World War would change all that. By 1937 the Reform rabbis, meeting in Columbus, Ohio, would reframe the system, expressing a world view quite different from that of the previous half-century.

Let me briefly summarize the program of urgent issues and self-evident responses that constituted the first of the new Judaisms of the nineteenth century. Questions we find answered fall into two categories: first, why "we" do not keep certain customs and ceremonies but do keep others; second, how "we relate to the nations in which we live." The system of Reform Judaism explained both why and why not: that is, why this, not that—the mark of a fully framed and cogent Judaism. The affirmative side covered why the Jews would persist as a separate group; the negative would account for the limits of difference. These two questions deal with the same urgent problem: namely, working out a mode of Judaic existence compatible with citizenship in (for these rabbis) America. Jews do not propose to eat or dress in distinctive ways. They do seek a place within "modern spiritual elevation . . . universal culture of heart and intellect." They impute to that culture the realization of the "messianic hope"—a considerable stake. And, explicit to the whole, the Jews no longer constitute a nation. They therefore belong to some other nation(s). If I had to specify a single self-evident proposition taken fully into account by Reform Judaism, it is that political change had changed the entirety of Judaism, but the Judaism at hand had the power to accommodate that change. So change in general formed the method for dealing with the immediate problem, which was change in the political and social standing the Jews were now enjoying. So, on the very surface, Reform Judaism formed a Judaic system that confronted immense political change and presented a world view and a way of life to an Israel defined other than as a political entity. Two questions demand attention: How did this Judaism come into being, and how did its intellectuals explain their system?

If I had to specify the single dominant concern of the framers of Reform Judaism, I should point to the Jews' position in the public polity of the several Christian, European countries in which they lived. After the political changes stemming from the American and French revolutions, the received system of the Judaism of the dual Torah answered the wrong questions. A new question, emerging from forces not contained within once-regnant Christianity, demanded attention from Jews affected by those forces. For those Jews, shifts in political circumstances defined the urgent question: change. Historians began to look for evidence of precedents for changing things because their own circumstance had already persuaded them that change mattered: change itself effects change (so to speak). They sought a picture of a world in which they might find a place—and, it went without saying, a picture that would outline a Judaic system—a way of life, a world view, and a definition of the Israel that would live the one and believe the other. The new Judaism was confronted with political change brought about not by Christianity but by forces of nationalism, which conceived of society as the expression not of God's will for the social order under the rule of Christ and his Church or his anointed king (emperor, tsar) but of popular will for the social order under the government of the people and their elected representatives—a considerable shift. When society does not form the aggregate of distinct groups—each with its place and definition, language, and religion—but consists rather of undifferentiated citizens (male, white, wealthy, to be sure), then the Judaism that Jews in such a society have to work out also will account for difference of a different order altogether. That Judaism has to frame a theory of who is Israel consonant with the social situation of Jews who wish to be different, but not so different that they cannot also be citizens.

The original and enduring Judaic system of Reform correctly appealed, for its intellectual foundations, to Moses Mendelssohn, an eighteenth-century Jewish philosopher and follower of the Enlightenment, who (in the words of Michael A. Meyer) called "for a pluralistic society that offered full freedom of conscience to all those who accepted the postulates of natural religion: God, Providence, and a future life."[2] The initial phrase presents the important component: a pluralistic society which, in the nature of things, constitutes a political category. Issues dominant from Mendelssohn's time on concerned "emancipation"—meaning the provision, for Jews, of the rights of citizens. Reform theologians took the lead in the struggle for such rights. To them it was self-evident that Jews not only should have civil rights and civic equality but also should want them. A Judaism that did not explain why the Jews should want and have full equality as part of a common humanity ignored the issues preoccupying those who found, in Reform Judaism, a corpus of self-evident truths. To those truths, the method—the appeal to historical facts—formed a contingent and secondary consideration.

To the Reform rabbis in Pittsburgh, Christianity presented no urgent problems. The open society of America did. The self-evident definition of the social entity, Israel, therefore had to shift. We recall how the fourth-century rabbis balanced Israel against Rome, Jacob against Esau, the triumphant political messiah, seen as arrogant, against the Messiah of God, humble and sagacious. So Israel formed a supernatural entity and in due course would enter into that final era in God's division of time, in which Israel would reach its blessing. The supernatural entity, Israel, now formed no social presence. Gone was the Christian world, where Christ ruled through popes and emperors, kings claimed divine right, and the will of the Church bore multiform consequences for society; and where, by the way, Israel, too, was perceived in a supernatural framework—if a negative one. So the world at large no longer verified the category of Israel as supernatural entity. Then came the problem of defining what sort of entity Israel did constitute, and what way of life should characterize that Israel, what world view should explain it: that problem produced a new set of urgent and ineluctable questions and inevitably self-evidently true answers, such as those in Pittsburgh later on.

To return to the birth of Reform Judaism, this Judaism dates its beginnings to Germany in the early nineteenth century. The reason for the development in Germany in particular was that German society, after the Napoleonic wars, underwent a process of change and reform. In tearing down the walls of the ghetto in Frankfurt, Napoleon had called into question the centuries-old status of the Jews. That small act formed part of a larger program of political change, and the momentum of that change persisted even after the defeat of Napoleon. For the forces of nationalism that were born in the German victory called into question many aspects of the established political settlement and brought about change on diverse fronts. The Jews, among other groups, now aspired to a position different from the one they had known for centuries. Some of them wished to find a place within the German polity, as citizens equal to other citizens. And, outside their community, forces for change of a political, as well as social and economic, character converged to produce that same result. Over the short term, change yielded dissolution of the Jewish community. For a fair proportion of Jewry simply left the community and adopted the dominant religion of the region in which they lived. This they accepted as the passport to Western civilization, civil rights, and, of course, career advancement. But those Jews who remained within the community determined on another path: that is, to change things in such a way as to accommodate Jewry to the requirements of citizenship. The earliest changes, called reforms and regarded as the antecedents of Reform, concerned trivial aspects of public worship in the synagogue.

These changes derived from the simple fact that many

Jews rejected the received system. People were defecting from the synagogue. Since, it was taken for granted, giving up the faith meant surrendering all ties to the group, the beginning of change required reform and ultimately Reform addressed two issues at one time: (1) making the synagogue more attractive, so that (2) defectors would return, and other Jews would not leave. The reform of Judaism as manifested in synagogue worship—the cutting edge of the faith—therefore took cognizance of something that had already taken place. And that was the loss for the received system—way of life, world view, addressed to a defined Israel—of its standing as self-evident truth. That loss manifested itself in two ways. First, people were simply leaving. Second and more important for the group, the many who were staying looked in a new way on what, for so long, had scarcely demanded examination. But, of course, the real issues involved not the synagogue but society at large. It would take two generations before Reform Judaism found the strength to address that much larger issue, and a generation further for the power of the ideas ultimately formulated in the Pittsburgh platform to be felt.

To begin with, the issue involved not politics but merely the justification for any change at all. But that issue asked the wrong question in the wrong way. The Reformers maintained that change was all right because historical precedent proved that change was all right. But change had long defined the constant in the ongoing life of the Judaism of the dual Torah. Generative causes and modes of effecting change marked the vitality of the system. The Judaism of the dual Torah endured, never intact but always unimpaired, because of its power to absorb and make its own the diverse happenings of culture and society. So long as the structure of politics remained the same, with Israel an autonomous entity, subordinated but recognized as a cogent and legitimate social group in charge of some of its own affairs, the system answered the paramount question. The trivial ones could work their way through and become part of the consensus, to be perceived in the end as tradition, too. A catalogue of changes that took place over fifteen hundred years, from the birth of Judaism to its death, would therefore list many more dramatic and decisive sorts of change than those minor revisions of liturgy—for example, sermons in the vernacular—that attracted attention at the dawn of the age of change-become-Reform.

What, then, made the difference so that change could be perceived as reform and transformed into the reform of Judaism—hence, Reform Judaism? When people could take a stance external to the received mode and effect change as a matter of decision and policy, for them Judaism in its received form had already died. For the received system no longer defined matters but now became subject to definition. And that change marks the move from self-evidence to self-consciousness.

We do not know what had brought about the demise of the received system as definitive and normative beyond all argument. Nothing in the earliest record of liturgical reform tells us. The constructive efforts of the first generation—only later recognized not as people who made changes or even as reformers but as founders of Reform Judaism—focused, as I have said, upon synagogue worship. The services were too long; the speeches were in a language (Hebrew) with which participants were no longer familiar; the singing was not aesthetic; the prayers were in a language no one now understood. Hence, some people recited them as a matter of duty, not in supplication; did not speak the language of the faith; formed other than received opinions on how to sing in synagogue; saw as alien what earlier had marked home and hearth. Those people no longer lived in that same social world that had for so long found right and proper precisely the customs now seen as alien.

When the heritage forms an unclaimed, unwanted legacy, out of duty people nonetheless accept it. So the reform that produced Reform Judaism introduced a shortened service, a sermon in the language people spoke, a choir and an organ, prayers in the vernacular. Clearly, much change had taken place prior to the recognition that something had changed. People no longer knew Hebrew; they no longer found pleasing received modes of saying the prayers. We look in vain to the subsequent reforms for answers to the question why people made these changes, and the reasons adduced by historians settle no interesting questions for us. The more interesting question concerns why the persistence of engagement and concern. For people always had the option, which many exercised, of abandoning the received Judaism. Among those for whom these cosmetic changes made a difference, much in the liturgy, and far more beyond, retained its powerful appeal. The premise of change dictated that Jews would say the old prayers in essentially the old formulation. And that premise carried much else: the entire burden of the faith; the total commitment to the group, in some form, defined by some indicators—if not the familiar ones, then some others. So we know that Reform Judaism, in its earliest manifestation in Germany in the early nineteenth century, constituted an essentially conservative, profoundly constructive effort to save for Jews the received Judaism by reforming it in some (to begin with) rather trivial ways.

The theory of the incremental history of a single, linear Judaism played a powerful role in the creative age of Reform Judaism. The ones who made changes (it is too soon to call them Reformers, or the changes Reforms) first appealed to the authoritative texts. Change is legitimate, and these changes in particular were wholly consonant with the law, or the tradition, or the inner dynamics of the faith, or the dictates of history, or whatever out of the past worked that day. The laymen who made the changes tried to demonstrate that the changes fit in with the law of Judaism. They took the trouble because Reform even at the outset claimed to restore, to continue, to persist in, the received pattern. The justification of change always invoked precedent. People who made changes had to show that their guiding principle was not new, even though the specific things they did were. So to lay down a bridge between themselves and their past, they laid out beams resting on deep-set piles. Change was founded on the bedrock of precedent. And more still: change restores, reverts to an unchanging ideal. So the Reformer claimed not to change at all, but only to regain the correct state of affairs, a state that others, in the interval, themselves had changed. That formed the fundamental attitude of mind of the people who made changes and called the changes Reform. The appeal to history, a common mode of justification in the politics and theology of the nineteenth century, therefore defined the principal justification for the new Judaism: it was new because it renewed the old and enduring, the golden Judaism of a mythic age of perfection. Arguments on precedent, as we shall see, drew the Reformers to the work of critical scholarship: they settled all questions by appeal to the facts of history.

We cannot find surprising, therefore, the theory that Reform Judaism stands in a direct line with the prior history of Judaism. Judaism is one. Judaism has a history; that history is single and unitary; and it has always been leading to its present outcome: Reform Judaism. Others would later challenge these convictions: Orthodox Judaism would deny that Judaism has a history at all; Conservative, or Positive Historical Judaism, would discover a different goal for history from that embodied by Reform Judaism. But the mode of argument, appealing to issues of a historical and factual character, and the premises of argument, insisting that history proved or disproved matters of theological conviction, characterized all the Judaisms of the nineteenth century. Not surprisingly, since the Judaisms of the age took shape in the intellectual world of Germany, with its profoundly philosophical and historical mode of thought and argument. So the challenge of political change carried with it its own modes of intellectual response: in the academic, scholarly framework.

In Germany, the method of the Judaism aborning as Reform exhibited a certain congruence to the locale. Whether Luther is demanding reversion to the pure and primitive faith of the Gospels or the earliest generation of Reform leaders are appealing to the Talmud as justification for rejecting what others saw as the Talmud's contemporary requirements, the principle remains the same. Reform renews; recovers the true condition of a faith; selects, out of a diverse past, that age and that moment at which the faith attained its perfect definition and embodiment. Not change, but restoration and renewal of the true modes, the recovery of the way things were in that perfect, paradigmatic time, that age that formed the model for all time: these deeply mythic modes of appeal formed the justification for change, transforming mere modification of this and that into Reform. The leaders of change took on the mantle of Reform, for they revised not only a few lines of a prayer but the entire world view expressed in the accepted liturgy.

The mythic being of the liturgy entailed the longing, in the imagination of the nation, for a return to Zion, for rebuilding of the Temple, for reconstitution of the bloody rites of animal sacrifice. In response to the Christian view that Israel's salvation had occurred in times past and ended with Israel's rejection of the Christhood of Jesus, the dual Torah had insisted on future salvation, at the end of time—which, self-evidently, had not yet arrived. For ages after the original exile, in 586 B.C.E., the Jews had appealed to a Scripture that explained why they had lost their land, their city, their Temple, their cult, and told them what they had to do to get them back. That scriptural message thus, as we have seen, formed a principal plank in the messianic platform of the Judaism of the dual Torah, since sages alleged that if Israel kept the Torah as they taught it, its promises—those of the Pentateuch and prophets alike—would come true. The Messiah-sage stood for exactly that outcome.

To Jews the condition of Israel in exile formed a self-evident fact of politics and culture alike. Speaking their own language, pursuing occupations distinctive to their group, living essentially apart from other peoples of the same time and place (who themselves formed not a uniform nation but a mosaic of equivalent social entities, that is, religion-nations, each with its language and its economy and its distinct society), Jews knew who they were. They were a nation in exile. The early changes, therefore, signaled that much else already had undergone revision and still more would have to change as well. Reform ratified change now a generation old, proposed to cope with it, and so to reframe and revise the received tradition as to mark out new outlines for self-evident truth.

The original changes, in the first decades of the nineteenth century, produced a new generation of rabbis. Some forty years into the century, these rabbis gave to the process of change the name of Reform and created those institutions of Reform Judaism that would endow the inchoate movement with a politics of its own. In the mid-1840s, several rabbinical conferences brought together this new generation. Trained in universities, rabbis who came to these gatherings turned backward, justifying the changes in prayer rites long in place, effecting some further, mostly cosmetic, changes in the observance of the Sabbath and in the laws covering personal status through marriage and divorce. In 1845, a decision to adopt for some purposes German in place of Hebrew led to the departure of conservative

Reformers, typified by Zacharias Frankel. But the Reformers found their apologia in the received writings, persisting in their insistence that they formed a natural continuation of the processes of the tradition. Indeed, that point of insistence—that Judaism formed, in the words of the eminent Reform theologian Jacob J. Petuchowski in regard to Abraham Geiger, "a constantly evolving organism"[3]—was the centerpiece of the nascent Judaism at hand.

Reform Theologian: Abraham Geiger

If we want to understand the new Judaisms of the age, we must turn to the leading intellect to show us how people reached their conclusions, not merely what they said or why they found self-evident the positions they took. Abraham Geiger (1810–74) enjoyed the advantage of the finest argumentative mind in Jewry in the nineteenth century, and his life presents facts of less interest than his work. In his work, his way of asking and answering questions tells us what matters in Reform Judaism: what people found self-evident, on the one side, and urgent, on the other. The urgency accounts for the questions, the self-evidence, the mode of discovering the answers. To those two matters, everything else takes second place. The question Geiger found ineluctable takes simple form: How can we explain what has happened to us? The answer: What has taken place—change become Reform—forms the natural and necessary outcome of history. In his emphasis upon the probative status and value of the facts of history, those self-evident principles lead us deep into the consciousness of the man and the Judaism he embodied. What Geiger took for granted—in our terms, held as self-evident—is that history proved propositions of theology. Whatever the particular matter of conviction or custom takes a secondary place. The primary source of verification, therefore, of appropriate and inappropriate traits in Judaism—that is to say, the origin of the reliable definition of Judaism—lies not in revealed records of God's will but in human accounts of humanity's works. To that principle—everywhere taken for granted, occasionally enunciated, but never systematically demonstrated—Geiger's mode of argument and inquiry took second place.

Since the earliest changes changed into reforms, and reforms of Judaism into Reform Judaism, to Geiger we address our principal questions: Old or new? And how did people explain themselves? Abraham Geiger presented in clearest form the argument that Reform carried forward the historical processes of Judaism. He took the position that there was a single, linear Judaism, and that it was affected by history—that is, by change. He appealed to the facts of history, beginning with the critical study of the Bible. Petuchowski summarizes his view as follows:

> Judaism is a constantly evolving organism. Biblical Judaism was not identical with classical rabbinic Judaism. Similarly, the modern age calls for further evolution in consonance with the changed circumstances. . . . The modern rabbis are entitled to adapt medieval Judaism, as the early rabbis had the right to adapt biblical Judaism. . . . He found traces of evolution within the Bible itself. Yet for Geiger changes in Judaism had always been organic. . . . The modern changes must develop out of the past, and not represent a revolutionary break with it.[4]

Geiger, therefore, recognized change as traditional: that is, changing represents the way things always have been and so legitimately now goes forward. The Jews change, having moved from constituting a nation to a different classification of social entity. The Messiah idea now addresses the whole of humanity, speaks not only of national restoration. Revelation then turns out to form a progressive, not a static, fact. In these diverse ways, Geiger—and with him, Reform Judaism through its history—appealed to history to verify its allegations and validate its positions. So facts turn into the evidence for faith.

Geiger grew up in Frankfurt and undertook university studies at Heidelberg, then Bonn, with special interest in philosophy and Semitics.[5] At that time, university study formed the exception, not the rule, for Jews. By definition, therefore, the change Geiger had to explain came about through the decision of the former generation. Geiger explained change; his parents made it. But among the intellectual leaders in Geiger's day, not only he, but his arch-opponent, Samson Raphael Hirsch, founder of Orthodox Judaism, also acquired a university education. So Orthodox Judaism, too, emerged as the result of the decision of the generation prior to the age of the founders (see chapter 3). To both sets of parents, the value of an education in the sciences of the West proved self-evident; the ways of harmonizing that education and its values with the education in the Judaic sciences were considerably less clear. Earlier generations had not sent their sons to universities (and, for a similar right, their daughters would have to wait until nearly our own day). Prior to the generation of the parents of Geiger and Hirsch, most parents found self-evident the value of education in the established institutions of the Judaism of the dual Torah—there alone. Knowledge of another sort, under other auspices, bore no value. Thus, before the advent of the reformer, whether the great intellect of Reform Judaism or the courageous leader of Orthodoxy, change had already affected self-evident truth.

Geiger served a parlous life in synagogue pulpits, not always appreciated for the virtues he brought to them: flawless German and his questioning of routine.[6] He spent most of his time, however, concerned not with the local synagogue community but with the constituency of Judaic learning. He began to produce a periodical, the *Scientific Journal for Jewish Theology*, in 1835. The purpose of scientific knowledge Max Wiener epitomizes in the following statement: "They were convinced that, given the historical facts, it would be possible to draw the correct practical conclusions with regard to the means by which their religion could best be served and elevated to the level of contemporary culture."[7] That is to say, through systematic learning Judaism would undergo reform. Reform Judaism rested on deep foundations of historical scholarship.

It was Geiger's aim to analyze the sources and the evolution of Judaism. If science (used in its German sense of "systematic learning") could uncover the sources of the Jewish "spirit," then, in Wiener's words, "the genius of his people and . . . its vocation" would serve "as a guide to the construction of a living present and future." Geiger's principle of Reform remained fixed. Reform had to emerge from *Wissenschaft*, "a term which he equated with the concept of the understanding of historical evolution." To him, "Judaism in its ideal form was religion per se, nothing but an expression of religious consciousness. Its outer shell was subject to change from one generation to another."[8] All things emerge out of time and of change. But when it comes to tracing the history of time and change, contemporary categories assuredly defined the inquiry. Thus Geiger produced, out of ancient times, portraits suspiciously congruent to the issues of his own day.

For example, in his account of the Sadducees and the Pharisees—the former enjoying a bad press; the latter, in Judaism, a good one—he identified the former with "the strict guardians of traditional institutions, while the latter spoke out in behalf of progress in both religion and politics."[9]* Geiger's principal point was: "What Geiger sought to prove by this demonstration [that the text of Scripture was fluid] is quite obvious. It was not the Bible that created and molded the religious spirit of Judaism; instead, it was the spirit of Judaism that left the stamp of its own form and expression upon the Bible—Life, and its needs and strivings, change from age to age."[11] Wiener and Petuchowski's accounts show what Geiger found to be self-evident: truths beyond all appeal that formed the foundation of his life's work as the first and best historian of Judaism. These premises we identify not in the propositions he proposed to demonstrate, but in the facts concerning change and the constancy of change which he took for granted.

At the outset I raised the question whether the framers of the Judaisms of the nineteenth century claimed to renew the received Judaism of the dual Torah or to invent a Judaism. And if they alleged that they stood as the natural next step in the tradition, does that claim stand? Geiger represents the answer of Reform Judaism in his day, a powerful and one-sided answer. Reform Judaism renews; it does not invent. There was, and is, only a single Judaism. In the current age, Reform undertakes the discovery of that definition. Reform clearly lays its foundations on the basis of history—that is, tradition. Propositions of a theological character, for example, concerning the dual Torah revealed at Sinai, the sanctified and therefore supernatural character of Israel, the holy people, the coming Messiah-sage at the end of time—these take their place in the line of truths to

* The Sadducees and Pharisees were sects in the Judaism of the period before the year 70. The Sadducees, who are regarded as upper-class figures, denied the existence of oral tradition. The Pharisees, who are described as influential, affirmed the existence of oral tradition, later called the oral Torah. These matters are placed into their own context in my *Self-Fulfilling Prophecy: Exile and Return in the History of Judaism.*[10]

be investigated through historical method, in historical sources. There may be an incongruity between the propositions at hand and the allegations about the decisive, probative character of historical inquiry in evaluating them. For the facts of history hardly testify, one way or another, concerning the character of revelation at Sinai (though we may know what people recorded in that connection), the status and sanctity of Israel (though the social facts and political issues surely pertained to this-worldly Israel), let alone that event at the end, on the other side, of history altogether—the coming of the Messiah.

The question whether the claim of Reform Judaism finds justification in the "facts" proves beside the point. The facts are what people make of them, whether discovered in history or imputed in revealed and holy writings, in a canon of truth. We can scarcely say that the position of Reform Judaism, as outlined by a brief sketch of Geiger's thought, even intersects or connects with what had gone before. Old or new? Not only new, but out of all relationship to the old. The appeal to the old—to history—turns out to come after the fact, the system, had already come to ample formation. Once the Judaism at hand had come into being, people knew what they wanted to find out from history: that is, whether things change. Geiger followed a far more sophisticated program since, knowing that things do change (to whom would the proposition have brought surprise?), he asked exactly how, in Judaism, change takes place, and in what direction. In his view, it was obvious that the Sadducees looked like the Orthodox of his day, and the Pharisees, like the Reformers.

The point of self-evidence, then, is that the categories defined in Geiger's day pertained a long time ago. That is the mark of the new Judaism called Reform Judaism: its powerful capacity without a trace of self-consciousness to impose anachronistic issues and categories. What changes is the repertoire of self-evident truths.

The Appeal to Historical Precedent: Abraham Cronbach and Jacob R. Marcus

Reform Judaism, once well under way, had to situate itself in relationship to the past. Geiger's powerful appeal to precedent left no choice. For not all precedents sustained contemporary choices—the system as it had already emerged; and some of the more recent choices surely called it into question. So as learning rolled forward, the question arose, Precisely what, in history, serves as a precedent for change-become-Reform? The answer sought the constants in change. To advance our understanding of Reform Judaism, we move once more to America, the country where Reform Judaism enjoyed massive success in the last half of the twentieth century, and where we see in full and articulate formulation the world view of Reform Judaism as it unfolded in a straight line from Geiger's day to our own. Our guide is Abraham Cronbach, a professor at Hebrew Union College during the first half of the twentieth century.

Specifically, in his preface to Abraham Cronbach's *Reform Movements in Judaism,* Jacob Rader Marcus, a principal voice in Reform Judaism in the twentieth century, provides a powerful statement of the Reform view of its place in history. Marcus recognizes that diverse Judaisms have flourished in the history of the Jews. What characterizes them all is that each began as a reform movement but then underwent a process we might characterize as "traditionalization." That is to say, change became not merely reform but tradition, and the only constant in the histories of Judaisms is that process of transformation of the new to the conventional or, in theological language, the traditional. This process Marcus describes as follows: "All [Judaisms] began as rebellions, as great reformations, but after receiving widespread acceptance, developed vested 'priestly' interests, failed their people, and were forced to retreat before the onslaught of new rebellions, new philosophies, new challenges." Nothing in Marcus's picture could have been a surprise to Geiger. So endures the fundamental theological method of Reform Judaism in its initial phase, the appeal to facts of history for the validation of theological propositions. But the claim that everything always changes yields a challenge, which Marcus forthrightly raises: "Is there then nothing but change? Is change the end of all our history and all our striving? No, there is something else, the desire to be free. . . . In the end [the Jew] has always understood that changelessness is spiritual death. The Jew who would live must never completely surrender himself to one truth, but . . . must reach out for the farther and faint horizons of an ever Greater God. . . . This is the meaning of Reform."[12]

Marcus thus treats as self-evident—obvious because it is a fact of history—the persistence of change. And, denying that that is all there is to Reform, at the end he affirms the simple point that change sets the norm. It comes down to the same thing. The something else of Marcus's argument presents its own problems. Appeal to the facts of history fails at the point when a constructive position demands articulation. "The desire to be free" bears a predicate: Free of what? Free to do, to be what? If Marcus fails to accomplish the whole of the theological task, however, he surely conveys the profoundly constructive vision that Reform Judaism afforded to its Israel.

For his part, Cronbach sets forth the five precedents for

the present movement: the Deuteronomic Reformation, the Pentateuchal Reformation, the Pharisaic Reformation, the Karaite Reformation, and the Hasidic Reformation. These reformations include important developments in the history of Judaisms. The Deuteronomic Reformation refers to the writing of the book of Deuteronomy, in two stages—first in 620 B.C., then in 570 B.C. The Pentateuchal Reformation speaks of the creation of the five books of Moses, the written Torah, in the time of Ezra, about 450 B.C. The Pharisaic Reformation draws on the then-established theory of the Pharisees as the founders of the Judaism after the destruction of the Temple in 70 C.E. The Karaite Reformation was a heresy that came to expression in the eighth and ninth centuries and flourished through the Middle Ages. It was a Judaism that rejected the belief in the dual Torah, specifically in the Talmud as the writing down of the oral Torah of Sinai, and maintained that God had revealed only one Torah, the written one. The Hasidic Reformation was a form of the Judaism of the dual Torah that laid great stress on direct encounter with God through prayer and mystical experience. In these reformations, as he called them, Cronbach found precedents for that of his own day and making—and he invoked the theory of a linear and incremental history of Judaism in so doing. His coming reformation appeals to social psychology and aims at tolerance: "Felicitous human relationships can be the goal of social welfare and of economic improvement. . . . Our Judaism of maturity would be dedicated to the ideal of freedom. Corollary of that ideal is what we have just observed about courtesy toward the people whose beliefs and practices we do not share."[13] We have now moved far from the position outlined by Geiger, in which a constant conversation with the received canon of the dual Torah yielded important propositions. But our interest in Reform Judaism hardly requires us to criticize the constructive efforts of its theologians. We want to know two things: First, is it old or new? It is new. Second, if a Judaism turns out to be new, as shown by its essentially distinctive principle of selection, then how does that Judaism establish its claim to form the natural, the necessary next step in the received Judaism? We find the answers to both questions in two further questions. First, does this Judaism ask the questions that for the Judaism of the dual Torah demanded answer, or does it ask other questions? That is a matter of fact. Second, does this Judaism find self-evidently valid the answers of the Judaism of the dual Torah, or do other propositions prove self-evidently true? That, too, is a matter of fact.

Urgent Questions, Self-Evident Answers

Two questions await attention. And the answers to both questions lie right on the surface. Given its intellectual strength, Reform Judaism had no difficulty saying precisely what it wished on classic issues. For this Judaism, the questions of the system of the dual Torah proved no more compelling than its answers. The whole turned from the self-evident statement of God's will to a source of precedents, available for selection and rearrangement. How to pick and choose formed the principal issue of method. The distinction between written and oral Torah provided the answer: choose the written; drop the oral. So the Reform theologians rejected the claim that the oral part of the Torah came from God. It was the work of men, time-bound, contingent, possessed of a merely advisory authority. Whatever precedents and antecedents Reform historians and theologians sought, they would not look in the rabbinic writings that, all together, fall under the name "Talmud," because there their opposition in orthodoxy found their principal ammunition. The Judaism from which Reform took its leave, the one that required the changes become reforms yielding Reform—that Judaism found its definition in the dual Torah of Sinai, as written down from the Mishnah on. So, quite naturally, when the Reformers addressed the issue of continuity, they leaped over the immediate past, represented by the Judaism of the dual Torah, and sought their antecedents in the processes of change instead.

But how did they express their judgment of the particular Judaism they proposed to revise? It was in clear and explicit statements that the Talmud at best preserved the wisdom of ordinary mortals, from which contemporary Jews might, if they wished, choose to learn.

A sequence of statements among nineteenth-century authorities expressed the entire consensus. So Joshua Heschel Schorr (1814–95):

> For as long as the Talmud is considered an inherently perfect, infallible monument of true divine tradition and is being accepted as such, no reform can take place through it. That being the case, why do we not get ready to expose the inner imperfections and the many irrefutably obvious faults from which the work suffers? This would clearly prove that what we possess here is a work created by humans, distorted by many errors, and that the writing of this volume is not imbued with one wholly integrated spirit.[14]

The study of history, therefore, carried a heavy freight of theological apologetics for Reform Judaism, a fact we have now confronted time and again. Here the very historical character of the Talmud made the case. It was the work of men, not of God. So its authority was no more than that of other men.

The Talmud will take its place among the works of mortals and lose its position as half of the one whole Torah of

Moses, our rabbi. Michael Creizenach (1789–1842) proposed to distinguish among parts of the Talmud:

> [The Talmud presents] a serviceable means for the interpretation of those ritual commandments which, according to the individual concepts of each man, are binding to this day. . . . We regard those portions of the Talmud which do not elucidate the Mosaic laws as merely humanly instituted decrees. . . . We consider those passages in the Talmud which are not consistent with the principle of the universal love of man, as outbursts of passionate hatred of which unfortunately quite often the best men cannot free themselves when they are oppressed in a disgraceful way and when they see that all considerations to which the dignity of human nature gives them undeniable claims are being violated against themselves.[15]

The upshot was that the changes-become-Reform took a clear and distinct step away from the received Torah. No one, even in the earliest generations of Reform, pretended otherwise. A new program of self-evident truths had taken the place of the old. As a new set of questions demanded responses, an established set of issues no longer mattered very much. So at the end we survey the questions people found they had, as a matter of life or death, to answer—and those answers that gave, and today still give, life.

Self-Evidence and Political Change

The urgent problem was, What is Israel in an age in which individual Jews have become something else, in addition to being Israel? Is Israel a nation? No, Israel does not fall into the same category as the nations. Jews are multiple beings: Israel in one dimension; part of France or Germany or America in a second. But if Israel is not a nation, then what of the way of life that had made the nation different, and what of the world view that had made sense of the way of life? These now formed the questions people could not avoid. The answers constitute Reform Judaism.

To close with the main point: Reform Judaism does not carry forward an unbroken tradition and does not claim to. This Judaism in advance knew as a matter of fact something that in the received Judaism one did not and could not have found out: that is, the simple fact the Jews' political standing could no longer be tolerated. But how to define a politics appropriate both to Jewry and to the hopes and expectations of Jews in nineteenth-century Europe and twentieth-century America? That issue required a fair amount of picking and choosing.

Finding reasonable evidence that Reform Judaism formed a new Judaism hardly challenges our imagination. The Reformers claimed no less. Assessing the claim of continuity presents more of a dilemma. Precedent for change hardly constitutes a chain of continuity, and the particular changes at hand scarcely recapitulate prior ones, either in substance or in social policy. But that is beside the point. Important is not whether the claim may find support in the facts of history, but what we learn about Reform Judaism from the definitive and indicative claim.

Once we know that the system, in all its components and proportions, had attained definition on its own terms, fully defining its program of pressing issues, we realize that the claim of continuity comes long after the fact of innovation. The claim, then, forms part of an apologia, rather than providing the generative force for the new system. That drew its strength elsewhere than from the received Judaism. The new Judaic system as a whole made its own points and, by the way, drew upon the received Judaism in adopting for its own texts held sacred in the established system. And the Judaism that resulted constitutes, therefore, something quite different from a continuous and ongoing tradition. We therefore can identify what the earliest generations of the new Judaism found self-evident: the truths that in their view demanded no articulation, no defense, no argument.

The questions they confronted and could not evade pertained to their understanding of themselves as citizens of a state other than an (imaginary) Jewish one, a polity separate from, and in addition to, Israel. When Petuchowski states simply that Reform Judaism came into existence to deal with political change in the status of Jews, he is leading us to the heart of the matter.[16] But what does that simple, to us self-evident, fact reveal about the incremental theory of Judaism, the notion that things move from point to point step by step? In my view, Reform Judaism presents an insuperable challenge to that theory. For it was not formed by incremental steps out of the received Judaism (the tradition), and it did not move along a path in a straight line from where Jews had been to where they wished to go. The system took shape on its own. Systems relate only in a common genealogy. But they cohere—for all Judaisms do contend with one another and regard one another as (unworthy) opponents within the same arena—because, after all, they address pretty much the same people about the same things.

I end not with analysis of a Judaic system but with recognition of what we learn, from Reform Jews, about the condition of humanity. The human achievement of Reform deserves a simple observation of what these people did and what they were. With acuity, perspicacity, and enormous courage, the Reformers, in the nineteenth and twentieth centuries alike, took the measure of the world and made ample use of the materials they had in hand in manufacturing something to fit it. And Reform did fit those Jews, and they were, and are, very many, to whom the issue of Israel as a supernatural entity has remained vivid. For, after all, the centerpiece of Reform Judaism remained its powerful notion that Israel does have a task and a mission, and thus should endure as Israel. Reform Judaism persuaded generations, from its beginnings to the present, of the worth of human life lived in its Judaic system. More than that we cannot ask of any Judaism.

CHAPTER 3

ORTHODOXY: PERFECT FAITH AND SELECTIVE PIETY

Orthodoxy and the "Tradition"

Orthodox Judaism came into being in Germany in the middle of the nineteenth century among Jews who, in rejecting Reform, were making a self-conscious decision to remain within the way of life and world view they had known and cherished all their lives. This statement will surprise people who reasonably identify all "traditional" or "observant" Judaism with Orthodoxy and who take for granted, furthermore, that all traditional Judaisms are pretty much the same. Here the distinction between those who adhered to the received system of the dual Torah and those who identified with Orthodox Judaism in mid-nineteenth-century Germany concerns such indicators as clothing, language, and, above all, education. When Jews who kept the law of the Torah—for example, as it dictated food choices and use of leisure time (to speak of the Sabbath and festivals in secular terms)—sent their children to secular schools, in addition to or instead of solely Jewish ones, or when, in Jewish schools, they included in the curriculum subjects outside the sciences of the Torah, they crossed the boundary between the received and the new Judaism of Orthodoxy. For the notion that science or German or Latin or philosophy deserved serious study, while not alien to important exemplars of the received system of the dual Torah, in the nineteenth century struck as wrong those for whom the received system remained self-evidently right. Those Jews did not send their children to gentile schools and, in Jewish schools, did not include in the curriculum other than Torah study.

What made Orthodoxy fresh becomes clear in the contrast to Reform Judaism. While the Reformers held that Judaism could change and was a product of history, their Orthodox opponents denied that Judaism could change and insisted that it derived from God's will at Sinai and was eternal and supernatural, not historical and man-made. In these two convictions, of course, the Orthodox were recapitulating the convictions of the received system. But in their appeal to the given, the traditional, they found more persuasive some of its components than others; and, as I have said, in the picking and choosing, in the articulation of the view that Judaism formed a religion to be seen as distinct and autonomous of politics, society, "the rest of life," they entered that same world of self-conscious believing that the Reformers also explored.

Let me, then, define Orthodox Judaism in more systematic ways, for mere knowledge of the circumstance, in public disputations with Reform, that gave birth to Orthodoxy does not allow the system its full and autonomous statement. Orthodox Judaism is that Judaic system that mediates between the received Judaism of the dual Torah and the requirements of living a life integrated in modern circumstances. Orthodoxy maintains the world view of the received dual Torah, constantly citing its sayings and adhering with only trivial variations to the bulk of its norms for everyday life. At the same time Orthodoxy holds that Jews adhering to the dual Torah may wear clothing that non-Jews wear and do not have to wear distinctively Jewish clothing; may live within a common economy and not practice distinctively Jewish professions (however, in a given setting, these professions may be defined: for instance, innkeeping in Russia, commerce in Poland); and may, in diverse ways, take up a life not readily distinguished in important characteristics from the life lived by people in general.

So for Orthodoxy a portion of Israel's life may prove secular, in that the Torah does not dictate and so sanctify all details under all circumstances. Since the Judaism of the dual Torah presupposed not only the supernatural entity Israel but also a way of life that in important ways distinguished that supernatural entity from the social world at large, Orthodoxy proved formidable in finding an accommodation for Jews who valued the received way of life and world view and also planned to make their lives in an essentially integrated social world. The difference between Orthodoxy and the system of the dual Torah was expressed in social policy: integration, however circumscribed, versus the total separation of the holy people.

Many Jews, Orthodox and non-observant alike, see Orthodox Judaism as the same as the tradition, as what is natural and normal, and hold that Orthodoxy now stands for how things always were, for all time. But since the term *Orthodoxy* takes on meaning only in contrast to Reform, Orthodoxy, in a simple sense, owes its life to Reform Judaism. The term first surfaced in 1795[1] and, in general, covers all Jews who believe that God revealed the dual Torah at Sinai, and that Jews must carry out the requirements of Jewish law contained in the Torah as interpreted by the sages through time. This position, of course, had for centuries struck as self-evident the generality of Jewry at large—centuries when Orthodoxy as a distinct and organized Judaism did not exist; it did not have to. Two events changed this situation: first, the recognition of the received system, the tradition as Orthodoxy; second, the specification of the received system as religion. The two go together. So long as the Judaism of the dual Torah enjoyed recognition as a set of self-evident truths, those truths added up to nothing so distinct and special as "religion," but to a general statement of how things are: all of life explained and harmonized in one whole account.

The former of the two events—the view of the received system as traditional—came first. (The matter of the self-aware recognition of Judaism as religion came later.) That identification of truth as tradition occurred when the received system met the challenge of competing Judaisms. Then, in behalf of the received way of life and world view addressed to supernatural Israel, people said that the Judaism of the dual Torah was established of old; was the right, the only way of seeing and doing things; was how things have been and should be naturally and normally: "tradition." But that is a category that contains within itself an alternative—namely, change, as in "tradition and change."

When the system lost its power of self-evidence, it entered, among other apologetic categories, that of the "tradition." And that came about when Orthodoxy met head on the challenge of change-become-Reform. We understand why the category of tradition, the received way of doing things, became critical to the framers of Orthodoxy when we examine the counter claim: that is to say, just as the Reformers justified change, the Orthodox theologians denied that change was ever possible. Thus, so Walter S. Wurzburger: "Orthodoxy looks upon attempts to adjust Judaism to the 'spirit of the time' as utterly incompatible with the entire thrust of normative Judaism which holds that the revealed will of God rather than the values of any given age are the ultimate standard." To begin, the debate was defined by the issue important to the Reformers: that is, the value of what was called "emancipation," or the provision to Jews of civil rights. When the Reform Judaic theologians took a wholly one-sided position affirming emancipation, numerous Orthodox ones adopted the contrary view. The position outlined by these theologians followed the agenda laid forth by the Reformers. If the Reform made minor changes in liturgy and its conduct, the Orthodox rejected even those that, under other circumstances, might have found acceptance. Saying prayers in the vernacular, for example, provoked strong opposition. But everyone knew that some of the prayers, said long ago in Babylonia in Aramaic were, in fact in the vernacular of the earlier age, the third century B.C. to the seventh century A.D. The Orthodox thought that these changes, not reforms at all, represented only the first step of a process leading Jews out of the Judaic world altogether; and, as Wurzburger says, "The slightest tampering with tradition was condemned."[2]

To discover where the received system of the dual Torah prevailed, and where, by contrast, Orthodoxy came to full expression, we have only to follow the spreading out of railway lines; the growth of new industry; the shifts in political status accorded to, among other citizens, Jews; changes in the educational system; in all, the entire process of political change, economic and social, demographic and cultural shifts of a radical and fundamental nature. Where these changes came first, there Reform Judaism met them in its way—and Orthodoxy in its. Where change came later in the century—as in Russian Poland, the eastern provinces of the Austro-Hungarian Empire, and Russia itself—there, in villages contentedly following the old ways, the received system endured. Again, in an age of mass migration from eastern Europe to America and other Western democracies, those who experienced the upheaval of leaving home and country met the challenge of change either by accepting new ways of seeing things or, articulately and in full self-awareness, reaffirming the familiar ones—once more, Reform or Orthodoxy. We may, therefore, characterize the received system as a way of life and world view wedded to an ancient peoples' homelands, the villages and small towns of central and eastern Europe, and Orthodoxy as the heir of that received system as it came to expression in the towns and cities of central and western Europe and America. That rule of thumb allows us to distinguish between the piety of a milieu and the theological conviction of a self-conscious community. Or, we may accept the familiar distinction between tradition and articulate Orthodoxy—a distinction, to be sure, with its own freight of apologetics.

Clearly, the beginnings of Orthodoxy occurred in the areas where Reform made its way—hence in Germany and in southern Hungary. In Germany, where Reform attracted the majority of not a few Jewish communities, the Orthodox faced a challenge indeed. Critical to their conviction was the notion that Israel, all of the Jews, bore responsibility to carry out the law of the Torah. But the community's institutions in the hands of Reform did not obey the law of the Torah as the Orthodox understood it. So, in the end, Orthodoxy took the step that marked it as a self-conscious Judaism, and separated from the established community altogether. The Orthodox set up their own organization and seceded from the community at large. The next step prohibited the Orthodox from participating in non-Orthodox organizations altogether. Isaac Breuer, a leading theologian of Orthodoxy, would ultimately take the position that "refusal to espouse the cause of separation was interpreted as being equivalent to the rejection of the absolute sovereignty of God."[3]

The matter of accommodating to the world at large, of course, did not allow for so easy an answer as mere separation. The specific issue—integration or segregation—concerned preparation for life in the larger politics and economic life of the country, and that meant secular education, involving not only language and science but history and literature, matters of values. Orthodoxy had two distinct wings: one rejected secular learning as well as all dealing with non-Orthodox Jews; the other cooperated with non-Orthodox and secular Jews and accepted the value of secular education. This latter position in no way affected loyalty to the law of Judaism—for example, belief in God's revelation of the one whole Torah at Sinai. The point at which the received system and Orthodox split requires specification. Proponents of the received system never accommodated themselves to secular education, while the Orthodox in Germany and Hungary persistently affirmed it. This affirmation points to a remarkable shift, since central to the received system of the dual Torah is study of Torah—Torah, not philosophy.

Explaining where we find the one and the other, Katzburg works with the distinction I have already made, between an unbroken system and one that has undergone a serious break with the familiar condition of the past:

> In Eastern Europe until World War I, Orthodoxy preserved without a break its traditional ways of life and the time-

> honored educational framework. In general, the mainstream of Jewish life was identified with Orthodoxy, while Haskalah [Jewish Enlightenment, which applied to the Judaic setting the skeptical attitudes of the French Enlightenment] and secularization were regarded as deviations. Hence there was no ground wherein a Western type of Orthodoxy could take root. . . . European Orthodoxy in the 19th and the beginning of the 20th centuries was significantly influenced by the move from small settlements to urban centers . . . as well as by emigration. Within the small German communities there was a kind of popular Orthodoxy, deeply attached to tradition and to local customs, and when it moved to the large cities this element brought with it a vitality and rootedness to Jewish tradition.[4]

These commentators authoritatively define the difference between tradition and Orthodoxy, between the received system accepted as self-evident and an essentially selective—therefore, by definition, new—system, called Orthodoxy. In particular, they tell us where to expect to find the articulated—therefore, self-conscious—affirmation of tradition that characterizes Orthodoxy but does not occur in the world of the dual Torah as it glided in its eternal orbit of the seasons and of unchanging time.

Old and New in Orthodoxy

I find it difficult to imagine what the urban Orthodox might otherwise have done. They experienced change, daily encountered Jews unlike themselves, no longer lived in that stable Judaic society in which the received Torah formed the given of life. The pretense that Jews faced no choices was scarcely a possibility. Nor did the generality of the Jews propose, in the West, to preserve a separate language or to renounce political rights. So Orthodoxy made its peace with change, no less than did Reform. The educational program that led Jews out of the received culture of the dual Torah, the use of the vernacular, the acceptance of political rights, the renunciation of Jewish garments, education for women, abolition of the power of the community to coerce the individual—these and many other originally Reform positions characterized the Orthodoxy that emerged, another new Judaism, in the nineteenth century.[5]

If we wonder how new the Orthodox system was, we find ambiguous answers. In conviction, in way of life, in world view, it was hardly new at all. For the bulk of its substantive positions found ample precedent in the received dual Torah. From its affirmation of God's revelation of a dual Torah to its acceptance of the detailed authority of the law and customs, from its strict observance of the law to its unwillingness to change a detail of public worship, Orthodoxy rightly pointed to its strong links with the chain of tradition. But Orthodoxy constituted a sect within the Jewish group. Its definition of the Israel to whom it wished to speak and the definition characteristic of the dual Torah hardly coincide. The Judaism of the dual Torah addressed all Jews, and Orthodoxy recognized that it could not do so. Orthodoxy acquiesced, however, in a situation that lay beyond the imagination of the framers of the Judaism of the dual Torah.

True, the Orthodox had no choice. Their seceding from the community and forming their own institutions ratified the simple fact that they could not work with the Reformers. But the upshot remains the same. That supernatural entity Israel gave up its place, and a natural Israel, a this-worldly political fact, succeeded to it. Pained though Orthodoxy was by the fact, it nonetheless accommodated the new social reality—and affirmed it by reshaping the sense of Israel in the supernatural dimension. Their Judaism no less than the Judaism of the Reformers stood for something new—a birth not a renewal, a political response to a new politics. True enough, for Orthodoxy the politics was that of the Jewish community, divided as it was among diverse visions of the political standing of Israel, the Jewish people. For the Reform, by contrast, the new politics derived from the establishment of the category of neutral citizenship in an encompassing nation-state. But the political shifts flowed from the same large-scale changes in Israel's consciousness and character; and, it follows, Orthodoxy as much as Reform represented a set of self-evident answers to political questions that none could evade.

Orthodoxy represents the most interesting challenge to the hypothesis I announced at the outset in claiming that no Judaism recapitulates any other. Each began on its own, defining the questions it wished to answer and laying forth the responses it found self-evidently true, and only then going back to the canon of received documents in search of proof-texts. To the proposed rule, then, that every Judaism commences in the definition, or the discovery, of its canon, Orthodoxy surely forms an enormous exception. For its canon recognized the same books, accorded them the same status and authority. Yet that was hardly the case. Orthodoxy produced books to which the received system of the dual Torah could afford no counterpart—and vice versa. Orthodoxy addressed questions not pertinent to the received system or to the world that that system had constructed, and found answers that violated important givens of that system. The single most significant trait of Orthodoxy, we shall now see, is its power to see the Torah as Judaism, the category shift that changed everything else (or that ratified all other changes).

Judaism Enters the Category Religion

The category *religion* recognizes as distinct from "all of life" matters having to do with the church, the life of faith, the secular as against the sacred—distinctions lost on the received system of the dual Torah, which legislated for matters we should today regard as entirely secular or neutral—for example, the institutions of state (king, priest, army). I have already noted that, in the received system as it took shape in eastern and central Europe, Jews wore garments regarded as distinctively Jewish, and some important traits of these garments indeed derived from the Torah. They pursued sciences that only Jews studied—for instance, the Talmud and its commentaries. In these and other ways, the Torah encompassed all of the life of Israel, the holy people. The recognition that Jews are like others, that the Torah falls into a category into which other and comparable matters fall—that recognition was long in coming.

For Christians it had become commonplace in Germany and other Western countries to see religion as distinct from other components of the social and political system. While the Church in Russia identified with the tsarist state, or with the national aspirations of the Polish people, in the German states two churches, Catholic and Protestant, competed. The terrible wars of the Reformation in the sixteenth and seventeenth centuries, which ruined Germany, had led to the uneasy compromise that a prince might choose the religion of his principality; and, from that self-aware choice, people understood that "way of life and world view" in fact constituted a religion, and that any one religion might be compared with some other. By the nineteenth century, moreover, the separation of church and state ratified the important distinction between religion, where difference would be tolerated, and the secular, where citizens were pretty much the same.

That fact of political consciousness in the West reached the Judaic world only in the late eighteenth century for some intellectuals and in the nineteenth century for large numbers of others. It registered, then, as a fundamental shift in the understanding and interpretation of the Torah. The Jews who formed the Orthodox Judaic system had the creative power to shift the fundamental category in which they framed their system, and thus made Orthodoxy a Judaism on its own, not simply a restatement, essentially in established classifications, of the received system of the dual Torah.

If we ask how Orthodox Judaism, so profoundly rooted in the canonical writings and received convictions of the Judaism of the dual Torah, at the same time made provision for the prevailing issues of political and cultural change, we recognize the importance of this shift in category. Orthodox Judaism took the view that one can observe the rules of the Judaic system of the ages and at the same time keep the laws of the state. More important, Orthodox Judaism took full account of the duties of citizenship, so far as being a good citizen imposed the expectation of conformity in certain aspects of everyday life. So a category, *religion*, could contain the Torah, and a counter category, *secular*, could allow Jews a place in the accepted civic life of the country. The importance of the shift in category therefore lies in its power to accommodate the political change so important, also, to Reform Judaism. The Jews' differences from others would fit into categories in which difference was (in Jews' minds at any rate) acceptable, and would not violate those lines to which all citizens had to adhere.

For example, Jews no longer wished to wear distinctively Jewish clothing, or to speak a Jewish language, or to pursue only Jewish learning and study solely under Jewish auspices. Yet the received system, giving expression to the rules of sanctification of the holy people, did entail wearing Jewish clothing, speaking a Jewish language, learning only, or mainly, Jewish sciences. Now clothing, language, and education fell into the category of the secular, while other equally important aspects of everyday life remained in the category of the sacred. Thus, Orthodox Judaism, as it came into existence in Germany and other Western countries, found it possible, by recognizing the category of the secular, to accept the language, clothing, and learning of those countries. And these matters served openly to denote a larger acceptance of gentile ways—not all, but enough to lessen the differences between the holy people and the nations. Political change of a profound order, which made Jews call into question some aspects of the received system—if not most or all of them, as in Reform Judaism—presented to Orthodox Jews the issues at hand: How separate? How integrated? And the answers required, as I have said, picking and choosing—different things, to be sure—just as much as, in principle, the Reform Jews picked and chose. Both Judaisms understood that some things were sacred, others not; and that understanding marked these Judaisms off from the system of the dual Torah.

Once the category shift had taken place, the difference was to be measured in degree, not in kind. For Orthodox Jews maintained those distinctive political beliefs in the future coming of the Messiah and in the reconstitution of the Jewish nation in its own land—beliefs that Reform Jews rejected. But, placing these convictions in the distant future, the Orthodox Jews nonetheless prepared for a protracted interim of life within the nation at hand, where like the Reform they differed in religion but not in nationality, for all were citizens. Thus, Orthodoxy, as much as Reform, signals remarkable changes in the Jews' political situation and—more important—in their aspirations. They did want to be different, but not so different as the received system would have made them.

Still, Orthodoxy in its nineteenth-century formulation claimed to carry forward, in continuous and unbroken relationship, the tradition. That claim assuredly demands a serious hearing, for the things that Orthodoxy taught, the way of life it required, the Israel to whom it spoke, the doctrines it deemed revealed by God to Moses at Sinai—all of these conformed more or less exactly to the system of the received Judaism of the dual Torah as people then knew it. So any consideration of the issue of a linear and incremental history of Judaism has to take at face value the character, and not merely the claim, of Orthodoxy. But we do not have to concede that claim without reflection. Each Judaism, after all, demands study in categories defined not by its own claims of continuity, but by its own distinctive and characteristic choices. For a system takes shape and then makes choices—in that order. But the issue here is whether Orthodoxy can be said to have made any choices at all. For is it not what it says it is: "just Judaism"? Indeed so, but the dual Torah of the received tradition hardly generated the base category *Judaism.* And any single Judaism, Orthodox or otherwise, is not Torah.

Here is where self-conscious choice enters discourse. For the Orthodoxy of the nineteenth century—that is, the Judaism that named itself "Orthodox"—exhibited certain traits of mind that marked its framers as distinctive, as separate from the received Judaism of the dual Torah as were the founders of Reform Judaism. To state the matter simply: the founders of Orthodoxy's act of choosing—that is, adopting for themselves the category *religion* and recognizing a distinction between religion and the secular, between the holy and other categories of existence—defines them as self-conscious: the received system was not for them self-evident.

The Torah was now transformed into an object, a thing out there, a matter of choice, deliberation, affirmation. In that sense, Orthodoxy both recognized a break in the line of the received tradition and proposed to repair that break: a self-conscious, a modern decision. The issues addressed by Orthodoxy, the questions its framers found ineluctable—these took second place. The primary consideration in my assessment of Orthodoxy's claim to carry forward, in a straight line, the incremental history of a single Judaism carries us to the fundamental categories within which Orthodoxy pursued its thought, but the Judaism of the dual Torah did not. How so? The Judaism of the dual Torah had no word for Judaism, and Orthodoxy did (and does).

Let me dwell on this matter of the category *Judaism*, a species of the genus *religion*. The fact is that those Jews for whom the received Judaism retained the standing of self-evident truth in no way recognized the distinctions implicit in the category *religion*. Those distinctions separated one dimension of existence from others—specifically, faith and religious action from all other matters, such as politics, economic life, incidental aspects of everyday life such as clothing, vocation and avocation, and the like. As I have stressed, the Judaism of the dual Torah, for its part, encompasses every dimension of human existence, both personal and public, both private and political. The Jews constitute a supernatural people; their politics form the public dimension of their holiness; and their personal lives match the most visible and blatant rules of public policy. The whole forms a single fabric, an indivisible and totally coherent entity, at once social and cultural, economic and political—and, above all, religious. The recognition, therefore, that one may distinguish the religious from the political, or concede as distinct any dimension of a person's life or of the life of the community of Judaism, forms powerful evidence that a fresh system has come into existence.

For nineteenth-century Reform and Orthodox theologians alike, the category *Judaism* defined what people said when they wished all together and all at once to describe what the Jews believe, or the Jewish religion, or similar matters covering religious ideas viewed as a system and as a whole. It constituted, therefore, a philosophical category, an -ism, instructing thinkers to seek the system and order and structure of ideas: the doctrine of this, the doctrine of that, in Juda*ism.* The nineteenth-century Judaic religious thinkers invoked the category *Judaism,* when they proposed to speak of the whole of Judaic religious existence. Available to the Judaism of the dual Torah are other categories, other words, to tell how to select and organize and order data: all together, all at once to speak of the whole.

To the Jews, therefore, who abided within the received Judaism of the dual Torah, Orthodoxy represented an innovation, a shift from the perceivedly self-evident truths of the Torah. For their word for Judaism was *Torah;* and when they spoke of the whole all at once, they used the word *Torah*—and for them also, the word *Judaism* encompassed different things than it did when used by nineteenth-century theologians. The received system not only used a different word but referred to different things. The two categories—*Judaism* and *Torah*—which were supposed to refer to the same data in the same social world, in fact denoted different data.

Judaism falls into a philosophical or ideological or theological classification: a *logos,* a "word"; while *Torah* falls into the classification of a symbol: that is, a symbol that in itself encompassed the whole of the system that the category at hand was meant to describe. The species *ism* falls into the classification of the genus *logos;* while the species *Torah,* while using words, transcends them and becomes a species of the genus *symbol.* How so? The *ism* category invokes not an encompassing symbol but a system of thought. Judaism is an it, an object, a classification, an action. Torah, for its part, is an everything-in-one-thing, a symbol. I cannot imagine a more separate and unlike set of categories than *Judaism* and *Torah*, even though both encompass the same way of life and world view and address the same social group. So *Torah* as a category serves as a symbol, everywhere present in detail and holding all the details together.* *Judaism* as a category serves as a statement of the main points: the intellectual substrate of it all.

The conception of Judaism as an organized body of doctrine—as in the sentence "Judaism teaches" or "Judaism says"—derives from an age when people further had determined that Judaism belonged to the category of religion and—of still more definitive importance—that a religion was something that *teaches* or *says*. That is to say, Judaism is a religion; and a religion, to begin with, is (whatever else it is) a composition of beliefs. The age at hand was the nineteenth century; and the category of religion as a distinct entity emerged from Protestant theological thought. For in Protestant theological terms, one is saved by faith. But the very components of that sentence—"one" (individual, not the people or holy nation), "saved" (personally, not in history, and saved, not sanctified), "faith" (not *mitzvot*)—prove incomprehensible in the categories constructed by Torah.† Constructions of Judaic dogmas, the specification of a right doctrine—an orthodoxy—and the insistence that one can speak of religion apart from such adventitious matters as clothing and education (for the Orthodox of Germany who dressed like other Germans and studied in uni-

* That is why I called my prime textbook *The Way of Torah*, and its companion-reader, *The Life of Torah*;[6] but I see other ways to compose an introduction to Judaism and am now experimenting with one of them. My tentative title says it all: *From Testament to Torah*.

† My more sustained critique of the Protestant definition of religion and its effects upon the academic study of religion is in my forthcoming article "Theological Enemies of Religious Studies," *Religion* (1987).

versities, not only in yeshivas) or food (for the Reform), testify to the same fact: the end of self-evidence, the substitution of the distinction between religion and secularity, the creation of *Judaism* as the definitive category.

In fact, in the idiomatic language of Torah speech, one cannot make such a statement in that way about, or in the name of, Judaism—not an operative category at all. In accord with the modes of thought and speech of the received Judaism of the dual Torah, one has to speak of Israel, the community, to address not only individual life but all of historical time. The word *saved* by itself does not suffice. The category of sanctification, not only salvation, must find its place. Most important, one native to the speech of the Torah will use the word *mitzvot*, or religious duties, not speaking of salvation by faith alone. So the sentence serves for Protestant Christianity but not for the Torah. Of course, for its part, Judaism, Orthodox or Reform, will also teach things and lay down doctrines, even dogmas.

The counterpart, in the realm of self-evidence comprised by the received Judaism of the dual Torah, of the statement "Judaism teaches" can only be "The Torah requires"; and the predicate of such a sentence would be not ". . . that God is one," but ". . . that you say a blessing before eating bread." The category *Judaism* encompasses, classifies, and organizes doctrines: the faith, which, by the way, an individual adopts and professes. The category *Torah* teaches what "we," God's holy people, are and what "we" must do. The counterpart to the statement of Judaism "God is one," then, is ". . . who has sanctified us by his commandments and commanded us to. . . ." The one teaches—that is, speaks of intellectual matters and beliefs; the latter demands—social actions and deeds of us, matters of public consequence, including, by the way, affirming such doctrines as God's unity, the resurrection of the dead, the coming of the Messiah, the revelation of the Torah at Sinai, and on and on: "we" can rival the Protestants in heroic deeds of faith. So it is true, the faith demands deeds, and deeds presuppose faith. But, categorically, the emphasis is what it is: Torah on God's revelation; the canon—to Israel and its social way of life, Judaism—on a system of belief. That is a significant difference between the two categories, which, as I said, serve a single purpose—namely, to state the thing as a whole.

Equally true, one would (speaking systemically) also "study Torah." But one studied not an intellectual system of theology or philosophy but rather a document of revealed Scripture and law. I do not mean to suggest that the theologians of Judaism, Orthodox or Reform, of the nineteenth century did not believe that God is one, or that the philosophers who taught that "Judaism teaches ethical monotheism" did not concur that, on that account, one has to say a blessing before eating bread. But the categories are different; and, in consequence, so too are the composites of knowledge. A book on Judaism explains the doctrines, theology or philosophy, of Judaism. A book of the holy Torah expounds God's will as revealed in "the one whole Torah of Moses, our rabbi," as sages teach and embody God's will. I cannot imagine two more different books, and the reason is that they represent totally different categories of intelligible discourse and of knowledge. Proof, of course, is that the latter books are literally unreadable. They form part of a genuinely oral exercise, to be cited sentence by sentence and expounded in the setting of other sentences, from other books, the whole made cogent by the speaker. That process of homogenization is how Torah works as a generative category. It obscures other lines of structure and order.

True, the two distinct categories come to bear upon the same body of data, the same holy books. But the consequent compositions—selections of facts, ordering of facts, analyses of facts, statements of conclusion and interpretation, and, above all, modes of public discourse, meaning who says what to whom—bear no relationship to one another, none whatsoever. Indeed, the compositions more likely than not do not even adduce the same facts or refer to them.

How is it that the category I see as imposed, extrinsic, and deductive—namely, *Judaism*—attained the status of self-evidence? Categories serve because they are self-evident to a large group of people. In Orthodoxy, therefore, the category *Judaism* serves because it enjoys self-evidence as part of a larger set of categories that are equally self-evident. The source of the categorical power of *Judaism* derives from the Protestant philosophical heritage that has defined scholarship, including category formation, since the time of Kant. *Juda* plus *ism* do not constitute self-evident, let alone definitive, categories. Judaism constitutes a category asymmetrical to the evidence adduced in its study; the category does not apply because the principle of formation is philosophical and does not emerge from an unmediated encounter with the Torah. Orthodoxy can have come into existence only in Germany—and, indeed, only in that part of Germany where the philosophical heritage of Kant and Hegel defined the categories of thought, also, for religion.

Creator of a New Judaism: Samson Raphael Hirsch

The importance of Samson Raphael Hirsch (1808–88), first great intellect of Orthodoxy, derives from his philosophy of joining Torah with secular education, producing a synthesis of Torah and modern culture. He represents the strikingly new Judaism, exhibiting both its strong tie to the received system but also its essentially innovative character. Sometimes called "neo-Orthodox,"[7] Hirsch's position, with its stress on the possibility of living in the secular world and sustaining a fully Orthodox life, rallied the Jews of the counterreformation. But he and his followers took over one principal position of Reform—the possibility of integrating Jews in modern society. What made Hirsch significant was that he took that position not only on utilitarian grounds, as Moshe Samet says, "but also through the acceptance of its [that society's] scale of values, aiming at creating a symbiosis between traditional Orthodoxy and modern German-European culture; both in theory and in practice this meant abandonment of Torah study for its own sake and adopting instead an increased concentration on practical halakhah [law]."[8] On that basis Orthodoxy is rightly identified as a Judaism distinct from the system of the dual Torah. Hirsch himself studied at the University of Bonn, specializing in classical languages, history, and philosophy.[9] So, as I noted, he did not think one had to spend all one's time studying Torah; and in going to a university, he implicitly affirmed that he could not define, within Torah study, all modes of learning. Gentile professors knew things worth knowing. But continuators of the Judaism of the dual Torah thought exactly the opposite: whatever is worth knowing is in the Torah.

In his rabbinical posts, Hirsch published works aimed at appealing to the younger generation. His ideal for the young was the formation of a personality that would be both enlightened and observant: that is, educated in Western knowledge and observant of the Judaic way of life. This ideal took shape through an educational program that included the Hebrew language and holy literature and also German, mathematics, sciences, and the like. In this way, he proposed to respond to the Reformers' view that Judaism in its received form constituted a barrier between Jews and German society, impeding the sort of integration they thought wholesome and good. Hirsch concurred in the ideal and differed on detail. Distinctive Jewish clothing, in Hirsch's view, was not important. He himself wore a Protestant ministerial gown at public worship, which did not win the approbation of the traditionalists; and when he preached, he referred not only to the law of the Torah but to other biblical matters, equally an innovation. He argued that Judaism and secular education could form a union, one that would require recognition of externals, which could be set aside, and emphasis on principles, which would not change. Thus, Hirsch espoused what, according to Jews wholly within the mentality of self-evidence, constituted selective piety and therefore, while details differed, fell within the classification of reform.

In his selectivity, Hirsch included changes in the conduct of the liturgy, involving a choir, congregational singing, sermons in the vernacular—a generation earlier, sure marks of Reform. He required prayers to be said only in Hebrew and Jewish subjects to be taught in that language. He opposed all changes in the Prayer Book. At the same time he sustained organizational relationships with the Reformers and tried to avoid schism. Halfway through his career, however, toward the middle of the century, Hirsch could not tolerate the Reformers' abrogation of the dietary laws and those affecting marital relationships, and made his break, accusing the Reformers of disrupting Israel's unity. In the following decades, he encouraged Orthodox Jews to leave the congregations dominated by Reform, even though, in a particular locale, the latter was the only synagogue. Separationist synagogues formed in the larger community.

In framing issues of doctrine, Hirsch constructed an affirmative system, not a negative one. His principal argument stressed that the teachings of the Torah constitute facts beyond all doubt, as much as the facts of nature do not allow for doubt. This view of the essential facticity—the absolute givenness—of the Torah led to the further conviction that human beings may not deny the Torah's teachings even when they do not grasp its meaning. Wisdom is contained within the Torah; God's will is to be found there. Just as the physical laws of nature are not conditioned by human search, so the rules of God's wisdom are unaffected by human search. The Torah constitutes an objective reality; and, in Simha Katz's words, its laws form "an objective disposition of an established order that is not dependent on the will of the individual or society, and hence not even on historical processes."[10] Humanity nonetheless may through time gain religious truth.

What makes Israel different is that the people gain access to the truth not through experience but through direct revelation. Gentile truth is truth, but derives from observation and experience. What Israel knows through the Torah comes through a different medium: the people stand outside history and do not have to learn religious truth through the passage of history and changes over time. Israel, then, forms a supernatural entity, a view certainly in accord with the Judaism of the dual Torah. But when it came to explaining the way of life, Hirsch went his own way, pursuing a theory of the practice of the religious life through concrete deeds—the commandments—in a highly speculative and philosophical way. He maintained that each of the deeds of the way of life represents something beyond itself, serves as a symbol, not as an end in itself. So when a Jew carries out a holy deed, the deed serves to make concrete a revealed truth. This mode of thought transforms the way of life into an exercise in applied theology and practical, practiced belief.

Specifically, in Katz's words, "the performance of a commandment is not determined by simple devotion but by attachment to the religious thought represented in symbolic form by the commandment. Symbolic meanings must be attributed . . . particularly to commandments which are described by the Torah itself as signs . . . and commandments which are established as pointing to historical events . . . and commandments whose entire content testifies to their symbolic character." The diverse commandments all together stand for three principles: justice, love, and "the education of ourselves and others."[11]

Hirsch's theory of who is Israel stood at the opposite pole from that of Geiger and the Reformers. To them, as we have seen, Israel fell into the classification of a religious community, that alone. To Hirsch, Israel constituted a people, not a religious congregation, and he spoke of "national Jewish consciousness": "The Jewish people, though it carries the Torah with it in all the lands of its dispersion, will never find its table and lamp except in the Holy Land." Israel performs a mission among the nations, to teach "that God is the source of blessing." Israel then falls between, forming its own category, because it has a state system, in the land, but also a life outside.[12] In outlining this position, Hirsch was reaffirming the theory of the supernatural Israel laid forth in the dual Torah. For him, the power of the national ideal lay in its polemical force against the assimilationists and Reformers, whom he treated as indistinguishable:

> The contempt with which the assimilationists treat David's [fallen] tabernacle and the prayer for the sacrificial service clearly reveals the extent of their rebellion against Torah and their complete disavowal of the entire realm of Judaism. They gather the ignorant about them to whom the Book of Books, the Divine national document of their Jewish past and future, is closed with seven seals. With a conceit engendered by stupidity and a perfidy born from hatred they point to God's Temple and the Divine Service in Zion as the unholy center of the "bloody cult of sacrifices." Consequently, they make certain to eliminate any reference to the restoration of the Temple service from

> our prayers. . . . The "cultured, refined" sons and daughters of our time must turn away with utter disgust from their "prehistoric, crude" ancestors who worship their god with bloody sacrifices.

Hirsch reviewed the long line of exalted leaders who affirmed sacrifice and were not crude—for example, Moses, Isaiah, Jeremiah, and on—and concluded:

> The Jewish sacrifice expresses the highest ideal of man's and the nation's moral challenge. Blood and kidney, head and limbs symbolize our service of God with every drop of blood, every emotion, every particle of our being. By performing the act of sacrifice at the place chosen by God as the site of His Law, we proclaim our determination to fulfill our lofty moral and ethical tasks to enable God to bless the site of the national vow with the presence of this glory and with the fullness of this love and grace.[13]

Hirsch's spiritualization of the sacrifices—with an ample tradition of precedent, to be sure—derived from the challenge of Reform. Demanding an acceptance at face value of the Torah as the revelation of God's wisdom, Hirsch nonetheless made the effort to appeal to more than the givenness of the Torah and its commandments.

On the contrary, he entered into argument in the same terms—spiritualization, lofty moral and ethical tasks—as did the Reformers, thus marking his thought as new and responsive to a fresh set of issues. As to the Reformers, he met them on their ground, as he had to; and his principal points of insistence, to begin with, derived from the issues defined by others. Hence, he belongs in the larger discourse among the Judaisms of the nineteenth century, each one a product of the end of self-evidence and the beginning of a self-conscious explanation for what had formerly, and elsewhere in that age, the authority of the absolutely given.

The Issue of Revelation and the Dual Torah

The Judaism of the dual Torah by definition maintained that not only the Hebrew Scriptures (Old Testament) but also the entire canon of rabbinic writings constituted that one whole Torah that Moses received at Sinai. The three Judaisms of the nineteenth century met that issue head on. Each of the possibilities—only Scripture; everything; some things but not others—found proponents. Any consequent theory of revelation had to explain the origin and authority of each component of the received canon. And, further, that theory of revelation had to explain what, precisely, revelation meant. The position of Orthodoxy on this matter takes on significance only in the larger context of the debate with Reform. Reform through Geiger took the view that revelation was progressive: the Bible derived from "the religious genius of the Jewish people." Orthodoxy through Hirsch as the example saw the Torah as wholly and completely God's word. A middle position, represented by Conservative Judaism, espoused both views: God revealed the written Torah, which was supplemented by "the ongoing revelation manifesting itself throughout history in the spirit of the Jewish people."[14]

Orthodoxy could not concur. The issue involved the historical identification of those responsible for the rabbinic writings. The Conservatives, in the person of Zechariah Frankel (see chapter 4), a contemporary of Hirsch, maintained that the whole of the rabbinic corpus derived from scribes and their successors, who had adapted the system of Scripture by inventing the notion of the oral Torah—a break the Orthodox could not concede. The Positive Historical School, in Katzburg and Wurzburger's description, held that "the religious consciousness of the Jewish people provided the supreme religious authority, [while] the Orthodox position rested upon the belief in the supernatural origin of the Torah which was addressed to a 'Chosen People.' "[15] So the theory of who is Israel joined the issue of revelation: how, what, when. The Orthodox position, as outlined by Hirsch, saw Israel as a supernatural people that has in hand a supernatural revelation. The entirety of the dual Torah and the writings flowing from it constitute that revelation. Quite how this notion of a long sequence of revealed documents differs from the conception of a progressive revelation is not entirely clear, but in context it made a considerable difference. For in his affirmation of the entirety of the Torah, written and oral, as the revealed will of God, Hirsch marked the boundaries of Orthodoxy and made them coincide with the precise ones of the received dual Torah. It is doubtful, however, whether those Jews to whom the supernatural character of Israel and the entirety of Torah formed self-evident truths understood Hirsch's careful explanations of matters outside the received modes of apologetics. For the one thing the traditionalist grasped—the absolute givenness of the whole—Hirsch could not concede. How do we know? Because he explained and explained and explained.

The Birth of a Judaism

Hirsch spent much energy defending the practice of the religious duties called "commandments"—such as circumcision, the wearing of fringes on garments, the use, in morning worship, of *tefillin* (commonly translated "phylacteries"), and the sacrificial cult and Temple. These he treated not as utter data—the givens of the holy life—but rather as transformed into symbols of a meaning beyond. And that exercise, in his context, testifies to the utter self-consciousness of the Judaism at hand; hence, to the formation of a new Judaism out of received materials, no less than Reform Judaism constituted a new Judaism out of those same received materials. For the sole necessity for making up such symbolic explanations derived from decision: defend these, at all costs. The contemporaries of Hirsch living in the villages of the East did not feel the need to defend these—to them, self-evidently holy—beliefs and practices.

When, therefore, Hirsch invoked the parallel, to which I have already alluded, between the study of nature and the study of the Torah, he expressed the freshness, the inventiveness, of his own system and thereby testified to the self-consciousness at hand. A sizable abstract provides a good view of Hirsch's excellent mode of thought and argument:

> One word here concerning the proper method of Torah investigation. Two revelations are open before us, that is, nature and the Torah. In nature all phenomena stand before us as indisputable facts, and we can only endeavor a posteriori to ascertain the law of each and the connection of all. Abstract demonstration of the truth, or rather, the probability of theoretical explanations of the acts of nature, is an unnatural proceeding. The right method is to verify our assumptions by the known facts, and the highest attainable degree of certainty is to be able to say: "The facts agree with our assumption"—that is, all the phenomena observed can be explained according to our theory. A single contradictory phenomenon will make our theory untenable. We must, therefore, acquire all the knowledge possible concerning the object of our investigation and know it, if possible, in its totality. If, however, all efforts should fail in disclosing the inner law and connection of phenomena revealed to us as facts in nature, the facts remain, nevertheless, undeniable and cannot be reasoned away.
>
> The same principles must be applied to the investigation of the Torah. In the Torah, even as in nature, God is the ultimate cause. In the Torah, even as in nature, no fact may be denied,

> even though the reason and the connection may not be understood. What is true in nature is true also in the Torah: the traces of divine wisdom must ever be sought. Its ordinances must be accepted in their entirety as undeniable phenomena and must be studied in accordance with their connection to each other, and the subject to which they relate. Our conjectures must be tested by their precepts, and our highest certainty here also can only be that everything stands in harmony with our theory.
>
> In nature the phenomena are recognized as facts, though their cause and relationship to each other may not be understood and are independent of our investigation. So too the ordinances of the Torah must be law for us, even if we do not comprehend the reason and the purpose of a single one. Our fulfillment of the commandments must not depend on our investigations.[16]

Here we have the counterpart, in his own argument, to Hirsch's theory of Torah and worldly learning. Just as he maintained the union of the two, so in the deepest structure of his thought he worked out that same union. Natural science dictated rules of inquiry—specifically, the requirement that one explain phenomena through a theory that one can test. The phenomenon is the given. Then, for the Torah, its requirements constitute the givens, which demand explanation but must be accepted as facts even when explanation fails. Clearly, Hirsch addressed an audience that had come to doubt the facticity of the facts of the Torah in a way in which none doubted the facticity of the facts of nature.

Once compared with nature, the Torah no longer defines the world view and the way of life at hand but takes its place as part of a larger world view and way of life, in which the Israelite–human being (in Hirsch's happy concept) has to accommodate both the received of the Torah and the given of nature. The insistence on the process of accommodation—"studied in accordance with their connection . . . and the subject to which they relate"—testifies to a world view essentially distinct from that of the received system of the dual Torah. In this new world view, the Torah demands explanation; its rules are reduced to the lesser dimensions of an apologia of symbolism, so that they form not givens in an enduring and eternal way of life but objects of analysis, of defense, above all, of reasoned decision. True, Hirsch insisted, "Our fulfillment of the commandments must not depend on our investigations."[17] But the investigation must go forward; and that allegation of Hirsch's, in and of itself, tells us we deal with a new Judaism.

Let me now summarize the argument, because what I have maintained runs contrary to the prevailing view of Orthodoxy. Orthodoxy never claimed to mark the natural next step in the history of Judaism, but saw itself as nothing other than Judaism. In its near-total symmetry with the received system, Orthodoxy surely made a powerful case for that claim. But the fact that the case had to be made, the context and conditions of contention: these indicate that another Judaism was coming into being. The asymmetrical points, moreover, demand attention, though, on their own, they should not decisively refute the position of Orthodoxy. What does refute it is the very existence of an Orthodoxy. The single most interesting instance of a Judaism of self-consciousness, Orthodoxy defends propositions that, in the received system, scarcely reached a level of articulate discourse: for instance, the absolute necessity to conform to the holy way of life of the Torah. The necessity for making such an argument testifies to the fact that people, within Orthodoxy, thought they confronted the need to choose and did choose. True, the choices, from the viewpoint of Orthodoxy, fell in the right direction. But Orthodoxy formed an act of restoration and renewal; therefore, an act of innovation. The modes of argument of Hirsch, representative as they are of the mentality of the Orthodoxy he defined, call into question the linear descent of Orthodoxy from what people called "tradition." An incremental progress, perhaps; but a lineal and unbroken journey, no. But even the incremental theory of the history of Judaism, which, in the case of Orthodoxy, identifies Hirsch's Orthodoxy with the system of the dual Torah, fails to take note of facts; and, as Hirsch himself argued, that failure sufficed. The facts were that people, Hirsch included, made clear-cut choices, identifying some things as essential, others not (clothing, for one important instance). If the piety of Reform proved selective, the selections that Hirsch made place him into the classification also of one who sorted out change and made changes. Just as the Reformers of the nineteenth century laid emphasis on the points of continuity they located between themselves and the past, so, of course, did the Orthodox (and, from their perspective, with better reason). Just as the Orthodox of the nineteenth century specify what mattered more than something else, so, of course, did the Reform (and, from their perspective, with greater relevance to the situation at hand).

The political changes that in the aggregate created an abyss between the Judaism of the dual Torah and the new, theological Judaisms of the nineteenth century affected both the Reform and the Orthodox of the age. They stood in a single line—one that broke off en route to (so to speak) Sinai—that is, to the Judaism of the dual Torah. So in Orthodoxy we find a system that is clearly incremental with the received system, but still more striking symptoms of a system formed afresh and anew.

Continuity or new creation? Both—but, therefore, by definition, new creation. Piety selected is by definition piety invented, and Hirsch emerges as one of the intellectually powerful creators of a Judaism. "Torah and secular learning" defined a new world view, dictated a new way of life, and addressed a different Israel. To those who received the Judaism of the dual Torah as self-evident, what the Torah did not accommodate was secular learning; nor did the Torah as they received it approve changes in the familiar way of life or know an Israel other than the one at hand. So the perfect faith of Orthodoxy sustained a wonderfully selective piety. The human greatness of Hirsch, and of the many Jews who found self-evident the possibility of living the dual life of Jew and German or Jew and American, lay in the power of the imagination to locate in a new circumstance a rationale for inventing tradition.

The human achievement of Orthodoxy demands more than routine notice. Living in a world that only grudgingly accommodated difference and did not like Jews' difference in particular, the Orthodox followed the rhythm of the week to the climax of the Sabbath, of the seasons to the climactic moments of the festivals. They adhered to their own pattern of daily life, with prayers morning, noon, and night. They married only within the holy people. They ate only food that had been prepared in accord with the rules of sanctification. They honored philosophy and culture, true, but these they measured by their own revealed truth as well. It was not easy for them to keep the faith when many within Jewry, and many more outside, wanted Jews to be pretty much the same as everyone else. The human costs cannot have proved trivial. To affirm when the world denies, to keep the faith against all evidence—that represents a faith that in other settings people honored. It was not easy for either the Orthodox of Germany or the immigrant Jews of America, whom an ocean voyage carried from the world of self-evident faith to one of insistent denial of that faith.

My grandmother was one of those Jews for whom the way of Torah defined the path of life. Raised as a Reform Jew, I know through her the pride, the dignity, the courage of the Judaisms of both the dual Torah and Orthodoxy. Challenged by the rabbi of our temple, advocate of Reform in its most vigorous formulation, that keeping the dietary laws involved violating the American Constitution, she did not answer; she did not think the argument important. At my bar mitvzah, held on Simhat Torah in 1945, when the Torah was carried about the sanctuary, the congregation remained seated, as was their custom, but she stood up all by herself—silently, without comment—as was hers. So we cannot miss the costs, but we recognize also the consequences, for humanity, of those who continued the received system and those who, come what may, sustained it and found in it sustenance for their lives. Each Judaism, Reform and Orthodox, demanded its price, but both richly rewarded those who paid that price. We the living inherit them all.

CHAPTER 4

CONSERVATIVE JUDAISM: ORTHOPRAXY AND ANACHRONISM

The order of the formation of the several Judaisms of the nineteenth century is first Reform, then Orthodoxy, finally Conservatism—the two extremes, then the middle. Reform defined the tasks of the next two Judaisms to come into being. Orthodoxy framed the clearer of the two positions in reaction to Reform; but, in intellectual terms, the Historical School in Germany met the issues of Reform in a more direct way. The Historical School comprised a group of nineteenth-century German scholars, who provided the principal ideas that were realized by Conservative Judaism, a twentieth-century Judaism in America. Each in its own setting took the middle position. We treat them as a single Judaism, because they share a single viewpoint.

The Historical School in Europe and Conservative Judaism in America stressed two matters: first, scholarship, with historical research assigned the task of discovering those facts of which the faith would be composed; and, second, observance of the rules of the received Judaism. A professedly free approach to what was called "critical scholarship" therefore would yield an accurate account of the essentials of the faith. But the scholars and lay people alike would keep nearly the whole of the tradition, just as the Orthodox did. The ambivalence of Conservative Judaism, speaking in part for intellectuals deeply loyal to the received way of life, but profoundly dubious of the inherited world view, came to full expression in the odd slogan "Eat kosher and think *traif*," meaning that people should keep the rules of the holy way of life but ignore the convictions that made sense of them. *Orthopraxy* is the word that denotes correct action and unfettered belief, as against orthodoxy, or right doctrine. Conservative Judaism in America could thus be classified as an orthoprax Judaism defined through works or practices, not through doctrine.

The middle position, then, derived equally from the two extremes. The way of life was congruent in most aspects with that of the Orthodox; the world view, with that of the Reform. Conservative Judaism saw the Jews as a people, not merely a religious community, and celebrated the ethnic as much as the more narrowly religious side of the Jews' common life. Orthodoxy took a separatist and segregationist position, leaving the organized Jewish community in Germany as that community fell into the hands of Reform Jews. Reform Judaism, for its part, rejected the position that the Jews constitute a people, not merely a religious community. Conservative Judaism emphasized the importance of the unity of the community as a whole and took a stand in favor of Zionism as soon as that movement got under way at the end of the nineteenth century.* What separated Conservative Judaism from Reform was the matter of observance. Fundamental loyalty to the received way of life distinguished the Historical School in Germany and Conservative Judaism in America from Reform Judaism in both countries. When considering the continued validity of a traditional religious practice, the Reform asked *Why?* and the Conservatives, *Why not?* The Orthodox, of course, asked no questions. Conservative Judaism for a long time enjoyed the loyalty of fully half of the Jews in the United States and today retains the center and the influential position of Judaism in this country.

The viewpoint of the center today predominates even in the more traditional circles of Reform and the more modernist sectors of Orthodoxy—even though the institutions of organized Conservative Judaism, the Jewish Theological Seminary of America, the Rabbinical Assembly, and the United Synagogue have faced various difficulties in the past decade and a half. The reason we distinguish institutions from systems is that a Judaism is not identical with the organizations and institutions that at one time or another serve that Judaism. Conservative Judaism as the Judaism of

* Since the Second World War, Reform Judaism has affirmed the ethnic aspect of the Jews' common life and become highly pro-Israel; and Orthodoxy, in its modern or Western mode, has entered into collaboration with Reform and Conservative Judaisms. The description at hand pertains to the situation characteristic of the first century of the three Judaisms, down to the Second World War, in Germany and America alike.

the center has never enjoyed a more paramount position than it does today throughout the world, even though the way of life and world view here identified as Conservative Judaism do not enjoy recognition as such elsewhere. In the State of Israel are many more who call themselves "traditional" than "religious," meaning Orthodox. That title, "traditional," in effect marks the Israeli who uses it as the equivalent of Conservative in America. In the Judaic life of many European Jewish communities, as well as those in Australia and South Africa and Canada, the basic situation of Conservative Judaism—observance of many basic rules by rabbis and of some by lay people, a moderate and rational reading of the received holy books, emphasis upon the ethnic as much as upon the narrowly religious side to things—characterizes the practiced Judaism. The rabbis are mainly Orthodox; the congregations mostly non-observant—just as in Conservative Judaism in America. So while calling themselves Orthodox and their Judaism, Orthodoxy, the religious sector of the Diaspora over all exhibits the distinctive indicators of Conservative Judaism, in its paradigmatic power the single most important Judaism of modern times.

The strength of the "Historical School,"[1] and therefore of Conservative Judaism, lay in that compromise defining the centrist position. The Historical School in Germany and Conservative Judaism in America affirmed a far broader part of the received way of life than Reform did, while rejecting a much larger part than did Orthodoxy of the world view of the system of the dual Torah. The Judaism at hand concurred with the Reformers that change was permissible, and claimed that historical scholarship would show what change was acceptable and what was not. But the proponents of the Historical School differed in matters of detail. The emphasis on historical research as a means of settling theological debates explains the name of the group. Arguing that its positions sprang from historical fact rather than theological conviction, Conservative Judaism maintained that "positive historical scholarship," joined to far stricter observance of the law than the Reformers required, would prove capable of purifying and clarifying the faith.

The history of Conservative Judaism in the nineteenth and twentieth centuries began in 1886, when rabbis of the centrist persuasion organized the Jewish Theological Seminary of America; and from that rabbinical school developed the Conservative Movement. For its part, as we have seen, the Historical School in Germany did not constitute a Judaism but a handful of scholars writing books, and a book is not a Judaism. In the United States and Canada, by contrast, the Conservative Movement in Judaism (as it sometimes called itself) or Conservative Judaism reached full realization in a way of life characteristic of large numbers of Jews; in a world view that, for those Jews, explained who they were and what they must do; and in a clearly articulated account of who is Israel—a Judaism. From the end of the First World War, Conservative Judaism became the dominant movement among American Jews. In *Conservative Judaism*, Marshall Sklare argued that that Judaism served to express the viewpoint of the children of the immigrants to America from eastern Europe who came at the end of the nineteenth century.[2] Those children laid emphasis on the folk aspect—the way of life—while rejecting the world view—the supernaturalism—of the received system of the dual Torah. That forms the counterpart in the life of ordinary people of the slogan, "Eat kosher and think *traif*." Sklare further identified Conservative Judaism with the area of second settlement, that is to say, the neighborhoods to which the Jewish immigrants or their children moved once they had settled down in this country. The enormous success of Conservative Judaism in the third generation beyond the initial migration—that is, among the grandchildren of the immigrants, from the Second World War to the

1970s—and the power of Conservative Judaism to establish itself in distant suburbs calls into question the thesis at hand. But in its own terms, Sklare's reading of the second generation assuredly illuminates matters.

The still greater attraction of Conservative Judaism for the third and fourth generations lay in two factors: first, its capacity to attract to a life of observance Jews who had grown up outside the religious world of Judaism; and, second, its power to mediate between the received tradition and the intellectual and social facts of the contemporary world. The center's fundamental definition of the urgent issues and how they were to be worked out, in both nineteenth-century Germany and twentieth-century America, therefore proved remarkably uniform and successful, from the beginning to the present.

The World View of Historical Scholarship: Zechariah Frankel and Heinrich Graetz

If history, the chosen discipline for Judaic theological argument in the nineteenth century, gave its name to the Judaism at hand, the particular area of history that defined discourse was by no means accidental. People made a deliberate choice in the matter. They did not study Scripture in the critical way, but they did study the documents of the oral Torah in accordance with the canons of contemporary academic scholarship. Why the difference? While no one argued about whether Moses gave the Ten Commandments, people did have to work out their relationship to the Judaism of the dual Torah—and, by definition, to the documents of the oral Torah. At issue was its origin and standing. The Orthodox answers, as we recall, left no ambiguity: The entirety of the Torah comes from God, not from mortal humanity; the entire Torah retains authority, such as it had from the very beginning; and, of course, the Talmud and the other rabbinic writings form part of the revelation of Sinai. The Reform answers took an opposite position: The oral Torah is an accident of history; it comes from human authors; it is not part of the Torah of Sinai. Now in addressing these issues, scholars thought that they could produce "positive" historical knowledge, which would secure reliable facts in answer to questions of faith.

The historians Zechariah Frankel (1801–75) and Heinrich Graetz (1817–91) founded the study of rabbinic literature, of the Talmud, as a historical source in Germany, in the 1850s, when Reform was well defined and Orthodoxy was coming to an articulate view of itself. Thus, the modern debate about the Talmud as history took shape in the single decade from 1851 to 1859. In less than ten years, four books were published that defined the way the work would be done for the next century: Leopold Zunz's posthumous publication of Nahman Krochmal's *Moreh nebukhe hazzeman* ("Guide to the Perplexed of Our Times" [1851], a title meant to call to mind Maimonides's *Guide to the Perplexed*); Heinrich Graetz's fourth volume of his *History of the Jews from the Earliest Times to the Present* (1853), which is devoted to the talmudic period; Abraham Geiger's *Urschrift und Uebersetzungen der Bibel* (1857); and Zechariah Frankel's *Darkhé hammishnah* ("Ways of the Mishnah" [1859]). These four volumes—Zunz and Geiger marking the Reform contribution; Graetz and Frankel, the Historical School's contribution (and Krochmal posthumously)—placed the Talmud into the very center of the debates on the reform of Judaism and addressed the critical issues of the debate: the divine mandate of rabbinic Judaism.[3] For three generations, there would be no historical work on the Talmud deriving from Orthodoxy; and what came later bore no constructive program at all.

In the struggle over reform, both Reform and Conservative theologians proposed that, by exposing the historical origins of the Talmud and of the rabbinic form of Judaism, they might "undermine the divine mandate of rabbinic Judaism."[4] As Ismar Schorsch points out, Geiger's work is the highwater mark of the attack on rabbinic Judaism through historical study. He treated it in a wholly secular way. Krochmal, Graetz, and Frankel presented a sympathetic and favorable assessment of rabbinic Judaism and, then, took their leave of Reform Judaism to lay the foundations for the Historical School of Conservative Judaism. In so doing, however, they adopted the fundamental supposition of the Reformers: the Talmud can and should be studied historically. They conceded that there is a history for the period in which the Talmud came forth. The Talmud itself was a work of men in history.

Both Graetz's and Frankel's method was essentially biographical. The two provided spiritual heroes, a kind of academic hagiography, imparting color and life to the names of the talmudic canon. One-third of Frankel's book is devoted to biographies of personalities mentioned in the Talmud. He collected the laws given in the name of a particular man and stated that he appears in such and such a tractate, and the like. Frankel's "card file," though neatly divided, yields no more than what is filed in it. Joel Gereboff comments on Frankel as follows:

> For Frankel Rabbi was the organizer and the law-giver. He compiled the Mishnah in its final form, employing a systematic approach. The Mishnah was a work of art; everything was "necessary" and in its place. All these claims are merely asserted. Frankel gives citations from Mishnaic and Amoraic sources, never demonstrating how the citations prove his contentions. Frankel applied his theory of positive-historical Judaism, which depicted Jewish life as a process combining the lasting values

> from the past with human intelligence in order to face the present and the future, to the formation of the Mishnah. The Mishnah was the product of human intelligence and divine inspiration. Using their intelligence, later generations took what they had received from the past and added to it. Nothing was ever removed. Frankel's work has little lasting value. He was, however, the first to analyze the Mishnah critically and historically; and this was his importance.[5]

What is important is not what Frankel proves but, as I said, what he implicitly concedes, which is that the Mishnah and the rest of the rabbinic literature are the work of men. Graetz likewise stresses the matter of great men. Schorsch characterizes his work:

> Graetz tried valiantly to portray the disembodied rabbis of the Mishnah and Talmud as vibrant men, each with his own style and philosophy and personal frailties, who collectively resisted the disintegrating forces of their age. . . . In the wake of national disaster, creative leadership forged new religious institutions to preserve and invigorate the bonds of unity. . . . He defended talmudic literature as a great national achievement of untold importance to the subsequent survival of the Jews.[6]

Now historians of the day in general wrote biographies. History was collective biography. Their conception of what makes things happen was tied to the theory of the great man in history, the great man as the maker of history. The associated theory was of history as the story of politics, of what great men have done. Whether the Jewish historians of the talmudic period were good, average, or poor historians in general terms I cannot say. The important point is that the beginnings of the approach to the Talmud as history centered on biography. But while most contemporary historians neither laid the foundations for religious movements nor engaged in vigorous debate on theological questions,

Graetz and Frankel strongly opposed Reform and criticized not only the results of Reform scholarship but the policies of Reform Judaism. The program of these two historians fitted more comfortably into a theological than a critical-historical classification, however much they invoked critical-historical and positive-historical knowledge to support their results. Thus, the Historical School, measured by the standards of its day, proved far less critical, far less historical, and far more credulous and believing than its adherents admitted—and, indeed, was methodologically obsolete.

For a broad range of critical questions concerning the reliability of sources escaped the attention of the Historical School. Specifically, in both classical and biblical studies, long before the middle of the nineteenth century, a thoroughgoing skepticism had arisen, formed in the Enlightenment of the previous century and not to be eradicated later. This critical spirit did not accept the historical allegations of ancient texts as necessarily true. So for biblical studies in particular, the history of ancient Israel no longer followed the paths of biblical narrative, from Abraham on. In the writing of the life of Jesus, for example—the contradictions among the several gospels, the duplication of materials, the changes from one gospel to the next between one saying and story and another version of the same saying and story, the difficulty in establishing a biographical framework for the life of Jesus—all of these and similar, devastating problems had arisen. The result was a close analysis of the character of the sources: for example, the recognition, before the nineteenth century, that the Pentateuch consists of at least three main strands—JE, D, and P. It was well known that behind the synoptic Gospels was a source (called "Q," for the German *Quelle*, "source") containing materials assigned to Jesus, upon which the three evangelists drew but which they reshaped for their respective purposes. The notion that ancient storytellers cannot be relied on as sources was thus well established. For the founders of talmudic history—Graetz, Frankel, and Krochmal—however, either did not know or did not find useful the discoveries of biblical and other ancient historical studies—and did not use them. The issues that concerned these scholars derived from a religious and not an academic or narrow scholarly debate, as is apparent when we examine the scholarly methods of the Historical School.

No German biographer of Jesus, for example, could, by the 1850s, have represented his life and thought by a mere paraphrase and harmony of the Gospels, in the way in which Graetz and Frankel and their successors down to the mid-twentieth century would paraphrase and string together talmudic tales about rabbis and call the result history and biography. Few were the scholars who, by the end of the nineteenth century, completely ignored the redactional and literary traits of documents, let alone their historical and social provenance. Yet the historians of positive-historical Judaism believed that whatever was given to a rabbi, in any document, of any place or time, provided evidence of what that rabbi really said and did in the time in which he lived. Thus, while the theologians of the Historical School claimed to present "mere" facts, as well substantiated as those of contemporary historians, the bulk of such facts derived from a reading of sources in as believing, not to say credulous, a spirit as the Orthodox brought to Scripture.

The middle position emerged in a simple way. On the one side, the historian-theologians of the Historical School chose to face the Orthodox with the claim that the Talmud was historical. On the other, they chose to turn their backs on the critical scholarship of their own day with that very same claim that the Talmud *was* historical. That formed a powerful weapon against Reform, and it was the weapon of the Reformers' own choice. Thus, as with the Reformers and the Orthodox, so for the Conservatives the place and authority of the oral Torah, embodied in the Talmud, formed the arena for debate. Facing the one side, the Historical School treated the Talmud as a document of history, therefore as a precedent for attending to context and circumstance, so as to admit to the possibility of change. But facing the other side, the Historical School treated the Talmud as a uniformly reliable and unerring source of historical information. The Talmud was the target of opportunity. The traditionalists trivialized the weapon, maintaining that history was essentially beside the point of the Talmud. But the real debate was not with Orthodoxy but with Reform.

Graetz set the style for such history as was attempted; Frankel, for biography of talmudic sages. Finally, let me quote Schorsch's judgment of Graetz, which constitutes an epitaph to the whole enterprise of talmudic history:

> Above all, Graetz remained committed to the rejuvenation of his people. His faith in God's guiding presence throughout Jewish history . . . assured him of the future. His own work, he hoped, would contribute to the revival of Jewish consciousness. He succeeded beyond measure. As a young man, Graetz had once failed to acquire a rabbinic pulpit because he was unable to complete the delivery of his sermon. There is more than a touch of irony in the remarkable fact that the reception accorded to Graetz's history by Jews around the world made him the greatest Jewish preacher of the nineteenth century.[7]

That none of this indicates a historical task scarcely requires proof. The reliance on precedent, of course, did not surprise proponents of the dual Torah, but they were surprised and deeply offended by the entire program, with its treating as this-worldly and matters of history what the received system of Judaism understood to form an entirely supernatural realm.

The Way of Life of Orthopraxy: Alexander Marx and Louis Ginzberg

We thus come to the question of who joined the Judaism of the Historical School in Europe and Conservative Judaism in America. It was in the way of life formed here that the world view was realized in a Judaism. Of particular interest are the system builders, the intellectuals: historians, talmudists, and other scholars. They are the ones, after all, who defined the ideas in concrete terms and expressed the values and the attitudes that made whole and complete all of the Judaisms I am considering, each with its world view, way of life, theory of an Israel—and each with its powerful appeal to an Israel as well. Since nearly all of the first generations of Conservative Jews in America and of the Historical School in Europe had made their way out of the received system of the dual Torah, the motivation for the deeply conservative approach to that system, the orthopraxy, requires explanation. For that motivation assuredly did not emerge from matters of doctrine. Indeed, once scholar-theologians maintained that the oral part of the Torah derived from mortals, not from God, disagreements with Reformers on matters of change can have made little difference. For by admitting to the human origin and authority of the documents of the oral Torah, the historian-theologians had accomplished the break with Orthodoxy, as well as with the received system. Then differences with Reform were of degree, not of kind. But these differences sustained a Judaism for a very long time, a Judaism that would compose its world view, its way of life, its audience of Israel, in terms that marked off that system from the other two successor Judaisms I have already considered.

Two Europeans-turned-American typify the first mature

generation of Conservative Judaism and show how the differences emerged: Louis Ginzberg and Alexander Marx, counterparts to Abraham Geiger and Samson Raphael Hirsch. Ginzberg and Marx, who were professors at the Jewish Theological Seminary of America for the first half of the twentieth century and important authorities in their fields of learning—Talmud and history, respectively—will serve as our interlocutors in pursuing the questions of this study. For what we want to find out—to remind ourselves of—is not the sociology, or even the theology, of the successor Judaisms of the nineteenth century, but where and how people made the passage from self-evidence to self-awareness, and how we may identify what changed, and specify what continued, within the received way of life and world view. The answers to these questions tell us how people identified and answered urgent questions and so constructed a social world in which to live out their lives.

In the case of the Historical School of Germany in the nineteenth century and of Conservative Judaism in the United States, the answers are clear. Keeping the way of life of the received tradition, to which the Conservatives felt deep personal loyalty because of upbringing and association, would define the way of life of Conservative Judaism. Ignoring the intellectual substance of the received system and striking out in new directions would define the method of thought, the world view. Conservative Judaism began—and for many years persisted—as a blatant orthopraxy—think what you like but conform to the law, as in the cynical apothegm I quoted earlier (page 149). The inherited way of life exercised profound power over the heart of the Conservative Jew of the early generation. The received viewpoint persuaded no one. So they decided to keep what could not be let go, and relinquish what no longer possessed value. To justify both sides, historical scholarship would find reassuring precedents, teaching that change is not Reform after all. But no precedent could provide verification for orthopraxy, the most novel, the most interesting reform among the Judaisms of continuation.

Of the two substantial figures who show us how Conservative Judaism actually worked in the lives of first-rate intellects, I turn first to Alexander Marx (1878–1953) who, in his *Essays in Jewish Biography* (1948), introduces scholars he knew and loved. His book presents a classic statement of the philosophy of the founders of Conservative Judaism. Marx teaches us where that Judaism came from—which, in his person, was out of the Westernized Orthodoxy of nineteenth-century Germany. He carried forward the legacy of his father-in-law, David Hoffmann, and of Hoffmann's father-in-law, Rabbi Azriel Hildesheim—two intellectual giants, after Hirsch, of Orthodoxy in Germany. Marx explains the choices of those whose biography he undertook: "The works of Rashi [a medieval Bible commentator] have attracted me since my early youth"; and, "My interest in Saadia [a philosopher] was aroused by the greatness and originality of his work and the unusual story of his life." As to the eight modern scholars whose work he describes, he says, "I had a personal reason for selecting these men. In one way or another each of them either affected my own scholarly career or was bound to me by ties of close friendship."[8] Hoffmann, for example, was his father-in-law; and Solomon Schechter, the founding president of the Jewish Theological Seminary of America just after the turn of the twentieth century, his friend. We see, therefore, how Marx's personal life affected his choice of heroic figures for biography.

But there is more to it than that. The notion that orthopraxy without a world view characterized Conservative Judaism is wrong. Marx expressed a system, and that system emphasized the same critical approach that characterized the Historical School. As I have already noted, the mode of scholarship in the study of the talmudic corpus, while different from that of both Orthodoxy and the system of the dual Torah called "traditional," in fact remained entirely within the programmatic and topical interests of Orthodox and traditionalists alike. In the case of Marx, this fact emerges clearly. His book, in its values and choice of heroes, is a party document—a work of theology masquerading as descriptive history. Orthopraxy contained its own world view, remarkably like that of Orthodoxy—except where it differed. There are deep convictions in his book, beliefs about right and wrong, not only about matters of fact. Hence, Marx proves more interesting than people who knew him in his day as a dry-as-dust factmonger might have predicted. He wrote an intellectual autobiography, expressed through the biographies of others—a powerful and subtle medium. In his pages, a reticent but solid scholar reflects on himself through what he says about others, reveals his ideals through what he praises in others. Here is an authentic judgment on the nineteenth and twentieth centuries and its principal intellectual framers: Marx's masters, friends, and heroes.

Marx himself was born in Eberfeld, in what is now East Germany. In his youth he served as a horseman in a Prussian artillery regiment—hardly a routine vocation for a rabbinical student, any more than was Hirsch's attendance at a university. Only later did Marx go to the Rabbinical Seminary in Berlin. There, in that center of Orthodoxy, he married the daughter of David Hoffmann, the son-in-law of the founder of that same seminary. So there was a continuity within the intellectual leadership of Western Orthodoxy: Hildesheim; Hoffmann; then, via the Jewish Theological Seminary of America, Marx. But then there was a break: while Hoffmann was an intellectual founder of Germany's westernized Orthodoxy, Marx in 1903 accepted Schechter's call to America. For Marx was one of the major European scholars Schechter brought to the Jewish Theological Seminary of America.

Perhaps Marx hoped that the Jewish Theological Seminary would reproduce the intellectual world of German Orthodoxy: intellectually vital and religiously loyal to tradition. In any case he became professor of history and librarian at the Jewish Theological Seminary. To be Conservative in Judaism then meant to make minor changes in the law but to make much of them, and at the same time to make major innovations in the intellectual life of Judaism and minimize them. Marx fit that pattern—as did many of those about whom he wrote. As a result, Marx's scholarship was erudite but not terribly original or productive. He embodied a Judaism that made much of facts—observances—but did little with them in a kind of intellectual counterpart to orthopraxy.

He carried on the intellectually somewhat arid tradition of Frankel and Graetz, collecting information and making up sermons about it, but engaging in slight analysis or sustained and sophisticated inquiry. He published in the areas of history and bibliography. His most popular work was his *History of the Jewish People* (written with Max L. Margolis), published in 1927.[9] The work, a one-volume history, must rank as among the most boring of its uninspired genre, but it does provide an accurate catalogue of important facts. So Marx's intellectual strength lay in his massive erudition, not in his powers of imagination and interpretation. To him history was a sequence of facts of self-evident importance and obvious significance—a theological, not merely an academic, conviction. For the theological data of the Historical School derived from historical facts, whose consequence was then self-evident.

But that view did not derive from Marx; it was commonplace then and is so even today that the facts of history bear self-evident theological meaning. That view would maintain, for instance, that if we know how a given belief or practice originated, we are guided as to the meaning of that belief, the legitimacy of that practice. If we can prove that the taboo against mixing milk with meat began in a Canaanite custom, or that the taboo against pork began because that meat spoiled so rapidly in the hot desert (as has been alleged), then we can dismiss those taboos as no longer valid, there being today no Canaanites but ample refrigeration. Called the "genetic fallacy," that position on the authority of history characterized the generation in which Marx did his work. Thus, Conservative and Reform theologians alike believed that people today should not feel compelled to do or not to do, to believe or to disbelieve—just because things once happened that way. To this view of theology Marx, with his entire generation of German and American scholars of Judaism, subscribed.

The important point, then, was the fact, and facts were to be defined one by one. Consequently, the episodic point, expressed in a brief article, formed the natural vehicle for scholarly expression. The alternative was a lengthy book, systematically working out and sustaining a proposition or problem with many implications. Marx wrote no such book, nor did many scholars in his day. Scholarship for Marx and his fellows was comprised of brief, topical, *ad hoc*, and unconnected papers—and, of such ideas, too. Graetz's history, made up of tales, and Frankel's biographies, thumbnail sketches based on paraphrases of talmudic stories, fall into the same classification. Given the stress on the self-evident meaning of facts, we can understand why the simple establishment of a fact allowed Marx and his generation to see in it a message and derive from it a meaning. But even as short essays, Marx's papers and those of his contemporaries contain important statements of broad significance. The modern figures of interest to Marx were at the center of the movement for the intellectual modernization of Judaism. All of them stood within the Western camp, but also took a traditionalist position in that camp. When we reflect on those Marx did not choose to write about—for example, Zunz and Geiger, founders of Reform Judaism; Zechariah Frankel, founder of the Positive Historical School that yielded Conservative Judaism—we see his points of sympathy and concern.

And that brings me to Louis Ginzberg (1873–1953), a still more typical and influential figure.[10] He typifies the entire group of theologian-historians, in that he grew up within the heartland of the Jewish world of eastern Europe, but left for the West. In that important respect, he stands for the experience of departure and of alienation from roots that characterized most of the early Reformers, the earliest generations of Conservative theologians, and the Orthodox of the age as well. Later some of these thinkers would lay down the rule that, to be a scholar in Judaism, one had to grow up in a yeshiva—and leave—a counsel that raised alienation to a norm. Conservative Judaism's world view bore no relationship whatsoever to the received system of the dual Torah. None of the representative men in the early generations found urgent the replication of the way of life and world view in which Ginzberg grew up.* The policy of orthopraxy, then, formed a mode of mediating between upbringing and adult commitment—that is, of coping with change.

Born and brought up in Lithuania, heartland of the intellectual giants of the received system, Ginzberg left it for Berlin and Strasbourg, where he studied with Semitists, historians, and philosophers—practitioners of disciplines unknown in the sciences of the dual Torah. Ginzberg's next move, from the central European universities, brought him to the United States, where, in 1899, he found employ-

* There were no women of note: A century would have to pass before women found their rightful place in the life of Judaisms.

ment at Hebrew Union College. But his appointment was canceled when it became known that he affirmed as valid the critical approach to the Hebrew Scriptures—a point of view, central to Reform and Conservative positive-historical scholarship, that made it impossible for him to be accepted by any Reform seminary.

In 1900, he found employment with the *Jewish Encyclopedia* and, in 1903, accepted an appointment in the Talmud at the Jewish Theological Seminary of America, yet another of the founding faculty collected by Solomon Schechter. Why Schechter found Ginzberg's views on biblical scholarship acceptable I do not know; but, of course, Ginzberg taught Talmud, not Scriptures. He taught at the Jewish Theological Seminary for fifty years, and has been called by Hertzberg simply "a principal architect of the Conservative movement."[11]

Ginzberg's scholarly work covered the classical documents of the oral Torah, with special interest in subjects not commonly emphasized in the centers of learning he had left. He studied the Talmud, just as he had done as a youth in Lithuania—but concentrated on the Talmud of the Land of Israel, which was not usual there, rather than on the Talmud of Babylonia, which was. And in the Talmud, he took a special interest not in legal problems but in folklore, and so compiled *The Legends of the Jews.*[12] Further, he offered a fresh and novel angle, hitherto unexplored entirely—namely, the issue of economic interest—claiming that sages had taken certain legal positions owing to particular class interests. In these striking ways, Ginzberg did something new with texts that were very, very old. The canon persisted, but the subject changed, and changed radically. Yet, despite the fresh questions and perspectives, the mode of learning remained constant. Ginzberg's work emphasized massive erudition, with a great deal of collecting and arranging, and was primarily textual and exegetical. When he entered into historical questions, the received mode of talmudic discourse—deductive reasoning, *ad hoc* arguments—predominated. For example, in the 1929 essay where he propounded the theory—famous in its day—that differences on issues of the law represented class differences, repeated enunciation of the thesis followed by examples of how that thesis might explain differences of opinion took the place of rigorous analysis and cool weighing of its implications.[13] Maintaining that liberals expressed the class interests of the lower classes, and conservatives of the upper classes, he then found in details of the law, as two parties debated it, ample exemplifications of this same theory. Just as in the yeshiva world Ginzberg had left, enthusiastic argument took the place of sustained analysis and critical testing, so in the world he chose to build, the same mode of thought persisted, changed in context, unchanged in character. For talmudists such as Ginzberg who acquired a university training, including an interest in history, and also continued to study talmudic materials, never fully overcame the intellectual habits ingrained from their beginnings in *yeshivot*.

Characteristic of talmudic scholarship is the search, first, for underlying principles to make sense of discrete, apparently unrelated cases; second, for distinctions to overcome contradictions between apparently contradictory texts; and third, for *hiddushim*, or new interpretations of a particular text. The exegetical approach to historical problems that stresses deductive thought, while perhaps appropriate for legal studies, produces egregious results for history, too often overlooking the problem of evidence: How do we know what we assert? What are the bases in actual data to justify *hiddushim* in small matters or, in large ones, the postulation of comprehensive principles (*shitot*) of historical importance? Ginzberg did not support, with archeological or even extratalmudic literary evidence, his theory that disputes reflect economic and social conflict. Instead, having postulated that economic issues are everywhere present, he proceeded to use this postulate to "explain" a whole series of cases. The "explanations," intended to demonstrate the validity of the postulate, in fact merely repeat and illustrate it. None of these theses in their exposition and demonstration bears much in common with then-contemporary humanistic learning: humanistic history, even then, was deriving its propositions from inductive, not deductive, proof. Ginzberg, for each of his hypotheses, failed to demonstrate that the data could not be equally well explained by some other postulate or postulates. At best he leaves us with "this could have been the reason" but provides no concrete evidence that this *was* the reason.

Ginzberg was more than a great scholar. He also provided for Conservative Judaism a full and systematic statement of its world view, clarifying its issues and methods and defining its attitudes. He explicitly stressed the orthopractic view that Judaism "teaches a way of life and not a theology." At the same time, he conceded that theological systems do "expound the value and meaning of religion in propositional form," but that doctrines follow practices: "Theological doctrines are like the bones of the body, the outcome of the life-process itself and also the means by which it gives firmness, stability, and definiteness of outline to the animal organism." So Ginzberg rejected "the dogma of a dogma-less Judaism." Religious experience—that is, observance of the way of life—comes first and generates all theological reflection. As for the role of history: "Fact, says a great thinker, is the ground of all that is divine in religion and religion can only be presented in history—in truth it must become a continuous and living history." This extreme statement of the Positive Historical School, which would not have surprised Frankel and Graetz, provides a guide to the character of Conservative Judaism in the context of the political changes of the nineteenth and twentieth centuries. The appeal to fact in place of faith, the stress on practice to the subordination of belief—these form responses to the difficult situation of sensitive intellectuals brought up in one world but living in another. To understand the reason orthopraxy proved appealing, we have to recall a simple fact. Growing up within the received way of life, the now-alienated Jews retained warm memories of home and family, joined to Sabbath, festival, the holy pattern of the life of the community. Facing the conflict between a way of life found affecting and appealing and a world view in conflict with "the facts," whether of history or science, the first generation beyond the tradition preserved what it valued and dropped what it did not. So it kept alive the way of life, while adopting positions contradicting the familiar premises of that way of life.* In line with the human problem solved by the appeal to orthopraxy, Ginzberg's judgment placed experience prior to thought: "Religious phenomena are essentially reactions of the mind upon the experienced world, and their specific character is not due to the material environment but to the human consciousness."[14] Ginzberg's capacity for a lucid statement of his own theological views belied his insistence that theology followed upon, and modestly responded to, what he called "religious experience" but was, in fact, simply the pattern of religious actions that he had learned in his childhood to revere.

So orthopraxy eased the transition from one world to another. The next generation found no need to make such a move; it took as normal, not to say normative, the stress on deed to the near exclusion of intellect that, for Ginzberg and the Historical School, as much as for Orthodoxy, ex-

* Modern Orthodoxy did no less, but it did so in a way that, in its view, would not at all violate the convictions of the received Judaism's world view.

plained why and how to keep in balance a world view now utterly beyond belief and a way of life very much in evidence. His address in 1917 to the United Synagogue of America, of which he served as president, provides a stunning statement of his system of Judaism:

> Looking at Judaism from an historical point of view, we become convinced that there is no one aspect deep enough to exhaust the content of such a complex phenomenon as Judaism, no one term or proposition which will serve to define it. Judaism is national and universal, individual and social, legal and mystic, dogmatic and practical at once, yet it has a unity and individuality just as a mathematical curve has its own laws and expression. By insisting upon historical Judaism we express further our conviction that for us Judaism is no theory of the study or school, no matter of private opinion or deduction, but a fact. . . . If we look upon Jewish History in its integrity as a simple and uniform power, though marked in portions by temporary casual parenthetical interruptions, we find that it was the Torah which stood forth throughout the history of Israel as the guiding star of [the Jews'] civilization.[15]

While some readers may find this statement gibberish, affirming as it does everything and its opposite, it is nonetheless a serious effort to state deeply held convictions. The key to much else lies in the capital *H* assigned to the word *History*, the view that history possesses "integrity as a simple and uniform power." What we have is none other than the familiar notion that history—fact—proves theological propositions.

That position cannot surprise us when we remember that the facts of the way of life impressed Ginzberg far more than did the faith that, in the context of the dual Torah, made sense of those facts and formed of the whole a Judaism. In fact Ginzberg did not possess the intellectual tools for the expression of what he had in mind, which is why he found adequate resort to a rather inchoate rhetoric. Assuming that he intended no merely political platform, broad enough to accommodate everyone whom he hoped would stand on it, we reach a single conclusion: Conservative Judaism, in its formative century from Frankel to Ginzberg, stood for the received way of life, modified in only minor detail, along with complete indifference to the received world view. To take the place of the missing explanation—of theology—"Jewish History" would have to make do. That history, of course, supplied a set of theological propositions; but these demanded not faith but merely assent to what were deemed ineluctable truths of history: mere facts.

The Birth of a Judaism

In its formative century, Conservative Judaism carried forward the received way of life—hence it was a Judaism professedly continuous with its past. But in its forthright insistence that no world view one could delimit and define accompanied that way of life, Conservative Judaism imposed on itself a still more radical break with the received tradition than did Reform Judaism. Above all, Conservative Judaism denied the central fact of its system—its novelty. The change effected by Frankel, Graetz, and Ginzberg involved not a scarcely articulated change of attitude, as with Hirsch, but a fully spelled out change of doctrine. For the one thing that Hirsch—all the more so his critics in the traditionalist world—could not concede proves central to Ginzberg's case: "Judaism" is everything and its opposite, so long as Jewish History defines the matter. So if we ask, incremental development or new beginning? the answer is self-evident. Conservative Judaism formed a deeply original response to a difficult human circumstance.

In its formative century, Conservative Judaism solved, not only for scholars and rabbis, the urgent problem of alienation. To people who had grown up in one place, under one set of circumstances, and now lived somewhere else, in a different world, the question of change proved urgent. They had to find ways of retaining ties to a past that, they knew, they had lost. They cherished that past, but they themselves had initiated the changes they now confronted. Some did so simply by emigrating from the old village in eastern Europe to a city in Germany, Britain, or America. That new circumstance imposed strains on the capacity to live in the familiar patterns. It certainly called into question the givenness of received attitudes, the established world view, as well. In the doctrine of orthopraxy, a generation in transit held on to the part of the past its memoirs found profoundly affecting and made space for the part of its present circumstance it did not, and could not, reject. A Judaism that joined strict observance to free thinking kept opposed weights in equilibrium—to be sure, in an unsteady balance. By definition such a delicate juxtaposition could not hold. Bridged with a fragile chain of words, the abyss between the way of life, resting on supernatural premises of the facticity of the Torah (as Hirsch rightly understood), and the world view, calling into question at every point the intellectual foundations of that way of life, remained. But the experience of change through migration affected only the founders. They produced a Judaism that served beyond their time and distinctive circumstance. We turn to a second-generation Conservative theologian to show us the more lasting statement of the system. He will indicate how the successor generation proposed to bridge the gap, to compose a structure resting on secure foundations.

The claim of Reform Judaism to constitute an increment of Judaism, we recall, rested on the position that the only constant in Judaism is change. The counterpart for Conservative Judaism was provided by the writings of Robert Gordis (1903–) which, for their day, set the standard and defined the position of the center of the religion. Specifically, we ask how Gordis viewed the Judaism of the dual Torah and how he proposed to relate Conservative Judaism to it. Here is his forthright account of the "basic characteristics of Jewish tradition":

> The principle of development in all areas of culture and society is a fundamental element of the modern outlook. It is all the more noteworthy that the Talmud . . . clearly recognized the vast extent to which rabbinic Judaism had grown beyond the Bible, as well as the organic character of this process of growth. . . . For the Talmud, tradition is not static—nor does this dynamic quality contravene either its divine origin or its organic continuity [all italics his]. . . . Our concern here is with the historical fact, intuitively grasped by the Talmud, that *tradition grows.*

Gordis's appeal is to historical precedent—a precedent that derives from a talmudic story, which by itself is scarcely historical at all. The story, as Gordis reads it, recognizes that tradition is not static. Let us read the story in Gordis's words and ask whether that is, in fact, its point:

> Moses found God adding decorative crowns to the letters of the Torah. When he asked the reason for this, the lawgiver was told: "In a future generation, a man named Akiba son of Joseph is destined to arise, who will derive multitudes of laws from each of these marks." Deeply interested, Moses asked to be permitted to see him in action, and he was admitted to the reason of the schoolhouse where Akiba was lecturing. To Moses' deep distress, however, he found that he could not understand what the scholars were saying and his spirit grew faint within him. As the session drew to a close, Akiba concluded: "This ordinance which we are discussing is a law derived from Moses on Sinai." When Moses heard this, his spirit revived![16]

While Gordis's view—that the story "clearly recognized

the vast extent to which rabbinic Judaism had grown beyond the Bible, as well as the organic character of this process of growth"—certainly enjoys ample basis in the sense of the tale itself, his interpretation of the story hardly impressed the Orthodox and traditionalists who read the same story. More important, if we did not know in advance that "the principle of development . . . is . . . fundamental," we should not have necessarily read the story in that context at all. For the emphasis of the story when it is not adduced as a proof-text for the Conservative position lies on the origin at Sinai of everything that came later. And that point sustains the principal issue at hand: the divine origin of the oral Torah, inclusive even of the most minor details adduced by the living sage. We know, of course, the issue urgent to the storytellers both of the Talmud of the Land of Israel and of Babylonia: namely, the place of the sages' teachings in the Torah. And that position, fully exposed here, was that everything the sages said derived from Sinai—precisely the opposite of the meaning imputed to the story by Gordis. It is not that Gordis has "misinterpreted" the story, but he has interpreted it in a framework of his own, not in the system that, to begin with, created the tale. This is evidence of creativity and innovation, of an imaginative and powerful mind proposing to make use of a received tradition for fresh purpose: not incremental but a new birth.

This small excursus on talmudic exegesis serves only to underline the fresh and creative character of Conservative Judaism. For without the slightest concern for anachronism, the Conservative theologians found in the tradition ample proof for precisely what they proposed to do, which was, in Gordis's accurate picture, to preserve in a single system the beliefs in both the divine origin and the "organic continuity" of the Torah: that middle ground, between Orthodoxy and Reform, that Conservative Judaism so massively occupied. For Gordis's generation, the argument directed itself against both Orthodoxy and Reform. In the confrontation with Orthodoxy, Gordis pointed to new values, institutions, and laws "created as a result of new experiences and new felt needs." But to Reform, he pointed out "instances of accretion and of reinterpretation, which . . . constitute the major modes of development in Jewish tradition."[17] That is to say, change comes about historically, gradually, over time, and does not take place by the decree of rabbinical convocations. The emphasis of the Positive Historical School upon the probative value of historical events serves the polemic against Reform as much as against Orthodoxy. To the latter, history proves change; to the former, history dictates modes of appropriate change.

Gordis thus argues that change deserves ratification after the fact, not deliberation beforehand: "Advancing religious and ethical ideals were inner processes, often imperceptible except after the passage of centuries." To his credit, he explicitly claims that Conservative Judaism is part of an incremental and continuous, linear history of Judaism:

> If tradition means development and change . . . how can we speak of the continuity or the spirit of Jewish tradition? An analogy may help supply the answer. Biologists have discovered that in any living organism, cells are constantly dying and being replaced by new ones. . . . If that be true, why is a person the same individual after the passage of . . . years? The answer is twofold. In the first instance, the process of change is gradual. . . . In the second instance, the growth follows the laws of his being. At no point do the changes violate the basic personality pattern. The organic character and unit of the personality reside in this continuity of the individual and in the development of the physical and spiritual traits inherent in him, which persist in spite of the modifications introduced by time. This recognition of the organic character of growth highlights the importance of maintaining the method by which Jewish tradition . . .

> continued to develop. This the researches of Jewish scholars from the days of Zacharias Frankel . . . to those of . . . Louis Ginzberg have revealed.[18]

The incremental theory follows the modes of thought of Reform, with their stress on the continuity of process, that alone. Here, too, just as Marcus saw the permanence of change as the sole continuity, so Gordis sees the ongoing process of change as permanent. The substance of the issues, however, accords with the stress of Orthodoxy on the persistence of a fundamental character to Judaism. The method of Reform, then, produces the result of Orthodoxy, at least so far as practice of the way of life would go forward.

While, like Orthodoxy, Conservative Judaism defined itself as Judaism pure and simple, it did claim to mark the natural next step in the slow evolution of the tradition, an evolution within the lines and rules set forth by that tradition itself. Appeals to facts proved by scholars underlines the self-evidence claimed in behalf of the system in its fully articulated form. Scholars could not see the anachronism in their reading the past in line with contemporary concerns. Everything was alleged to be self-evident. But, of course, it was not. What truths Conservative theologians held to be self-evident they uncovered through a process of articulated inquiry. The answers may strike them as self-evident; but they themselves invented the questions.

The appeal to an incremental and linear history, a history bonded by a sustained method and enduring principles that govern change, comes long after the fact of change. Assuredly, Conservative Judaism forms a fresh system, a new creation, quite properly seeking continuity with a past that has, to begin with, been abandoned. For processes of change discerned after the fact, and in the light of change already made or contemplated, are processes not discovered but defined, then imputed by a process of deduction to historical sources that, read in other ways, scarcely sustain the claim at hand. The powerful scholarship of Conservative Judaism appealed to a reconstructed past, an invented history: a perfect faith in a new and innovative system, a Judaism discovered by its own inventors.

Conservative Judaism solved a profound human problem, rather than answering an urgent question. The problem was how to make a graceful and dignified exit from a world view and a way of life that people had come to find alien. As between the two, the Conservatives abandoned the world view—ideas are cheap, words do not have to mean much—but sustained the way of life, imparting to it all sorts of fresh meanings, as best they could. The insistence on continuity yielded a certain cynicism, a going through motions. But the human anguish for a generation deeply loyal to a world it rejected cannot escape our notice. For Conservative Judaism in its formulation as orthopraxy was transient. Ginzberg kept the cultic laws of the Torah. The next generation did not. The future of Conservative Judaism lay in its serving as a road not out, but into, the Judaic system of the dual Torah—as by the mid-1950s, it had begun to do.

A Challenge to Orthodoxy

EMANUEL RACKMAN

I

A GROUP OF ISRAELI INTELLECTUALS, ORTHODOX in practice and commitment, addressed an inquiry to one of the world's most pious and learned of rabbis. In their work and thought they had embraced scientific theories which appeared to contradict passages of the Bible when literally interpreted. The age of the earth was one example. From another rabbi they had heard that Orthodoxy requires that one believe the earth to be only 5728 years old. Were they to be regarded as heretics because of their disagreement with this view?

The twenty-five-page reply prepared for them is not yet published. Its author (who prefers to be unnamed) sought the concurrence of three colleagues who had occasionally expressed progressive views. One declined to become involved because of advanced age and poor health; another declined concurrence because of fear of what he himself calls "McCarthyism" in Jewish Orthodoxy; the third felt that his status in the traditionalist community was not yet sufficiently secure to be of any value to the scholar soliciting approval, especially since the latter himself enjoyed so much more prestige than he.

The reply—with copious references to authorities—indicates that Orthodoxy is not monolithic: it requires acknowledgment of the divine origin of the Commandments and firm resolve to fulfill them; however, it also permits great latitude in the formulation of doctrines, the interpretation of Biblical passages, and the rationalization of *mitzvot*. It is not difficult to demonstrate that the giants of the Tradition held widely divergent views on the nature of God, the character of historic revelation, and the uniqueness of the Jewish faith. Not all of these views could possibly be true, and yet not one of them may be deemed heretical, since one respected authority or another has clung to it. The only heresy is the denial that God gave the Written and Oral Law to His people, who are to fulfill its mandates and develop their birthright in accordance with its own built-in methodology and authentic exegesis.

Often in the past, upon encountering new cultures or philosophical systems, Jewish scholars re-examined the Tradition and discovered new insights and interpretations. Their contemporary colleagues of a more conservative temperament resisted and attacked the creative spirits

---

EMANUEL RACKMAN *is the rabbi of the Fifth Avenue Synagogue in New York and assistant to the president for university affairs at Yeshiva University.*

as heretics, though the impugned protested that they were deeply committed to the Tradition and had said nothing which was not supported by respected authorities who had preceded them. The resulting schisms were often no credit to the Jewish people and, in modern times, even yielded groupings among American Jews which are not based altogether on ideological differences.

Unfortunately, however, it is the reactionaries in Orthodoxy who bear much of the guilt for this tragic phenomenon. Their heresy is that they regard their own Biblical and Talmudic interpretation as canonized in the same measure as the texts themselves—which was never true. They are repeating this heresy again, in Israel and the Diaspora, so that already Jewish sociologists detect the possibility of further schisms in Orthodoxy. At least four groups are even now discernible,* and the "rightists" are exercising pressure to brand the "leftists" as heretics and to force them either to create a new sect or to identify with Conservative Judaism. The founder of Reconstructionism did break with the Tradition, and his views, insofar as they deny the divine origin of Torah and *mitzvot,* are heresy. But this was unequivocally clear to his own colleagues on the faculty of the Jewish Theological Seminary fifty years ago, and Solomon Schechter must have had him in mind when he poked fun at those who observe the *mitzvot* and yet deny their God-given character. However, this does not mean that all who have new approaches are *ipso facto* non-Orthodox and must affiliate elsewhere.

In more recent times Rabbi Abraham Isaac Kook, of blessed memory, was regarded as having expressed dangerous opinions. Dr. Joseph B. Soloveitchik and Dr. Samuel Belkin today are experiencing the same fate. The late Rabbi Aaron Kotler, dean of the "rightists," denied that those who receive a secular education can express authentic Torah views. The students of the Rabbi Isaac Elchanan Theological Seminary of Yeshiva University, whose graduates Dr. Belkin and Dr. Soloveitchik ordain, are taught by rabbis who are rightist, leftist, and centrist; and, while academic freedom is enjoyed by all, there prevails an uneasy tension among both faculty and seminarians which is also reflected in the rabbinical associations they subsequently join together with graduates of other Orthodox seminaries. Milton Himmelfarb has detected and written of this tension as it appears in the periodicals of Orthodox thought and opinion, like *Deot, Amudim, Jewish Observer, Tradition,* etc. It is even more pronounced in Israel in the sundry factions of several religious political parties and their daily, weekly, and monthly publications. The politicians there clamor for unity

* See Charles S. Liebman, "A Sociological Analysis of Contemporary Orthodoxy," JUDAISM, Summer 1964, p. 285 ff.

among the Orthodox, but the ideologists, especially in the religious collectives, insist that, before there can be unity even on an election slate, religious parties must at least unite on mutual respect for the legitimacy of their divergent religious views. But this is not forthcoming.

Two questions must needs be considered. Is the "right" correctly representing the Tradition? And is it wise even for them, from their point of view and certainly from the point of view of the survival of the Tradition, to deal with the "left" as they do?

One who undertakes to answer these questions must do so with fear and trepidation. Since he must deal with the totality of the law and creed known as Judaism, he ought not be so presumptuous as to regard himself as so much the master of the entire Tradition that he can offer definitive views on virtually every aspect. Furthermore, some of the views he must, of necessity, express will incur the wrath of colleagues and cause their exponent to share the fate of the very people whom he wants properly to reclaim as members of the community of the devout and committed. Like them he will be called a heretic whose ideas jeopardize the future and integrity of Torah.

Nonetheless, silence is not the alternative when one is convinced that precisely a measure of candor is the *desideratum,* not only because God wills that we speak the truth as we see it—for His name is Truth—but also because silence and its concomitant smugness are estranging Jewish intellectuals. Jewish intellectuals are becoming interested in the Tradition, but they will not accept the rigidity of most contemporary exponents of Orthodoxy. They crave more autonomy of the soul. Moreover, some effort ought to be expended to reaffiliate those who, principally because of the way in which Jews have organized themselves politically in Israel and socially and institutionally in the English-speaking countries, find themselves identified with groups whose ideology they do not truly share. For many reasons they cannot identify with the present leadership of Orthodoxy anywhere in the world, and yet they regard themselves as wholly within the Torah tradition. The time is ripe for a candid re-examination of fundamentals and a challenge to those whose principal claim to authority is that they have closed minds and secure their leadership by exacting a comparable myopia from their followers. One may not deny them their freedom of worship, but even as they want their views tolerated and respected so must they be prevailed upon to recognize that others are as devout and as committed as they, and that the Tradition has always permitted a considerable amount of diversity in thought and action. It was never proper to consolidate ranks by substituting fixity for dynamic religious creativity, and certainly in the contemporary open society with its emphasis on the open mind, it is hardly propitious to commit the error occasionally committed in the past when one group of Jews withdrew from their co-religionists, regarded the others as heretics, and sought to save themselves by severing contact with those with whom they disagreed.

Rightly or wrongly, one Jewish sociologist has named me as an ideologist of "modern Orthodoxy." However, one can hardly regard modern Orthodoxy as a movement: it is no more than a coterie of a score of rabbis in America and in Israel whose interpretations of the Tradition have won the approval of Orthodox intellectuals who are knowledgeable in both Judaism and Western civilization. None of the rabbis feels that he is articulating any position that cannot be supported by reference to authentic Jewish sources. None wants to organize a separate rabbinic body, and several have rejected an attempt to publish an independent periodical, because they did not want the remotest possibility that this form of separatism be interpreted as a schism in Orthodoxy. I, no less than they, deny any claim to innovation. Our choice of methods and values in the Tradition, our emphases, and our concerns, may be different. But the creation or articulation of shades and hues hardly warrants dignifying our effort with the terms "ideology" or "sect." We know that the overwhelming majority of Orthodox rabbis differ with us and that the faculties of most Orthodox day schools and rabbinical seminaries disapprove of some of our views and so instruct their pupils. It is not our mission to have them join our ranks. Rather do we seek to help Jewish intellectuals who are being alienated from the Tradition to realize that they can share a commitment to the faith which is acceptable to them and at least as authentic as the one they have received from their teachers but which they feel impelled to renounce. We reject the multiplication of dogmas and their precise formulation. Among Christians this notion is presently popular as "reductionism." In Judaism, however, "reductionism" is very ancient: the Midrash tells us of different prophets who sought to encapsulate the tradition in seven, three, or even one principle. Ours is a commitment which invites questioning and creativity in thought and practice, as applied not only to the Law but also to theology.

II

ONE MUST BEGIN WITH THE MEASURE OF FREEDOM permitted in Jewish Law and commitment by the Tradition itself. When do one's thought and action place one beyond the circle of the devout? We discover that the range of diversity in creed, ritual, and law is so great that, no less than in a democracy, consensus is required on much less than is usually thought—in order to claim rightful status as an Orthodox Jew.

Must one who professes Orthodoxy be committed to the retention of the total Halachah insofar as it deals with civil law—the law of property and obligations, corporations, partnerships, sales, trusts, estates? According to the Halachah itself, there is a residual power to alter all property relationships in the *bet din* (court), and especially in a supreme legislative and judicial body such as the Sanhedrin once was and many hope will soon be reconstituted. The principle is known as *hefker bet din hefker.* A *bet din* has the power to declare property ownerless and in that way to divest a man of his rights, vesting them in another. This power was exercised whenever changes were made in the Halachah with regard to economic affairs. A man may thus be Orthodox and yet actively propagate changes in the law for the promotion of capitalism or socialism, bigness or smallness in economic enterprise, curbs on strikes, or greater freedom for organized labor.

The Halachah has many ethical norms and insights to offer on these subjects, but any Jew—committed to the Halachah—enjoys, on the basis of his interpretation of the Halachah, unlimited freedom to propose changes; if he were fortunate enough to be a member of the Sanhedrin and to prevail on his colleagues to embrace his point of view, he would be the creator of new Halachah. There may be instances where the changes are so radical that resort would have to be taken to legal fiction. Thus, when Hillel saw that Jews were not lending money to each other because of the fear that the sabbatical year would nullify the debts, he could have changed the rule by exercising the power of *hefker bet din hefker,* divesting debtors of their money and vesting it in their creditors, but this would have been an unequivocal nullification of a Biblical mandate. Instead he instituted the *pruzbul*—a legal fiction whereby the debts incurred prior to the sabbatical year were transferred to the court for collection. Perhaps he also hoped thereby to keep alive some memory of the Biblical rule and that one day it would be revived in practice. To alter the Biblical rule of inheritance in order to establish the equal rights of daughters to inherit with sons, or to abolish the last vestige of primogeniture in Jewish law, may also require resort to legal fictions—as the late Chief Rabbi Herzog once unsuccessfully proposed. In any case, one cannot be regarded as a heretic because of one's dissatisfaction with the present state of the Halachah with regard to economic matters and one's determination to effect change and development. Such change and development have always been, and must needs continue to be, achieved.

Is the Orthodox Jew any less free in connection with criminal law? Whether he wants to diminish the number of crimes and mitigate punishments or whether he wants to increase them, he can do so within the frame of the Halachah. He must be most circumspect, it is true, with regard to capital offenses—but even here he is by no means without power. Again, there are residual powers in the *bet din* and even in the king (the executive authority) which can be exercised to safeguard peace and order and promote the general welfare. Centuries after capital punishment had virtually been abolished, the Jewish community protected itself against informers by reviving capital punishment. It also altered the rules of evidence to make convictions more feasible. A devotee of the Halachah, therefore—even as he tries to fathom its spirit and especially the enormous regard it has for human life and freedom by comparison with its lesser regard for the right of property —need not feel impotent to propose and press, in fulfillment of that spirit, for the adoption of a new criminal law for a modern state, even for a state that professes to be committed to the Halachah.

Nor need he feel inhibited as he seeks within the spirit of the Halachah to urge upon his fellow citizens the consideration of specific proposals for the constitutional structure of the state. He will be able to justify unicameral and bicameral legislatures, proportional representation, popular election of judges and their appointment by the executive, a parliamentary and a presidential form of government, and sundry other forms of government which may be found in modern states. The more profound his commitment to the Halachah, and the more preoccupied he is with what God would have willed for a new Jewish State, the more tolerant will he be of all the proposals and the more will he resort to the will of the people except when that will flouts basic norms and ethics with regard to which majority rule is not to be countenanced. Thus, as neither civil nor criminal law is fixed and immutable in the Halachah, public law in general is an area in which commitment to the Halachah requires no general agreement among the devout.

Israel's victory in the Six-Day War made this abundantly clear. Shortly after the occupation of the new territory, Chief Rabbi Nissim held that, according to the Halachah, it would be forbidden to negotiate for peace as the *quid pro quo* for the return of any of these areas. Rabbi Joseph B. Soloveitchik questioned this decision and indicated that perhaps for an enduring peace it would be necessary to relinquish some of the land and that statesmen might be in a better position to render such a decision, which would be binding on rabbis precisely as the opinion of a doctor is binding on a rabbi in connection with the breaking of a fast on the Day of Atonement. Rabbi Nissim countered with the suggestion that there are certain commandments for which martyrdom is required. He was certainly justified in making that suggestion, since almost every conquest in the history of humanity has involved the loss of blood, and Jews, too, have been commanded to conquer. (In at least one situation this was even a *mitzvah.*) In a recent essay, a pupil of Rabbi Kook, Rabbi Yehuda Gershuni, documented his support of Dr. Soloveitchik's view. In any event, it is obvious that on so historic an issue, one so vital to the future of the people of Israel, a radical difference of opinion prevails among giants in the world of Halachah. And who will deny that all are Orthodox in commitment and practice!

In family law we encounter a more circumscribed area. Yet here, too, as a devotee of the Halachah one can propose and agitate for changes that will nullify almost every rule of the past. It might be the sheerest folly to do so. But the question under consideration is not whether one should write a new code for Jewish domestic relations but rather whether the power resides in the duly constituted authorities to do so. And it does. Therefore, he who thinks that changes are in order and proposes them for promulgation by the *bet din* or Sanhedrin cannot be regarded as a heretic. As in the case of property, the Rabbis ruled that all marriages have an implied condition that their validity and continuance are based on rabbinic consent. Rabbis in the past have differed as to how extensive this power is, but one cannot be deemed a heretic when he agrees with the most liberal views heretofore entertained. Exercising the power that rabbis have, they may one day reintroduce the annulment of Jewish marriages and the abolition of the last vestige of illegitimacy (except in the case of unequivocal proof that the child was born of an incestuous relationship). They may find ways to legislate an Enoch Arden law and make the incidence of the levirate law impossible. There are some limitations; but for any Orthodox group to brand as a heretic one who feels keenly that changes should be made—within the Halachic frame and by its own methodology—is to define heresy as it was never defined in the past. One can argue with the proponents of change because of policy considerations, but one may not challenge their loyalty to the faith. Indeed, they may be its most passionate champions as they try to relieve human distress.

III

THE AREAS OF PERSONAL RELIGIOUS OBSERVANCE and congregational or temple practice are quite different. There the *bet din* is not so free to act as in other spheres of the Law. And he who would, for example, say that a Jew need not don the phylacteries or eat kosher food could be regarded as a heretic. However, one should not underestimate the extent to which rabbis may, in good faith, differ with each other within the frame of the Halachah without even recommending change. They may differ on policy considerations; they may differ on the steps that are required to nullify or modify earlier rabbinic legislation; they may differ on programs that are designed to guide people back to the Torah way of life. Even when they agree on what Orthodoxy requires in terms of normative practice, they can differ on policies and programs to achieve the goal they all envisage.

A few timely illustrations are in order. Should a rabbi use the microphone on the Sabbath in a synagogue where its use is required? The prohibition may be Biblical in origin. Others maintain that it is only rabbinic. Still others argue that the microphone may be used. Which is the better course for a rabbi to take—to rely on the more lenient view and serve the congregation so that it will not align itself with the non-Orthodox camp, or to decline to serve, thereby avoiding the compromise of one's own convictions and firmly presenting to that congregation a strict pattern of Jewish observance? In the final analysis, considerations of policy will dictate what one's decision will be, and Orthodox rabbis have been known to hold either view.

Similarly, Halachah dictates that men shall be separated from women in the synagogue. Some authorities hold that the most that can be Biblically supported is that they shall sit in separate sections. At least one authority holds that there is a Biblical requirement for a divider seventy-two inches high. But Biblical rules are also sometimes suspended in the face of greater needs of the community, especially in times of stress. Most often the suspension is temporary, but not necessarily so. Perhaps this explains why some of the policy-makers at Yeshiva University's theological seminary permit rabbis to serve congregations with mixed seating, in the hope that these congregations may one day revert to the traditional practice. They may be in error, but they are acting within the frame of a well-established Halachic principle that for God's sake one sometimes flouts Torah mandates. They are not to be regarded as diminished in their commitment. On the contrary, they may be more prophetic, and as they venture they may reclaim many, while others are saving only a remnant.

My last illustration is perhaps the one on which rabbinic opinion is most sharply divided. Most prohibitions are rabbinic in origin—they constitute the "fence around the Law." In modern times many of these rules have become onerous, and often meaningless. There are many ways to modify and even nullify their impact. Some rabbis seek the re-establishment of a Sanhedrin to accomplish this desired result. Others rely on a well-known principle that when the reason for the "fence" has disappeared the rule, too, automatically dies. What right does one have to question the integrity or commitment of an Orthodox Jew who proposes one way or the other? All have ample authority on which to rely. To what extent, for example, may electric power be used on the Sabbath, since the prohibition is at most rabbinic? Perhaps the use of musical instruments can also be liberalized. I personally may not agree, and in several instances I should like to see more "fences" added to safeguard Biblical rules (such as the prohibition against usury), but I cannot deny that there are reasons for modifying some established prohibitions. One ought not, in any case, pronounce bans against those who are pressing for conclusions with which one differs, provided that they make their proposals out of their commitment to the Law rather than their rejection of it.

If heresy is to be found anywhere, therefore, it must be in the areas of doctrine and creed rather than of law and practice.

IV

EVEN WITH REGARD TO DOCTRINE, such a divergence of opinion has prevailed among the giants of the Tradition that only one dogma enjoys universal acceptance: the Pentateuch's text was given to the Jewish people by God. However, what its mandates are, their number, application, and interpretation—this is part of the Oral Law, also God-given, but its guardians were rarely unanimous on its legal norms and less so on matters theological. That a majority prevailed on any particular issue in the past does not necessarily mean that the minority view is heretical, for, while one must continue to fulfill the law as the majority decided, one may propagate the minority point of view in the hope that it will one day be accepted by a new Sanhedrin. Maimonides is less liberal on this point than his critical glossator, Rabbi Abraham Ben David, but even Maimonides accords this power to a Sanhedrin greater than its predecessors in quality and quantity. Therefore, how can one brand as a heretic anyone who in matters theological differs with his contemporaries and seeks to make normative a point of view once rejected or proscribed but for whose acceptance he continues to hope?

How many are the dogmas of Judaism? Maimonides said thirteen, but other scholars held that there were fewer. Even on so basic a point as to whether there can exist more than one divine law Albo differed with Maimonides. He denied that there is any evidence for Maimonides' contention that the immutability of the Mosaic Law is a pillar of the faith and opined that there may be a succession of divine laws, so that even Mosaic law is not beyond change or repeal.* Jews generally have agreed with Maimonides—at least until the Messiah will come, and upon his coming they believe with Albo that new divine laws may be promulgated. The collective experience of the Jewish people may warrant the conclusion that the Maimonidean

* *Book of Roots* I, 3, 25; III, 13-16.

view is the more prudent—pragmatically to be regarded as true—but who can gainsay the right of a dissenter to agree with Albo or even a modification or extension of Albo's view and yet regard himself as a member of the family of the committed?

Agreement or even consensus is still more difficult to find in connection with such matters as the nature and mission of angels, the character of "the world-to-come" and how it differs from immortality of the soul, the precise role the Messiah will play when he comes and what events will be the most dependable credentials of his legitimacy, the form final judgment will take in a hereafter and the reward and punishments to be dispensed, the transmigration of souls, and a score of other issues with which ancient and medieval scholars were concerned. One discovers in their writings virtually every opinion known to man, ranging from the purest rationalism to the wildest fancy. Few Orthodox Jews try to be specific in formulating their own creeds. They are content with a few generalizations: that God endows every human being with a soul, which is His eternal spark within us and immortal; the human being—body and soul—is responsible and accountable for his performance on earth; one day nature will be made perfect, and as God fulfills His promise to make it perfect He will also have to do justice to the dead, who are the most helpless victims of nature's imperfections. Details are not only avoided, they are unthinkable. Except in most elusive form these sentiments can hardly be regarded as dogmas; they leave too much room for the play of the imagination of the individual believer. Therefore, it is incredible that moderns, who are committed to faith and the Law, should be excluded from the fold because of limited credulousness in this sphere. Indeed, it would be impossible for reactionaries to ignore the giants of the past who were equally skeptical. (Only recently did I come upon a note of Strashoun proving that the Talmud did not subscribe to Kabbalistic notions of the transmigration of souls.)

But the range of the diversity involves doctrines even more basic to the faith. To what extent, for example, is there any binding authority on the nature of God and His attributes? Here, too, Maimonides and Rabbi Abraham ben David differed so radically on God's corporeality that, were Jews prone to create sects because of doctrinal disputes, as Protestants do, each would have been responsible for a new sect in Judaism. Even with regard to so integral a part of Judaism as God's role as Creator, Maimonides retained an open mind. He believed that the correct interpretation of the Bible required a belief in *creatio ex nihilo,* but he admitted that if it could be proven conclusively—as Aristotle had failed to do—that this was impossible, one would then only be required to re-examine and correct one's interpretation of the Bible to make it consonant with the demands of absolute truth. Judaism is very much at peace with a host of antimonies regarding God's nature—His imminence and His transcendence, His prescience and His becoming, His absolutism and His vacillation. To deny that God is a personal God who communicates with all men, and especially with Israel, would be heresy according to Judaism, but any description of Him by rationalists, empiricists, intuitionists, or existentialists would hardly be without some warrant in the writings of the Sages.

Similarly, there is no substantial agreement with regard to the manner in which God communicated with Israel, its Patriarchs and Prophets. Somehow the Tradition preferred never to demand of Jews more than that they believe the text of the Pentateuch to be divine in origin. Otherwise, the widest latitude in interpretation was not only permitted but often encouraged. Even the authorship of the Five Books of Moses was not beyond the scope of the diversity. Several Sages held that Moses himself wrote the book of *Deuteronomy* but God dictated its inclusion with the earlier books. Moreover, much in the earlier books started also as the work of man. In their dialogues with God the Patriarchs spoke their own words. Jacob composed his own prophecy for his offspring. Moses sang his own song of trumph on the Red Sea. In the final analysis, then, the sanctity of the Pentateuch does not derive from God's authorship of all of it but rather from the fact that God's is the final version. The final writing by Moses has the stamp of divinity—the kiss of immortality. So stated, the dogma is a much more limited one than one would be led to believe it is when one listens to many an Orthodox teacher today.

If this is the situation with regard to the Pentateuch, is it wise to add dogmas that the books of the Prophets and the Writings were all authored by the men to whom the Tradition attributes them? The Talmud itself was not dogmatic, but contemporary Orthodoxy always feels impelled to embrace every tradition as dogma. The Talmud suggests that perhaps David did not write all the Psalms. Is one a heretic because one suggests that perhaps other books were authored by more than one person or that several books attributed by the Tradition to one author were in fact written by several at different times? A volume recently published makes an excellent argument for the position there was but one Isaiah, but must one be shocked when it is opined that there may have been two or three prophets bearing the same name? No Sage of the past ever included in the articles of faith a dogma about the authorship of the books of the Bible other than the Pentateuch. What is the religious, moral, or intellectual need for adding dogmas now when it is well known with regard to many such issues that there always prevailed *noblesse oblige* among scholars? It may be heresy to deny the possibility of prophetic prediction, but it is not heresy to argue about authorship on the basis of objective historical and literary evidence. How material is it that one really believes that Solomon wrote all three Scrolls attributed to him? Is the value of the writings themselves affected? And if the only purpose is to discourage critical Biblical scholarship, then, alas, Orthodoxy is declaring bankruptcy: it is saying that only the ignorant can be pious —a reversal of the Talmudic dictum.

True, a pious man has *emunat ḥakhamim,* faith in the dicta of the Sages. Yet Orthodox Jews do not rely on this principle in connection with their physical well-being. They are willing to be treated in illness by physicians who hold views that differ radically from those expressed in the Talmud for the treatment of disease. Certainly the Tradition condones this. Is it less forgiving of one who in his study of the Bible feels impelled to arrive at conclusions on the basis of evidence unavailable to his forebears?

No more than with regard to the authorship of the Biblical books did the Sages canonize interpretations of the Bible. For the purpose of the Halachah one interpretation may have to be followed until the Halachah, within its own processes, is altered; but the Sages recognized, offered, and delighted in many alternative, frequently contradictory interpretations which had significance for their spiritual living. Especially was this true when they interpreted narrative portions of the Bible. Maimonides was the most revolutionary of all when he held that most Biblical history is allegorical. Whether Jacob only dreamed that he wrestled with an angel or actually did so was debated by sundry Sages. Nahmanides even held that it was God's intention that the *mitzvot* of the Torah were given for ultimate fulfillment in the Land of Israel, and our observance of them in the Diaspora is only preparation for our sojourn in the land of our fathers. Hardly any Orthodox rabbi aggrees with him today—and perhaps none agreed with him in his day. Was he, therefore, deemed a heretic?

Even the historic fact of revelation was not specifically delineated. Whether God as much as spoke all the Decalogue so that everyone could hear it was controversial. One Rabbi dared to say that God did not descend to earth. Summing up the Talmudic and Midrashic texts available and the opinions of medieval philosophers, one modern scholar said that the best that could be said for the Jewish conception of revelation is that it is "elusive." Perhaps it is. But the net effect is a consensus on which the faith is founded. *Something* extraordinary happened—and the Jew begins with a text that is God's word. He may not always understand it. He may often question why God approved of much that He gave. Unlike Martin Buber, the Orthodox Jew does not reject any part of the text. If he finds it difficult to explain why the very God who ordered us never to take revenge also demanded the extermination of the Amalekites, he does not delete from the text the lines he does not fathom; he ponders them until divine illumination comes to him. He may discover that the Amalekites—unlike the Egyptians—merited destruction and continuing hate; he may regard Amalek as the symbol of militarism for the sake of militarism; or he may even conclude that what is meant is the id in every human being. Heresy begins not when interpretation is challenged but when the text is no longer considered divine. That is why Franz Rosenzweig did not consider himself un-Orthodox because of his theory of revelation but only because he could not bring himself to obey all the *mitzvot* until they spoke to him personally and became meaningful to his own existential situation. Unlike him, the Orthodox Jew obeys and does not wait. Obedience to God's will by itself is meaningful to his existential situation, and the more he obeys the more he discovers meaning and relevance.

If Jews differed with regard to their interpretation of the texts of Scripture, certainly they differed with regard to their interpretation of history. It has been demonstrated, for example, that Ashkenazim and Sephardim differed with regard to their positions on eschatology and the warrant that historical situations might provide for either activism or quiescence with regard to the coming of the Messiah.

Thus, even with respect to creed, the diversity is as legion as it is with respect to Law. To be counted among the devout and the committed never required unrelenting conformity in matters of the mind and heart. Judaism did not suffer as a result. On the contrary, it remained one of the most dynamic and spiritually satisfying of all religious traditions. In the last century and a half this magnificent Tradition was abandoned: in its encounter with the enormous diversity of the winds of doctrine prevailing in the modern world, Orthodoxy sought to guarantee its survival by freezing the Halachah and its theology. As a result, it now cannot realize its full potential in an age when more and more intellectuals are prepared for the leap of faith but hardly for a leap to obscurantism.

V

ARE THE "RIGHTISTS" JUSTIFIED from a practical point of view? They argue that only the "freeze" will save Judaism and that it is better to weed out those whose outlook on the faith and the Law is liberal, to retain only the hard-core of loyalists who never question. Some of them would even prefer to insulate their followers against all secular learning. If secular learning there must be, let it be held to a minimum, and that minimum should be restricted to "safe" disciplines such as mathematics, accountancy, business. Even natural science may be "safe." Social science is more hazardous; biology, psychology, anthropology and archaeology are most dangerous of all. Where possible, the loyalists seek to live in isolated, self-contained communities. For their right to do all of these things even the liberal must fight. Their freedom should not be curtailed because one disagrees with them. But one must question the wisdom of their program as well as the correctness of their perspectives. At the same time, one must demonstrate to them that Orthodoxy's future is bright if, instead of resorting to self-containment, it is true to its historic destiny to be ecumenical vis-à-vis the total Jewish community.

Perhaps the liberals have been too decent in their hesitancy to expose the sordid situation that prevails in the rightists' camp. Personal vilification and even journalistic blackmail are ruthlessly in vogue. An Anglo-Jewish weekly that consistently spoke the views of the reactionaries is attacked by a more extreme Hebrew monthly for being mildly sympathetic with the plight of the State of Israel. The same magazine heaped abuse on a day school that is Agudist, not even Mizrachi, in its orientation. Needless to say, it would be sheerest folly to expect that such extremists would heed an appeal to reason made by a rabbi whose liberal sympathies are well-known. However, the overwhelming majority of Orthodox Jews, who are not only devout and committed but also generous in their support of institutions dedicated to the survival of the Torah tradition, are decent people. They are not organized in any kind of "citizens' union" to cleanse their own movement, and they support no one party or publication. To them an appeal for Jewish ecumenism must be made. Jewish intellectuals also must be cautioned against identifying Orthodoxy with a committed but fanatical minority who, alas, because they were themselves in Europe the victims of so much hate, have lost the capacity to be tolerant and to love.

It is the nature of the extremist that he cherish extremes: the more extreme a position is, the better it suits his temperament and outlook. For that reason there are so many defections, for example, by more moderate Klausenberger Hasidim to the virulently anti-Zionist *Rebbe* of Satmar. For that reason also the most extreme group in Israel, which was never Hasidic—the *Neturei Karta*—affiliated with Satmar. If a *Rebbe* more extreme than the Satmar were to enter upon the scene, there would be many defections to the new "right." Would that be regarded as the new Orthodoxy, while the other Hasidic movements would be "conservative"? Jewish sociologists have studied with justifiable admiration what Hasidic communities are achieving, but they have respectfully ignored the strife, the hostility, and the unmistakable ugliness of the manner in which several of the groups react to others. However, unless the spirit of mutual respect and toleration is nurtured, deepened and propagated, many more Orthodox youth will not only detect the malaise of Orthodoxy but reject the entire Tradition precisely because it can breed such unhealthy psyches. This is a practical reason for ecumenism. One distinguished Israeli rabbi and popular author was so distressed by the bitter, almost savage-like, factionalism that prevails that he initiated a movement for truth and peace. His effort aborted, and he was speedily silenced. If one talks about peace and truth and, above all, respect for differences, one becomes supect and loses status in extremist Orthodox circles.

It would, therefore, be wise for Orthodox Jews frankly to reject extremism not only as ideologically inconsistent with the Torah tradition but as pragmatically untenable for survival. Moreover, there must be mutual respect if Orthodoxy is to mobilize all of the committed in a common effort to achieve adequate representation in the organized American Jewish community and in government circles. It is to the credit of Orthodoxy that on many national and international issues it has expressed original and courageous positions. There is a growing respect everywhere for its new strength and refreshing insights. However, its adherents still constitute such an amorphous community that its spokesmen are not accorded prestige positions or merited allocations from available funds by the leadership of the general Jewish community. The intolerance of Orthodox Jews vis-à-vis each other is matched by at least a comparable intolerance vis-à-vis non-Orthodox Jews, and the leaders of the general Jewish community cannot be gracious when their graciousness is less than reciprocated. Thus many of them, for example, who are profoundly impressed by what Yeshiva University has accomplished for both America and Jewry still find it difficult to give as generously to it as they do to other universities—Jewish and non-Jewish—only because they equate the name "Yeshiva" with obscurantism and fanaticism. In academic circles, on the one hand, Yeshiva University's reputation continues to soar, while in the circles of Jewish Federations and philanthropists there is resistance because of mistaken images.

Most important of all, only a liberal approach can help youth who are groping to discover that Orthodoxy is an exciting quest and not always the oracle for final answers. Only the liberal approach can help them see that the quest is one which involves a creative partnership between God and man not only in the conquest of the earth but also in fulfillment of God's will for both nature and man. Youth are too sophisticated to believe that any man is the master of the ultimate. They are much more prone to accept the meaningfulness of process even in creed, not only in law, and will cherish the tension of the Orthodox who are profoundly committed to the fact of revelation at the same time that they seek to unravel that revelation and make it progressively significant for human thought and action.

With a respectful ecumenical approach Orthodoxy has much to gain. It is to be hoped that it will not miss its opportunity.

VI

IN ALL FAIRNESS TO THOSE WHO SHARE MY VIEWS, it should be said that they are not alumni of any one Yeshiva but of virtually all. If half of them or more are alumni of Yeshiva University, it is only because half or more of all Orthodox rabbis ordained in America have studied there. They are all individuals who have not hesitated to expose themselves to the totality of humanity's accumulated learning. Indeed, they deem it an insult to the revealed word of God that the validity of what God gave can only be maintained by remaining oblivious of other disciplines. What is more, it is they who maintain that the Torah will be valid no matter what the test to which it is subjected and no matter what the circumstances in which one is called upon to live.

This is why they are most militant champions not only of a viable Halachah but also of the Torah's revelance to every issue one encounters in a modern state. They recognize that final decisions in many instances involve questions of policy, and often in policy questions the opinions of the knowledgeable laymen are at least as sound as those of the "doctors of the Law." In this way they also help to revive an ancient Jewish tradition that gives the layman a real voice in many matters confronting the Jewish community. They seek less of a dictatorship of the rabbinate and more the combined action of the community of the devout and committed. In an age when Hasidism is on the march, and thousands yield obedience to a chosen *Rebbe* or *Rosh Yeshiva,* their position can only be that of a few. But they are an influential few and do not want to separate from their brethren. Their brethren, too, should not cavalierly dismiss what need all have of each other, if Orthodoxy is to meet the challenge of the age.

AMERICAN ORTHODOXY— RETROSPECT AND PROSPECT

EMANUEL RACKMAN

The earliest Jewish settlers on American soil brought with them the only Judaism they knew—Orthodox Judaism. Two centuries later Reform Judaism took root and still fifty years thereafter Conservative Judaism was born. Under the circumstances, one would have expected that Orthodox Judaism would be the first to meet the challenge of the American scene, ideologically and institutionally. In fact, it was the last to do so. Paradoxically enough, it is only in the last few decades that Orthodoxy seriously came to grips with the problem of its own future.

For too long a time Orthodoxy relied upon the fact that the preponderant number of American Jews professed to be its adherents. Majorities supporting the status quo in many social situations often rely upon the force of their numbers and their inertia, while well organized and dedicated minorities make gains for change. The Orthodox Jewish community once was such a majority. It was slow to realize the extent to which it was losing its numerical advantage. Second, the ranks of American Orthodoxy were ever replenished with thousands of immigrants from abroad. The new arrivals more than compensated for the defections to other groups. Now the loss of the European reservoir of Jews has caused American Orthodoxy to become concerned. It must find the way to command the loyalty of American born Jews. Third, Orthodoxy by its very nature compromises less easily with new environments and new philosophies, so that it could not avail itself of that flexibility which aided the growth of the Reform and Conservative movements. The challenge of the American scene had to be met differently and the solution was later in its formulation and implementation. Nonetheless, significant and many were the contributions of Orthodoxy to our dual heritage as Americans and as Jews.

It fell to the lot of Orthodoxy to establish the legal status of Jews and Judaism in American democracy. To the everlasting credit of our pioneering forbears it must be said that they were not content with second-class citizenship in the United States. George Washington confirmed this attitude in his now famous letter to the Orthodox congregation in Newport, Rhode Island. However, the false dictum that America is a "Christian state" must be challenged again and again, even in the twentieth century, and while the battle is now waged by all Jews, and especially the defense agencies, it is usually one Orthodox Jew or another who creates the issue. The right of Sabbath observers to special consideration where "Blue Sunday" laws are in effect; their right to special treatment in the armed forces; their right to unemployment insurance benefits when they decline employment because of religious scruples—these are typical of many problems that Orthodox Jews raise in the hope that their resolution will insure maximum expansion of the American concept of equality before the law. In many instances, bearded Orthodox Jews who retain their eastern European dress are also a challenge to the sincerity of most Americans who boast that their way of life spells respect for differences. The resistance of many of our co-religionists to the levelling character of American mores, and its inevitable discouragement of diversity, is a healthy contribution to our understanding and practice of democracy. Altogether too often American Jews require the reminder even more than American Christians.

In the same spirit it was American Orthodoxy that bore, and still bears, the lion's share of the resistance to world-wide calendar reform. Though all Jewish groups have cooperated, it is Orthodoxy alone that regards any tampering with the inviolability of the Sabbath day fixed at Creation as a mortal blow to Judaism and in the name of the religious freedom of minorities it seeks to alert the American conscience to desist from prejudicial action.

It was, however, in the establishment and construction of thousands of synagogues throughout the country that Orthodox Jews made manifest not only their loyalty to their ancestral heritage but their appreciation of their grand opportunity in this blessed land of freedom. How truly pauperized immigrants managed, in cities large and small, to rear beautiful edifices for worship is a saga worthy of more attention than it has heretofore received. What is particularly noteworthy is that no central agency guided or financed the movement. In every case it was individual Jews who banded together and performed the feat, a remarkable tribute to the effectiveness of our tradition in inducing in individual Jews the capacity to act on their own initiative for the greater glory of God. Even today no central body guides or directs the establishment of Orthodox synagogues. Orthodoxy's synagogue organization—the Union of Orthodox Jewish Congregations of America—is still totally ineffective in this kind of work. The initiative must always come from Jews who desire an Orthodox synagogue, and not from any resourceful, missionary, national or international body. In part, this is also one of the weaknesses of Orthodox Judaism which its leaders want to correct on the threshold of its fourth century on the American scene. However, it remains to be seen whether it will be the Union of Orthodox Jewish Congregations or Yeshiva University that will blaze the new path.

The extent to which Orthodox Jews gave of their wordly goods for the establishment and construction of synagogues was exceeded only by their willingness to sacrifice for the cause of Jewish education. Their first venture in this direction, even before the era of the public school, was a Jewish all-day school under the auspices of Congregation Shearit Israel in New York. The more usual approach to the problem, however, was via the Talmud-Torah, the afternoon school in which children spent from five to ten hours weekly. In some instances the Talmud Torahs were successful, and many distinguished

American Rabbis and scholars received their earliest instruction in Judaica in such schools. Yet altogether too often because of incompetent instructors, bizarre methods, and inadaquate facilities, the Talmud Torahs failed to induce either a love or an understanding of Judaism. In the twentieth century, therefore, Orthodox Judaism countered with the Yeshiva movement. This movement has enjoyed a phenomenal growth. In the ranks of Conservative Judaism, too, it is receiving sympathetic attention and support, and even among Liberal Jews one occasionally hears it suggested that the all-day school is the most effective answer to Jewish illiteracy.

Three organizations of Orthodox Jewry now propagate the Yeshiva program and supervise the establishment of new schools. The Vaad Hachinuch Hacharedi of the Mizrachi Organization of America also deals with Talmud Torahs, while Torah Umesorah whose program and goal were conceived by the saintly Rabbi Faivel Mendelowitz, is concerned with Yeshivoth alone. The Lubavitscher Hasidim have their own unit for identical work. The Vaad Hachinuch Hacharedi is more Zionist in its outlook than the latter two groups; the latter two groups even regard the knowledge of Yiddish as important for the survival of Torah. Together, however, they stress the importance of a thorough background in Bible and Talmud at the same time that secular studies more than meet the standards of the American public schools. With the increase in the number of schools on the elementary level, there came also an increase in the number of schools on the secondary level. Beyond the high school level there was also established a network of schools which ordain Rabbis. At one time the Rabbi Isaac Elchanan Theological Seminary in New York (still the largest) and the Hebrew Theological College, founded by the late Rabbi Saul Silber of Chicago, were the only two Orthodox seminaries in America. Now there are at least a dozen. Unfortunately, however, these schools are not even federated with each other; there is no joint action whatever. Even their graduates are not affiliated with one Rabbinic body, although the Rabbinical Council of America has the largest percentage of all the graduates, while the Rabbinical Alliance of America, and the oldest of all, the Union of Orthodox Rabbis of the United States and Canada, get a fair measure as well. These three Rabbinic groups have recently sought some areas for joint action but as yet the results are meagre. And this is perhaps the greatest weakness of Orthodox Jewry—its inability to consolidate, or even coordinate, its educational institutions and their alumni.

Nonetheless, the enrollment of about thirty thousand Jewish boys and girls in the all-day schools constitutes Orthodox Jewry's proud achievement at the close of the third century of American Jewish history. The financial burden has been indescribably great. And the financial problem will be insoluble in times of economic depression. For that reason many supporters of the Yeshiva movement hope for state support of parochial schools. Heretofore Jews have been quite unanimous in their support of the defense agencies' position on the complete separation of church and state in America. However, with most welfare funds denying aid to the Yeshivoth of their own communities, or at best making niggardly allocations, one can predict that in the not too distant future, the sponsors of the Yeshivoth will be desperate enough to join with representatives of the Roman Catholic Church in an effort to obtain state or federal aid. Such a move may make for a further cleavage between Orthodox and non-Orthodox Jews. But Orthodox Jews feel that they have more than vindicated the right of the Yeshiva movement to be hailed as a major contribution to the survival of Judaism in America and that the time has come for welfare funds to abandon their hostility to the cause. New York City's Federation of Jewish Philanthropies, for example, has already begun to see the light.

One interesting by-product of the Yeshiva movement has been the remarkable financial success that publishers have enjoyed in their republication of classics in Judaica. The Union of Orthodox Rabbis republished the Babylonian Talmud about thirty-five years ago. Thereafter business firms have done it profitably several times and they have added many other works. Orthodox Judaism does not yet adequately subsidize its scholars nor provide for the publication of their original contributions to scholarship. Yet enough of a demand for books has been stimulated to make many a reprinting financially worthwhile.

Another interesting by-product of the Yeshiva movement has been the effect of the presence of a Yeshiva in many a mid-western city upon the Orthodox group within that city itself. Within the Orthodox community, where only chaos and anarchy reigned before, the Yeshiva became the great cohesive force, and the Yeshiva leadership inspired greater control over kashrut supervision, the construction of better facilities required by Orthodox Jews for all ritualistic observances, and even more cooperation in fund-raising for local and overseas religious needs.

How the Yeshiva movement served more than the cause of Torah, narrowly conceived, can be gleaned from the fact that it was a Yeshiva, led by the brilliant and visionary Dr. Bernard Revel, that established on American soil the first Jewish college of arts and science; later it became America's first Jewish University. More recently it undertook the construction of a medical and dental school. Furthermore, that Orthodoxy in America was prepared to abandon its historic indifference to the education of women, was made manifest not only by the fact that a large percentage of the children enrolled in the Yeshivoth are girls, but that Yeshiva University headed by the resourceful and indefatigable Dr. Samuel Belkin, now has a secondary school and college for them.

In the area of overseas relief Orthodoxy was always impatient with the general agencies because of their neglect of religious institutions, and as a result during and after World War I the Central Jewish Relief Committee and Ezrath Torah Fund were organized to bring aid and succor to European Yeshivoth. The Union of Orthodox Rabbis deserves special commendation for this achievement. With regard to Palestine, too, Orthodoxy was preoccupied with religious development. Within the framework of the World Zionist Organization, American Orthodoxy advanced the program of the Mizrachi and Hapoel Hamizrachi parties. Rabbi Meyer Berlin (Bar-Ilan), who was also the founder of the Teachers' Institute which became affiliated with the Rabbi Isaac Elchanan Theological Seminary and later was one of the larger schools of Yeshiva University, was the ideological spokesman and administrative head of every phase of the work. With the new wave of immigration immediately prior to, and after World War II, the separatist Agudath Yisrael party gained an appreciable following in the American Jewish community and created a very marked cleavage between the traditionalists who hoped for some synthesis of western thought with our ancestral heritage and the traditionalists who hoped to reestablish on American soil replicas of Eastern European Jewish communities. The former are also more cooperative with non-Orthodox Jewish groups and participate in the work of the Synagogue Council of America even as they are represented in the Commission on Jewish Chaplaincy of the National Jewish Welfare Board and organizations like the New York Board of Rabbis. The profund ideological differences between the two groups came to the fore with respect to the issue of the conscription of women in Israel. However, the same lack of unity that has weakened Orthodoxy's achievement in the fields of synagogue and Yeshiva organization has also undermined the esteem in which Orthodoxy's significant achievments for Israel ought be held. Nonetheless, it is American Orthodoxy that has always borne the brunt of the responsibility for the preservation of almost all of Israel's religious life.

Orthodox Judaism has maximalist objectives not only for religious education in America and abroad but also with regard to religious observances. Unfortunately, in this area too it has failed to achieve any measure of unity or coordination. Kashrut supervision for example, is under the aegis of no central body, and even the cooperation of states that have laws on the subject has not eliminated the anarchy that prevails. The most progressive step forward was taken by the Union of Orthodox Jewish Congregations, in cooperation with the Rabbinical Council of America, when it registered its "U" as a guarantee of kashrut and made the label available to firms that meet the strictest requirements. This helped to popularize Kashrut and the Union not only advertised the products it endorsed but published brochures on the significance of the dietary laws generally. The ultimate hope is to divest individual Rabbis of the right to act on their own for personal gain. The resistance of members of the Union of Orthodox Rabbis is great and even the Rabbinical Council of America had to pass resolutions censuring its members who flout the policy and give *Hechsherim* as individuals. In the area of Sabbath observance there has been less success although the number of professional and business firms that observe the Sabbath has been increasing. The Young Israel movement has helped to find employment for Sabbath observers but as yet the future of the Sabbath depends principally upon the establishment of the five day week in the American economy. The Young Israel movement, on the whole, not only helped to dignify orthodox religious services, and create social and economic opportunities for observant youth, but also made a magnificent contribution to Jewish adult education all over the country. Modern Mikvehs are being built in many communities and though the laws pertaining to *Taharat Hamishpacha* have suffered the greatest neglect, Orthodox Judaism has sought to improve the situation by constructing more attractive and inviting facilities for their observance and by publishing literature on the subject in English.

In the area of English publications and public relations generally, Orthodox Judaism must meet new challenges.

Its Halakhic and scholarly journals, such as *Talpioth*, of Yeshiva University, have a limited circle of readers while most American Jews have only the vaguest notions of the nature of Orthodoxy and its spiritual and intellectual vitality. True, within the ranks of Orthodox Judaism there are many to whom the modern scene and western thought constitute no challenge. These elements are to be found principally among the recent immigrants to the United States. And they often intimidate the more progressive Orthodox elements who recognize that Jewish law was always dynamic and that Judaism never required an ostrich-like indifference to currents of thought that prevailed in the world about. A sad illustration of the dangers of such intolerance was recently afforded Orthodox Jews when an Orthodox Rabbinic Journal—which was never noted for its progressive approach, and even delighted in attacking the younger Rabbis of the Rabbinical Council of America—found itself under attack by an even more "rightist" journal because it published an article suggesting that the redactors of the Babylonian Talmud did not see the Palestinian Talmud! The tendency to canonize each and every view of the past with absolutely no critical or historical evaluation is strong among these "rightists." Some of them even favor the social and economic isolation of Orthodox Jews. They propose the establishment of Orthodox Jewish communities with Sabbath observing vendors of the necessities of life, Sabbath observing professional and service personnel, etc.

The position of these "rightists," however, is not typical. Most American Orthodox Rabbis are not isolationists. They admit that for at least another generation or two most American Jews will not be observant. Nevertheless, they want these Jews to appreciate their moral obligation to support the totality of their ancestral heritage as Jews that it may be transmitted intact to later generations whose knowledge of Judaism and whose spiritual climate may be more conducive to the development of Judaism in consonance with its historic philosophy and pattern rather than as a compromise with Jewish illiteracy and the materialistic, "sensate" values of the present era. The prevailing values of our day are antithetical to most of the values of Judaism. They, therefore, believe that to adjust Judaism to the values of today is to forfeit the role of religion as a goal and aspiration for a more spiritual tomorrow. Our posterity should not be prejudiced by us and receive from us only truncated conceptions or patterns of Jewish thought and practice. With this approach, most Orthodox Rabbis are urging even the non-observant to identify themselves with Orthodox synagogues and send their children to Yeshivoth. Serious problems do arise when such children are confronted with the contrast between what they are taught in school and what they see at home. However, the leaders of the day-school movement are trying to solve these problems through their publications, their conferences with parents, and their day-by-day contact with the children.

Most Orthodox synagogues now have English-speaking Rabbis who preach in English. Prayer-books and copies of the Pentateuch with English translations are the rule, not the exception. Especially noteworthy among the English translations of the traditional prayer-book is Dr. David de Sola Pool's add, recently sponsored by the Rabbinical Council of America. Under the auspices of the

Union of Orthodox Jewish Congregations, Dr. Leo Jung edited a number of excellent volumes on Jewish information. Several of the essays have become classical expositions of Orthodox Judaism. At least one, "Study as a Form of Worship," by Professor Nathan Isaacs of Harvard University, has gained a world-wide currency among Jews. Rabbi Herbert S. Goldstein translated selections from Rashi's commentary on the Pentateuch for family use on the Sabbath, and more recently a linear translation was made available by a commercial publisher.

Orthodox Judaism is endeavoring to recapture the loyalty of American Jews. However, it cannot "adjust" to the American scene. The term "adjust" too often implies man's right to trim religion to meet his personal desires. Such a right Orthodoxy denies any Jew, and notwithstanding even Dr. Kinsey, the sixth commandment of the Decalogue is binding no matter how high the percentage of spouses who flout it. Nonetheless, most American Orthodox Rabbis recognize that there has always been, and still are, different modes of Orthodox Jewish thought and practice, and that Orthodoxy has always admitted a great measure of innovation. The innovation, however, is always within the Halakhic process and pursuant to its revealed norms. The result, therefore, is organic development of God's will, not man's.

In order to communicate this point of view to American Jews Orthodoxy must have leaders who are not only articulate in English but also masters of western thought and its temper. That is why Yehiva University and the Hebrew Theological College advocate the mastering of all western thought in order to create an ultimate synthesis with Jewish learning. This goal will be achieved as more of the graduates of these schools and other Yeshivoth become expert in the natural and social sciences.

There already exists a society of Orthodox Jewish scientists which is dedicating itself to the solution of problems created for Orthodoxy by modern technology. Many a Halakhic point of view is receiving support from the natural sciences, and what is more important, these scientists are demonstrating that there is no conflict between natural science—which has abandoned the notion that it can attain any absolute truths whatever—and religion which calls for faith in given absolutes. The greater challenges to Orthodoxy, however, come from the social sciences and an impressive group of Orthodox leaders, lay and Rabbinic, are coping with them.

Orthodoxy's position vis-a-vis the Higher Criticism of the Bible is one such area. While Orthodoxy is committed to no one conception of Revelation, all Orthodox Jews regard the Pentateuch as divinely revealed. Moses wrote it while in direct communion with God. Moreover, with Moses too, the Oral Law had its beginnings and its process was ordained by God. German Jewish Orthodoxy perhaps made more progress in its defense of this position than has American Jewish Orthodoxy to date. However, Orthodoxy relies heavily on the fact that modern archaeological research has bolstered the historicity of the Biblical narrative and Orthodoxy is confident that further progress in philology will precipitate the same kind of retreat from anti-Orthodox viewpoints that the Bible's erstwhile plastic surgeons have suffered. Rabbi Chayim Heller, at Yeshiva University, is stimulating both the confidence and the type of research necessary to sustain the Orthodox position. Moreover, many Orthodox thinkers believe that with a retreat from humanism generally, humanism will no longer be the vantage point from which the revealed Word of God will be arrogantly evaluated. Man will not be the measure of God.

The greatest challenge of all, however, lies in the realm of Halakhah; first, the importance of its study, and second, the importance of living by its prescriptions. Is the Halakhah viable in the modern age? Can it and does it enrich our spiritual existence? Is it relevant to our yearnings and aspirations and can it edify and fulfill them? Only a small percentage of even Orthodox Jews are content with the mandate, "The Law is the Law and must, therefore, be obeyed." Philosophical approaches to Halakhah and philosophical analyses of the Halakhic process must be articulated. The undisputed leader of the Orthodox Jewish community in this domain is Dr. Joseph B. Soloveichik, of Yeshiva University, who is now also Chairman of the Halakhah Commission of the Rabbinical Council of America. In addition to his brilliant resolution of many involved Halakhic problems of the modern age, and his equally masterful analyses of Talmudic texts, he is demonstrating the viability of the Halakha, the relevance of its insights to abundant and adventurous spiritual living, and the intellectual harvests to be reaped from preoccupation with its study. Most of the great Halakhic scholars who adorn the faculties of America's Yeshivoth, and most of the distinguished Orthodox Rabbis who founded and still lead the Union of Orthodox Rabbis of the United States and Canada, deserve credit for their benign influence upon the loyalty of thousands of American Jews to our ancestral heritage. But they have done little more than transplant the Orthodoxy of Eastern Europe on American soil. It is to Dr. Soloveichik, his co-workers and students, that American Orthodoxy looks for the ideological content, the techniques and the conclusions required to stem the tide of defections to other groups by making it abundantly clear that Halakhic Judaism is eternal and has naught to fear from the challenges of western thought, present and future.

First, however, it wants to stimulate a renascence of Torah learning on American soil. Orthodoxy feels that until Jews are learned they cannot be pious. It insists that it sustained its greatest set-back in America because of Am ha-Arazuth, Torah illiteracy. For more than two and a half centuries America could not boast of a score of men learned in the Law. How could Orthodoxy then achieve here that synthesis that was once the glory of Spanish Judaism? The first task, therefore, is to spread the knowledge of Torah. As tens of thousands become masters of the Halakha, the Halakha will have a new birth in the new world.

Second, Orthodoxy does not believe that the modern contribution to progressive revelation can come until the modern age recaptures basic religious experience. The commitment of our age to material values has deadened our capacity for religious experience. Yet, there is evidence that as we face the atomic era in human history, there will be a resurgence of religious values and a reawakening of religious experience. In such atmosphere, Judaism will thrive. Particularly will Halakhic Judaism thrive as more and more Jews seek to apprehend God's will rather than merely indulging their own.

TRUTH AND WISDOM: AN ORTHODOX APPROACH

EMANUEL RACKMAN

I

Notwithstanding popular opinion to the contrary, Orthodox Judaism does not give its adherents unequivocal answers to the basic questions of life. Nor does it even prescribe for every situation in which the Jew may find himself. While it does have religious, philosophical and ethical imperatives, these are often antithetical in character and man is rarely spared the onus of deliberate choice and decision. It is important to point this out for the benefit of those who are already committed to the Law as well as for those who are about to embrace it.

Judaism affords no escape from the awareness of reality or the exercise of reason. Indeed, the divinely revealed must be true—in the absolute sense—and what is absolutely true can be an anchor for emotional and intellectual security. But the divinely revealed is limited in word and scope. Life, on the other hand, is complicated, nuanced and calls for cautious application of divinely revealed norms to an endless diversity of situations. To make this application the Jew must constantly muster all of the resources of heart and mind available. And for this he has his Oral Law and the sea of the Talmud. Most appropriately has it been said that while truth is to be found in the Decalogue, the Talmud has wisdom. The former is absolute; the latter is qualified, antithetical, even unsure of itself.

As simple an imperative as "Thou shalt not steal" cannot be treated as an absolute. Is man's right to the ownership of things divinely protected? When can his neighbors, or his fellow-citizens, invade the right and subject ownership to the requirements of the public weal? What is the nature of the higher good, or how many of its beneficiaries, that in its name the public—a state or a community—may expropriate an individual? The Talmud suggests that the prohibition against the theft of things may not even be part of the Decalogue—the theft of things is too unimportant an evil to be given equal status with prohibitions against murder, incest and adultery. The Oral Law, therefore, regards the com-

Since the beginnings of modern times, the relationship between the Written and Oral Law has formed one of the crucial foci of both Jewish historical research and ideological discussion. Offering a plethora of interesting illustrations culled from the Talmud, the writer sets forth the thesis that the relationship is to be seen as a constant antiphony between divine, universal truth, beyond the accidents of time and the exigencies of circumstance, and its growing, modulated application to the stubborn uniqueness of life's actualities. The Talmud, the author maintains, by the exercise of reason turns the divine truth of revelation into wisdom and thus rends it life-directing and life-enhancing.

mandment as directed against kidnapping. As murder and incest and adultery are crimes involving personality, not property, so must the prohibition against stealing involve humans, not things.

Is the prohibition against murder, however, any more absolute than the one against theft? Apparently, judicial punishment, even when capital, is not murder. Is killing in self-defense murder? And what of the killing of one's enemies in war, or after their conquest? As murder must be defined, so must adultery and incest. Even the mandate to tell the truth may have exceptions, and certainly envy—though generally reprehensible—is often encouraged when it stimulates rivalry in righteous and scholarly living.

Thus, even the revealed truth of the Decalogue becomes qualified and nuanced in life and the simplest revelation provides none of the absolutism that so many moderns associate with Orthodoxy. Man retains a creative role in the very process of applying revelation itself. He cannot altogether abdicate the autonomy of his reason. Nor can he, in Judaism, altogether delegate this responsibility, to others. Even his choice of an authority is ultimately an act that calls for deliberation and decision.

However, if with regard to the commands of the Decalogue, there remains an area for interpretation, then *a fortiori* with regard to the remainder of the Law, one can anticipate an uncertainty or ambiguity. Many texts of the Pentateuch—in the narratives and in the codes—invite a multiplicity of exegeses. Saadiah Gaon argued that the lack of clarity is deliberate, for thereby God stimulated understanding by man on many different levels—literal, mystical, allusive. This diversity in interpretation could also help to make diverse the application of Torah to many different situations. Revelation's importance is then due as much to the process it initiated and continues to mold as to its fixity. Indeed, its poles are many, even antithetical, and the Jew must learn to live by the light of these many suns. Simple and stark truth he may never achieve, but at least wisdom is within his reach. This wisdom is contained in the Oral Law, which helps us cope with the ambiguity and lacunae of revelation. And Moses, who taught the Law to all Israel, could not evade his own part in the process. That is why tradition must regard him as the lawgiver of both that which is written and that which is oral.

II

One of the most elementary functions of reason when applied to revealed materials is classification. In revelation itself there is no classification—there are only particulars upon which an inductive operation must be predicated. Without classification, an evolving body of law becomes incapable of transmission to succeeding generations. Moreover, in the very process of classifying the rules, new insights are born and the creative role of man is seen again. An isolated, revealed truth, becomes part of an organized body of wisdom.

Thus, for example, the Oral Law, as based on revelation, could not subscribe to the distinction which most modern states make between civil and criminal law. According to Torah, all conduct is either proper or improper, righteous or sinful. Consequently Halakhic analysis was not troubled, as modern legal philosophy is, with the problem of defining a crime, as differentiated from a tort. The Jew either did or did not do what God had sanctioned. If he did what God sanctioned, he could not be summoned before the court. If he did what God had not sanctioned, or failed to do what God had ordained, then how could one regard his act of omission or commission as culpable only from a civil point of view and not from a criminal one? Judaism's classification, therefore, was exclusively functional. It focused attention on the remedy which the court could grant. And the classification of cases was predicated on whether the court could grant a monetary award or a corporal punishment: flogging, imprisonment or execution. The nature of the court's judgment determined the qualifications and number of judges, the nature of the proof required, and the immunities of the persons against whom claims were asserted. That which was intended to be done to the defendant was definitive. If only his assets were to be reached, then the Law was less concerned about the possibility of error. Greater caution had to be exercised when it was his limb or his life that was in jeopardy. The state, however, played no more and no less of a role in the one case than in the other.

Thus, a court of three sat in a suit which involved the payment of money, and a court of at least twenty-three when his life was at stake. In the latter type of case the judges invariably had to be duly ordained masters of the Law; in the former type, the requirement was not so rigid. Decisions were arrived at by a majority vote, but for an execution more than a simple majority was necessary.

In cases involving only money, self-admissions were countenanced to a limited extent; in cases involving corporal punishment, confessions were utterly disregarded—they were absolute nullities. Furthermore, proof normally required two competent eye-witnesses; some circumstantial evidence was valid in cases involving money. In cases involving corporal punishment no circumstantial evidence whatever was considered. Even the thoroughness with which the court interrogated the witnesses differed in both types of cases, for the interrogation of witnesses was by the court, not by attorneys. Some judges in capital cases played their role as cross-examiners so devastatingly that they virtually abolished capital punishment altogether—for this the Halakhah became famous. The judicial procedure of Judaism clearly manifests how much higher was the evaluation placed on life and limb than that placed on property.

With regard to the competency of witnesses there were also different standards. Some persons might be competent to testify in a lawsuit involving only money but not for a trial involving corporal punishment. Moreover, in the latter typeof case it was necessary that the testimony be of such a character that the witnesses might not only be impeached generally but also be subject to the special form of impeachment as a result of which they could become liable because of their perjury to the same punishment that they sought to mete out to the accused.

It was because the classification of the Oral Law concentrated on the difference between property and life that the eighth commandment of the Decalogue was interpreted as involving kidnapping. The Rabbis understood that all of the last five commandments of the Decalogue involved a hierarchy of values pertaining to human personality—the integrity of one's life (the prohibition against murder); the integrity of one's family (the prohibition against adultery); the integrity of one's freedom (the prohibition against kidnapping); the integrity of reputation (the prohibition against bearing false witness); and immunity from being begrudged in what one has (the prohibition against coveting). The prohibition against stealing property is found in Leviticus and it involved no corporal punishment—at most, the return of the theft with double or quadruple or quintuple damages (which excess was a fine).

The preoccupation of the Law with the nature of the court's judgment resulted in many an anomaly. Thus, for example, a tort which was substantial enough to warrant a judgment in the amount of one cent or more, was tried by less rigorous rules than a tort which was so inconsequential that it involved damages of less than a cent. Because in the latter case, the court could award no money but could order the flogging of the defendant, the more stringent rules applicable to cases involving corporal punishment had to be followed.

On no issue, however, is the contrast so great as with respect to the measure of responsibility. When a money judgment is involved the defendant is usually held accountable without regard to his fault, for no legal system was ever committed more extensively to the theory of strict liability than the Halakhah. The only situations in which the defendants might not be liable for the immediate consequences of their acts were either when they were minors or incompetents, or when the acts were not theirs —when their bodies were used by others. Otherwise, they would be liable for torts committed even in their sleep. If the defendant, however, was to suffer corporal punishment, then his act must not only have been wilful but he must also have been forewarned in advance by two competent witnesses that if he proceeded with the act, he would suffer the punishment that is involved, and he must nonetheless have defiantly committed the act. Ignorance of the Law in such case is not only regarded as a defense but the witnesses who bring the crime to the attention of the court bear the burden of proof that they themselves apprised the defendant of the law involved. Needless to say, this was the way in which all corporal punishment was abolished—for who but an insane person would commit an unlawful act in the presence of two competent witnesses who were forewarning him and preparing to testify against him! Furthermore, how could any of the laws against adultery and incest be enforced when the very act of coitus that constituted the offense had to be performed in the presence of two warning witnesses. It was thus that most of the laws which called for corporal punishment became exclusively hortatory. They constituted moral norms for social and educational purposes. Undoubtedly, the leniency of the Law increased the incidence of behavior that was frowned upon by the Law. The Talmud records this argument. When the incidence was too high, emergency measures had to taken. One such instance is recorded with regard to the practice of witchcraft and necromancy which the Pentateuch had forbidden. Moreover, a court of twenty-three, it would appear, had a reserved power to get rid of evil-doers, and if someone offended too brazenly, they could resort to a ruthless form of punishment with torture, to accomplish the result. However, there is no recorded case where this was done. The power remained a reserved power of the judiciary.

Moreover, the greater concern of the Law for human personality, rather than property, prompted the rabbis to develop the law of stealing, that what was uppermost in their minds was the reform of the thief and not the return of the theft. Owners who sought to reclaim their property were frowned upon for thereby they deterred thieves from confessing their sin and doing penitence. Those owners, on the other hand, who waived their rights, helped to rehabilitate anti-social beings into honest men. How different the situation today when the criminal law and the threat of prosecution become the principal means whereby stolen goods are recovered, and in exchange for restitution, the offender is released!

It can hardly be claimed that any modern state, including Israel, could base its criminal law on the Halakhah. Indeed, few if any rabbis in almost two thousand years have thought that the Halakhic system could be restored in its entirety in any period other than the messianic era. Nonetheless, Jews studied the rules as part of Torah and hoped thereby to learn more about God, Who is the Source of their Law, and some of their ethical insights might very well receive more attention in all legal systems of today.

III

The second major function of reason in the Oral Law is to resolve ambiguities in the revealed truths. No ambiguity in the Pentateuch, for example, has attracted more attention in Christian and Jewish history than the *lex talionis*—"an eye for an eye and a tooth for a tooth." Christian scholarship has generally assumed that the Pentateuch required the physical removal of the limb of the person who thus offended against another. The Talmudic rule—that the tort be compensated for with money—was considered a later development. Modern scholarship has exposed the error of this assumption. Some scholars have even demonstrated that the payment of money for the tort antedates the *lex talionis* in the development of some legal systems. Others maintain that the two rules are to be found in force at the same time. Perhaps either the offender or his victim had a choice of remedy. Certainly, Talmudic sources indicate that both remedies were known among Jews and were regarded as normative by one group or another. And the least that could be said about the revealed rule is that it was ambiguous. It remained for the Oral Law to resolve the ambiguity by reason, as well as tradition.

"An eye for an eye" might mean that an eye is to be removed for an eye even as the phrase "a life for a life" means precisely that when it is used in connection with the crime of murder. There the phrase is understood as requiring a life to be taken to atone for a homicide. However, "an eye for an eye" might also mean that a monetary equivalent shall be paid, as the phrase "a life for a life" used in Leviticus in connection with the killing of another's cattle, whereupon it is unequivocal that the tortfeasor pays the value of what has been destroyed, and does not forfeit his own life or the life of his cattle. Furthermore, in Exodus, only a few verses before the so-called *lex talionis*, there is a rule calling for the payment of medical expenses and loss of earnings in the event of bodily harm imposed upon another, which contradicts the phrase "a bruise for a bruise" a few verses thereafter. In Numbers it appears that the punishment for murder cannot be compounded with money but other torts may be thus compounded.

The ambiguity prompted the rabbis

of the Talmudic era and a preponderance of medieval commentators to articulate what is in essence the difference between the simple, stark truth of revelation and the qualified, nuanced wisdom of its application. He who takes another's eye merits the loss of his own. Measure for measure is the principle of divine, absolute justice. But no human tribunal can administer measure for measure. What executioner can remove the eye of an offender with absolute assurance that he will not kill and thus do more damage than he was authorized to do! Or how can one achieve exact equivalence when eyes are not all of the same size or vigor! God may articulate in revelation what is absolutely just but only He could administer it. Judges on earth can only permit themselves a limited retribution—full payment for every manner of loss sustained—in ultimate earning capacity, in pain, embarrassment and healing costs, and also loss resulting from one's unemployment during recovery from the tort inflicted.

The *lex talionis*, however, is not the only instance in which punishments are revealed vindictively only to indicate the extreme displeasure of God with the persons offending while, in fact, human tribunals are incompetent to administer the penalties prescribed, and can only mete out less severe ones. The simple, stark, truths of revelation are absolute norms in God's justice but mortal man must be content to leave it to God to bring the full measure of His wrath to bear upon the sinner. A human court shall only punish mildly. In this category are to be found scores of commandments with regard to whose violation Scripture says either "He shall die" or "That soul shall be cut off from his people," and the rabbis said that only God will decide how and when. The most that they would do in such cases is to decree lashes against the offender, provided that all the technical prerequisites for any form of corporal punishment had been fulfilled. This applied to many of the prohibitions against incest—particularly those involving collateral consanguinity rather than forbears or descendants—and most of the commandments pertaining to ritual observance.

The dialectic of the Oral Law involved two sets of antithetical norms. On the one hand there were God's exacting standards of justice and the unquestioning obedience. He was entitled to receive from the people whom He had taken out of Egypt that they might be His people and receive His Law. On the other hand there were God's compassion and love and His mandate that man be equally merciful. Where the revealed command appeared harsh or vindictive—primarily because the Jews were less likely to obey unless the Torah used fervent exhortation or vituperation —the Oral Law veered in the direction of mitigation. Thus, the provisions for the complete extermination of all the seven nations of Canaan, as well as Amalek, were understood as binding only if these pagans refused to make peace with Jews and fulfill the Noahide code, without which they could hardly be deemed safe to live with. Similarly, the almost inhuman commands of Deuteronomy with regard to the wayward son and the idolatrous city were so understood by the Oral Law that they were virtually nothing but exhortations, with at least one rabbi contending that the laws were never actually applied and another rabbi claiming to have had hearsay knowledge of the application of the Law. To such an extent had the laws become purely academic that no one is reported ever to have beheld an actual trial!

On the other hand, a provocateur for paganism—who thereby endangers Israel's covenant with God—was not regarded by the Oral Law as adequately condemned by the revealed word. His crime is so heinous that he is not entitled to the privileges and immunities of other offenders in capital cases. Moreover, if the Torah did not adequately punish the usurer the Oral Law added to his grief, and according to one rabbi, he forfeits the principal of, as well as the interest on, his loan. Again, revealed laws are qualified and nuanced in the dialectic of the Oral Law.

In no instance does the ambiguity of the revealed word beg for resolution more than in connection with the problem of individual versus collective responsibility. Repeatedly the Torah ascribes guilt to the group for the sins of the few at the same time that it ordains that "a man shall die for his own sin." The prophets wrestled with the problem and no less so did the Oral Law. For the prophets the problem was theological—for the rabbis, legal. And since theologians do not have to arrive at conclusions while jurists must pronounce verdicts, we find both groups accentuating antithetical views. In Jewish philosophy and ethics it was the principle of collective responsibility that was of paramount importance. The righteous suffer for the sins of their generation and all Jews are mutually responsible for each other. In Jewish jurisprudence, on the other hand, the principle of individual responsibility was carried to such an extreme that an accessory before the fact was not liable to punishment. Only he who does the actual killing or stealing bears the brunt of the law. In his commission of the crime, he has no partners and he cannot look forward to even that modicum of comfort that others who cooperated with him—before or after—will share his plight before the bar of justice.

In life it is a fact that the good suffer because of the bad, and the innocent are placed in jeopardy because of the guilty. The Torah recognizes this truth. It is, however, also given to individual men to choose between good and evil. This is a fact of the moral life and the Torah states it unequivocally. That because of those who choose evil, the righteous are denied their reward, remains a problem of theodicy for philosophers and theologians. However, man cannot claim a right to do evil and rely upon the argument that God Himself breaches His own covenant when He denies them their due. Human justice can only reckon with individual responsibility and act accordingly. On the level of absolute truth there is dilemma, contradiction, paradox. On the level of life and experience, there must be decision.

IV

The third major function of reason in the Oral Law is to fill the lacunae in the revealed word. In Numbers, for example, the Jewish law of inheritance is set forth. A decedent's estate, it is said, passes to his children, and if he has no children, to his brothers. The Oral Law ordains, however, that the father has a prior right to that of the brothers. The revealed word is silent with regard to the father. It is reasonable that the father's right should be antecedent to that of the brothers since the latter inherit only by the virtue of the common ancestor whose claim ought therefore be superior to theirs. Yet why the omission in the revealed word? Because, it is argued, for a father to inherit a child is a tragedy and the Torah preferred in such a case to leave a lacuna and let reason fill the gap.

Many phrases and words of Scripture are also illusions to practices or things whose character is known only through the Oral Law, such as the manner of slaughtering cattle, the nature of the fair fruit used on the Sukkoth festival, the composition of phylacteries. However, there were significant sections of the Law with regard to which there were only the most meager references in the Biblical texts, while it must have been anticipated that there would be a high incidence of litigation involving them. Of these none is more exciting than the field of contracts—the enforcibility of a promise made by one person to another. Here, too, the Oral Law compensated for the lacuna, deriving from a few verses a multitude of insights that reveal the tradition's unrelenting concern for equity, the dignity of human speech, the need of the economically disenfranchised, and other values which are of paramount importance in a system of jurisprudence that is theocentric and not rooted only in history, economics, and power.

The Bible did ordain that a man should fulfill "what comes forth from his lips." At least one entire tractate of the Talmud deals with vows and, as one medieval commentator suggested, the goal of its study should be the signification and sanctification of speech. It is of interest that the sages associated this goal with marital harmony, so important was guarded speech to the cultivation of a proper relationship between husband and wife. But apart from the moral and social implications of all kinds of intemperate talk and broken promises, did persons aggrieved have any basis on which to sue? Since "talk is cheap," when may persons have reason to believe that a legally binding promise was made in their behalf so that they may enforce its fulfillment?

It would be too much for any legal order to insist upon the performance of every promise. Friends may agree to take a walk or play a game of golf and disappoint each other with impunity. Men also make exaggerated statements as to what they intend to do for others. They offend against ethics but it would be too much to set legal machinery in motion to enforce every foolish utterance of mortals. Needless to say, if there has been reliance upon a promise earnestly made, and injury follows a breach of the promise, the promisor should make good the loss. Jewish law concurs. But what of a promise to make a gift which few legal systems ever enforce? Should not such promises be a matter of "honor," with only social, not legal, sanctions to protect them?

Students of jurisprudence know how all legal systems wrestled with this problem. The Romans and Continentals came forth with a doctrine of *causa,* and the Anglo-Americans with a doctrine of *consideration,* two symbols to indicate that the parties to a contract intended to consummate an agreement of which the law should take cognizance. At least two interesting problems emerged in England and America. Pledges to charity were not enforcible since these were gratuitous gifts. Moreover, persons who did not themselves participate in the agreement could not complain that the promises were not performed since they were not principals.

The Oral Law of Judaism generally assumes that only deeds, not words, could create legal rights in others, and thus "nude" promises were a nullity. A formal act accompanied by words, such as a transfer of title to property with a formal possessary act, would be effective.

Nonetheless, with words alone one could obligate one's self to give charity. With regard to the poor, and with regard to the Temple, one could not pretend that one was merely jesting. The maxim was, "A verbal declaration in God's behalf was the equivalent of delivery," and the beneficiaries of the promises could themselves recover the gifts even though the words may have been uttered to another. Curiously enough, another type of promise enjoyed the same privileged status —promises of dowry. A marriage was too significant an event to permit of any kind of idle speech.

Another interesting exception was the unexecuted commitment of a person in acute illness. In most legal systems the trend is to impose additional formalities in such cases, as in the case of wills, in order to make certain that there is no undue advantage taken of the plight of the donor or testator. The fears of the Oral Law were quite to the contrary. Unless the patient could really be assured that his desires were being effectuated, he might die sooner as a result of the distress of frustration. In his condition, greater laxity prevailed and the value of saving human life yielded to the value of certainty in legal transactions. Again, the simple truth of revelation evoked in life a pattern of regulation that was complex and nuanced.

And what is true of revelation is true of all profound religious experience. The mystic's awareness of God induces certainty, perhaps salvation. But continuing to live with a constant awareness of God does not necessarily involve certainty. Nor does it relieve one of all perplexity and doubt. The religious experience is only the beginning of wisdom. Its maturation and fulfillment require the Law, which in Judaism is endless—as endless as the sea. Indeed, the Talmud is a sea. It may have shores but it has no termini.

Conservatism and the Orthodox Resurgence

SHLOMO RISKIN

DURING THE PAST TWELVE YEARS THAT I have served as rabbi in mid-Manhattan, a significant change seems to have taken place within the Conservative movement or, at least, in the manner in which the movement regards itself and how it is perceived by others. From my perspective as a student in the Rabbi Isaac Elchanan Theological Seminary of Yeshiva University, it seemed as though the Conservative movement was to be the major Jewish religious force on the American scene. Throughout suburbia new Conservative Centers were mushrooming, generally relegating the Orthodox *shul* to a small number of old men too poor to leave the run-down urban center; USY directed a youth movement, Ramah conducted summer camps virtually without competition, and the Solomon Schechter Day Schools promised to be the intensive educational vehicle of the future.

What has occurred, instead, is an unexpected resurgence of a vital Orthodoxy, which appears to be holding the keys for the future survival of Judaism. To be sure, there is, at the same time, massive ignorance of, and apathy towards, the Jewish tradition on the part of the largest segment of American Jewry. Our students on college campuses are intermar-

---

SHLOMO RISKIN *is rabbi of Lincoln Square Synagogue and dean of Manhattan Hebrew High School.*

rying at the rate of 49%, and the consumption of kosher meat has dropped precipitously during the last decade. Nevertheless, Torah Umesorah has spawned a proliferation of Day Schools in every major Jewish population center, Lakewood and Lubavitch have inspired the establishment of many Yeshiva High Schools, *batei medresh* and *kollelim*, Yeshiva University's Albert Einstein College of Medicine boasts of a daily minyan Torah *shiurim*, the Orthodox Union disseminates *glatt kashrut* on our airlines and the influence of the National Conference of Synagogue Youth and the *baalei t'shuvah* yeshivot have inspired many *meḥiẓah* synagogues, sometimes even as the youth minyan in a separate room of a Conservative synagogue. Indeed, it is precisely between the horns of these polarized phenomena that the Conservative movement faces its dilemma. The synagogue building boom has all but disappeared—our youth create *shtiblakh and ḥavurot*—, the Solomon Schechter Schools are generally considered a watered-down compromise to their Orthodox counter-part, and the movement sees its successes entering Orthodoxy while its failures wander into assimilation. Even Marshall Sklare, the sociologist-author who wrote a definitive study of Conservative Judaism, described the crises of confidence within the Conservative camp, in a recent *Midstream* article, in terms reminiscent of the cliché that "the operation was successful but the patient died." What has actually occurred? How can we best understand what appears to be the "identity crisis" of the Conservative movement?

In a recent *Commentary* article entitled "The Dilemma of Conservative Judaism," Lawrence Kaplan suggests that its "tradition and change" ideology has been split into two antagonistic camps: the "tradition" group, which would be most comfortable within Modern Orthodoxy (David Feldman and the Talmud faculty of the Jewish Theological Seminary), and the "change" group, which is virtually identifiable with Reform. In essence, argues Kaplan, the movement has yet to decide whether its future will be determined by contemporary societal values or by time-honored halakhic absolutes, for it is on this issue that it is now divided.

I believe that there is another element which must be understood in evaluating the present condition of the Conservative movement. The success of any movement must be determined, in large measure, by the committed Jewish community for which it speaks, just as every leader must ultimately be judged by the quality of the students-disciples whom he directs. There can be no king without a nation, no *rebbe* without *ḥasidim*. Especially in the absence of a central Sanhedrin or even a religio-political ruler, the normative in Judaism has been determined, to a great extent, by what was accepted by the committed Jewish community. Within the Talmud one frequently finds the phrase: "Go out and see how the nation is behaving," and rabbinic authority had to accept the final veto of the observant community with the dictum: "No decree may be instituted for the community unless the majority of the community will abide by it."

The responsa literature throughout the ages bears eloquent testimony to the need of each generation to interpret halakhah in accordance with the specific exigencies of the hour; nevertheless, these responsa were written for, and accepted by, individuals and communities who understood the authority of a tradition larger than themselves, and were ready to abide by the decision, whether stringent or lenient. The halakhic authorities of each generation profoundly understood that, whatever their conclusion, they could not leave the mainstream of observant Jews behind if they wished to be a link in the great chain of Jewish being. Those who study the *Shulḥan Arukh,* a guide for Jewish living written during the sixteenth century and quoted and commented upon until this very day, will recognize that it is more descriptive than prescriptive, that it is truly authoritative because it expresses the manner in which the observant Jewish community lived and, in many communities, still lives. There can be no meaningful Jewish ideology within our traditional framework unless it speaks for an observant Jewish community which lives by its precepts.

In many respects, the Orthodox Jewish community owes a great deal to the Conservative movement. It taught the importance of interpreting Judaism while utilizing the contemporary idiom, and it established the synagogue as being more than a place of prayer alone. The summer camp as a vehicle for Jewish education and the intense *ḥavrusah* experience as a substitute for the large, sterile congregation are all ideas which emanated from the Conservative movement. Its chief failure, however, lies in its inability to create Jewish communities which are committed to Jewish tradition in accordance with the Conservative ideology, or of Jewish masses who see Conservatism as being more than compromise between Orthodoxy and Reform. In the main, the phrase "I belong to a Conservative synagogue" becomes a ready excuse for religious inconsistencies, and has come to temper religious commitment with the pragmatic realities of American culture. Perhaps the problem is rooted in the lack of clear ideology which will define the movement and help its adherents to define themselves vis-à-vis our tradition. Unless this definition is forthcoming, it will be difficult for the movement to retain its most idealistic and sensitive youth.

Orthodoxy Resurgent

DAVID J. SCHNALL

I

THE EUROPEAN JEW WHO CAME TO THESE shores at the turn of the century arrived with high expectations. Gold would lie in the streets, he believed, and diamonds hang from every branch. No more the poverty of the *shtetl*, the oppressive political system preventing mobility from without or the often equally harsh social system preventing mobility from within. This was a new world with open values.

The perspective was reinforced by every cousin, uncle or brother-in-law who had made the journey first. No matter that they had met with little of the expected success. No matter that their living conditions were little improved over what they had left behind. No matter that they even lacked the small bit of status, the great bit of security that the *shtetl* had afforded. They certainly were not about to admit that to their greenhorn relatives who would only chorus: "I told you so!" After all, appearances are also important.

And the new arrival was equally prepared to accommodate himself to his adopted environment. A new world required a new name, new clothes, a new language and, most of all, a new outlook. The old ways, the old observances, perhaps they were functional in Europe. In any event, there was little choice back there. But not here . . . not in America. Here one had to be a *Yenkey*. The beard, the long black coat, the *ẓiẓit*, they all must go. Working on the Sabbath was often not even a matter of choice. And how better to insure the successful assimilation of one's children into the new culture than to see that their rearing, their education was inundated with the new American values?

In most ways, the Jewish immigrant was little different from those of other persuasions. This country is largely a secular and pragmatic affair, still much imbued with the great melting pot ideology. Strict religious observance, imported from the old country, is an obstacle at best. At worst, it is suspect.

In response, American Jewish theology, and the institutions created in its support, sought means by which to recognize — even legitimate — these secularist and assimilationist impulses within the context of the faith. For a previous generation of immigrants, the tenets of Reform appeared most appropriate. Relatively unsuccessful in Central Europe during the early and mid-19th century, Reform found fertile ground

---

DAVID J. SCHNALL *is associate professor in the graduate school of public administration, Long Island University*

among early American Jewish communities. Notably, German-Jewish immigrants saw this theology as a reasonable compromise with their new environment and their steady economic and social rise after the Civil War.

Aspirations and observances met — both structurally and intellectually. Temples were built on the order of high-church, with separate pews eliminated and organ recitals introduced. Those beliefs and practices that appeared to prevent one's involvement in secular society were dropped officially — even as they had already long been dropped from usage by the congregants. It is no surprise, therefore, that early calls to a nationalist revival and Zionist activism were largely rebuffed by those who saw them as a threat to new-found status and upward mobility. Even the word "Jew" was considered in poor taste and replaced with the softer, more classical "Hebrew."

But these newer arrivals from Eastern Europe, always more pious and less socially aware, were not quite prepared to go that far . . . at least not initially. Probably less from theological commitment and more from unease, they would not attend the grand services at Reform temples, nor could they afford the social amenities that such society required. They were, after all, poor cousins. They would be cared for by their wealtheir co-religionists if only they'd stay downtown, quiet and deferentially out-of-sight. Conflicts between these *OstJuden* and the uptown *Yahudim* were legion, and inherent in the relationship.

The circumstances served as catalyst to the birth of yet another theological form whose very *raison d'être* was to be compromise, and whose direction would be lay rather than rabbinic, whether traditional or radical. There would be accommodation to the new environment but within the context of loyalty to the faith. There would be the middle-ground sought by the new immigrant and his children who still felt a tie to the "God of their fathers" but had been raised in the American milieu. As its name implies, this religious form would be "conservative" in its approach, as it sought to make peace with the New World.

The sensibilities of the founders aside, however, traditionalism, piety, strict observance were soon left behind or relegated to the poor and the lower classes. Large, powerful and fairly cohesive units were created or extended to serve as the lay, communal and rabbinic arms of American Jewry's more liberal branches. As these replaced the founders, values became institutionalized and soon found their way into doctrine. What may have begun as a search for a medium in the context of flexibility was to become a full-blown theology.

Everything else, particularly everything to the right of these new incarnations, was heaped together in yet a third form: Orthodoxy. The *kollelim*, the *yeshivot*, the *Ḥassidishe welt*, the religious Zionists, the Agudah, "modern" Orthodoxy . . . a motley crew, indeed — were all heaped into the same pile, identified more in terms of what they were not than what they were.

The lack of clarity or cohesion in this third category bothered liberal theologians and analysts little because, at best, these were no more than vestiges. Surely one could not expect that traditional religious belief and observance, by whatever name, would survive the pressures and strains of an open society. Surely, groups noted for their obscurantism and, by their nature, isolationist, parochial and backward-looking, would neither take root nor prosper in the American environs. Orthodoxy would soon die, meld into one of the other two branches of Judaism or remain the identity of those few pietists who would live at the periphery of modern society.

II

Somehow, it just didn't happen that way. What was assumed to be a death rattle was little more than a groan in response to the pains of adjustment. Dormancy was mistaken for expiration. Those very factors perceived as reactionary may well have been stabilizing and there seems to have been more vitality in the authoritative consistency provided than was earlier imputed. Its tenacity was impressive.

Part of the picture was framed by external events. The Holocaust, in itself as well as in its ramifications, had a profound effect. The very attack on the legitimacy of the Jew, upon his humanity, served as a shock to many who took their Jewishness for granted, indeed, to those who saw it as passé. The post-war arrival on these shores of east European sages and the remnants of once flourishing Hassidic communities offered graphic support for this reconsideration of one's heritage. It also reinforced already existing — though not yet self-conscious — Orthodox strongholds.

While these bastions of the right were regrouping, Orthodoxy's more liberal elements (yes, Virginia, they do exist) took great strength from the birth of the State of Israel in the wake of the Holocaust. While most Zionists were quite secular, the very concept of Zionism and its renaissance on the ancestral homeland was, at its base, highly traditional. It fulfilled messianic longings earlier repudiated by Reform Judaism. It represented the Jew acting on Biblical prophecies and rabbinic dicta, long eradicated from the world-view of liberal Jewry. It expressed an unwillingness to negotiate with the pressures of an alien environment — no matter how hospitable. Traditional Jewish practice would be written into the basic laws of the infant polity and its religious establishment would eschew liberalism. Zionism could do little other than vitalize the "modern" Orthodox, even as they perceived it to be *reshit ẓmiḥat geulatenu*, the first blossom of the Redemption.

It would be one more generation, however, before these early seeds would bear fruit. The move to professionalize, on the part of more secular and liberal Jewish elements during the forties and fifties, would not be visible among the Orthodox until the sixties and seventies. Today, however, traditionalism — and its institutional manifestation as Orthodoxy — has returned with a passion.

Witness: the growth of affluent, professional, Orthodox, suburban Jewish communities — complete with *mikveh, eruv*, (*glatt*) kosher butcher, *yeshivah* and *shomer shabbat* tennis club;

Witness: the increasing numbers of *yarmulkeh*-wearing interns, residents, house staff and attending physicians at major metropolitan hospitals and medical centers;

Witness: the broad presence of similarly attired university professors, attorneys and accountants in all phases of their callings;

Witness: the proliferation of thriving institutions and programs of study, prayer and support services geared toward the *Ba*ᶜ*alei Teshuvah*, those who would return to the tradition in both practice and outlook. The spectrum extends from the Lubavitcher Rebbe through Steven Riskin to Shlomo Carlebach;

Witness: the growing traditionalism within the Reform and Conservative establishments, reflecting a restive element (of longing?) within their laity;

Witness: (and this may be the most telling signal of all) the growing number of Orthodox professionals in positions of authority within well-established Jewish communal and defense organizations of clearly non-Orthodox bent. In the words of one old-timer surveying the attendance and affiliations of those at a recent meeting of the Conference of Presidents of Major Jewish Organizations: "Only in America . . ."

In a sense, this marked renewal and vitality of Orthodoxy has emerged in inverse qualitative proportion to the apparent difficulties within American Jewry's other branches. One need not belabor to this readership the growing rate of secularism, assimilation and intermarriage. Little needs yet to be added regarding the shocking threats posed by cultism and evangelical appeals. It is no secret, however, that these problems are far more pronounced among those whose ties to tradition, Judaic spirit and culture are tenuous, limited and confused. This is not to say that the issues are unknown within Orthodox circles or that there are none there who suffer from disaffection and confusion. It is to say that they are far less known.

As a corollary, one might view the matter pragmatically. It may be that liberal and progressive theology is not the wave of the future for America's Jews — if, indeed, it ever was. Compromise and accommodation was initially struck in the hope of stemming the very tides of which we speak: attract the youth, make the better-educated and the acculturated more comfortable in their religious environment. The compromises were made, but it seems that neither the young nor the upwardly-mobile stormed the gates of the synagogues nor did they flood the study halls as a result. And as for their children. . . .

The exodus from tradition, therefore, is fast losing even the utilitarian imperative and attraction that it once claimed. Editorially, the present convulsions within Conservatism over the ordination of females may fall into the same category. Theology/Halakhah aside, those who feel — and there are many, particularly within the laity — that affording female ordination and greater female religious particpation generally is a strategy for attracting or "keeping" their younger and more progressive elements, may well be in for a shock. Perhaps there is truth in the insight offered by the contemporary humourist, George Carlin. An Irish Catholic, Carlin claims that he did not leave the Church for reasons of deep moral principle. He left because he dislikes getting up early on Sundays. The moral issues came later.

Yet, these changes, introduced originally to accommodate the environment but unsuccessful in battling the forces of secularism and disaffection, have now been institutionalized past their utility. If by nothing other than the measure of pragmatism, they may be compared to the European-imported Orthodoxy of two generations ago. Both appear unsuited to their environment, yet claim the allegiance of devotees who cling out of sincere, if misguided, principle.

III

In this sense, it must be borne in mind that what has developed as American Orthodoxy of the seventies represents, as well, a variety of compromises, which derive from the very values of professionalism and mobility that motivated liberals a generation earlier. One cannot attend a university and professional school without being affected. One cannot participate actively in the secular arena and not be influenced. One cannot partake of the material benefits of affluence and not undergo change. Surely the Orthodoxy of today, particularly but not exclusively its non-Hassidic elements, is far removed from that of the Elders.

If anything, though, its transplantation, its grafting upon the American root, has given it an unexpected vitality and flexibility. It appears to be confronting many of the challenges of modern and material values, both directly and indirectly. While neither defeating nor eliminating them, today's Orthodoxy seems to be demonstrating that it is not, per se, incompatible with traditional observances and beliefs. The proliferation of Continental or Oriental eateries, Caribbean cruises and Passover vacation packages, all under strict rabbinic supervision, serve witness to the fact that an upwardly-mobile, (conspicuous) consumer need not compromise his religious principles. The presence of regular services and classes in the chapels of metropolitan hospitals, university campuses and in the financial districts of many cities, makes the same point. One need not live in seclusion nor deny the world.

As might be expected, many of these developments are quite fluid. Most noticeable is a sense of insecurity in the changes that have been adopted and a general rightward stance that is reflected in observance as well as in the training and selection of clergy and teachers. Well within the best familial traditions of the past lies the desire of parents to provide better for their children than they had for themselves. This aspiration is usually defined in material terms, but here it has taken an educational and cultural bent as well. Perhaps disturbed by lacunae in their own training, perhaps disaffected by the often heavy-handed methods which they encountered, these parents seek to provide for their children a better Jewish education than they themselves may have received.

Many are profoundly distraught by the insufficient preparation afforded them as students at full-time primary or secondary Jewish schools. The issues that they were to confront on the campus and in the "real world" were dealt with peripherally, if at all. The commitment to Jews elsewhere, as well as to the State of Israel, was rarely explored. Ethical values were under-emphasized by comparison with time spent on the rudiments of ritual observance and practice. The events of history — especially contemporary history — and the role of the Jew within them was a matter of ad hoc treatment and general indifference.

At the same time, many parents have become disenchanted with their experiences in the world of professional and higher education. They are less impressed with modernity and sophistication, perhaps for not having had to fight the ideological battles of the past. The very cosmopolitanism and progressivism that higher education is designed to instill has become passé. They would like to prepare their children better or, alternatively, to shield them altogether from such conflicts and tensions.

In some instances, this has resulted in an active involvement in local day schools and *yeshivot* for the purpose of introducing more sophisticated and socially-aware curricular materials and the engagement of instructors better able to convey them. In the best examples, its results are new programs of Holocaust studies, Zionism, Jewish life abroad, Jewish philosophy and Jewish history as well as actual study in Israel. While some of this is yet a bit trendy and faddish its introduction is promising.

In other instances, parents have been moved to send their children to primary and secondary schools far to the right of their own training, indeed far to the right of their life-styles. They hope to provide, thereby, a stronger and more secure Jewish foundation for their children, a less vulnerable *Weltanschauung*, a more comprehensive and complete commitment. Truth-to-tell, the results are ironic and often barely short of humorous and bizarre. Well-dressed suburban parents walk to *shul* with teen-age sons whose attire, complete with black suit, tie-less white shirt, and broad-brimmed black hat, makes them appear quite incongruous; children of professionals opt out entirely and decide that any form of secular higher education is not for them; affluent and upwardly-mobile parents have daughters who marry young men studying at a *kollel* and depending upon small stipends, parental largesse and the efforts of their wives. Parents who regret these developments should recognize that, whatever the motivation, these new conflicts are largely of their own making.

Finally, it appears that the new Orthodox generation and its institutions have often accepted a relatively insular position regarding those Jews who do not share their values. There is frequently lacking a willingness to participate in broader councils of Jewish welfare and concern if it will be necessary to share the podium with spokespeople of competing theological doctrine. There is a more profound unwillingness to proffer any form of implicit legitimacy to those of other branches of Judaism, even when the issues are neither theological nor ideological. In short, a sense of *klal yisrael* is often absent.

This lack is counter-productive from general, as well as self-interested, perspectives. Most issues that confront the Jews in America do not divide easily by the degree of one's religious observance or doctrinal purity. Those outside the Jewish community do not, and will not, understand the nature of that which separates us, and the already free proliferation of public dissent need not be given further impetus.

By the same token, the powerful and well-established Jewish organizations that make important fiscal and monetary policy regarding issues of vital importance to the Orthodox Jewish community will not easily be moved from without. Certainly, they will not be moved by external indifference. Concern about lending passive legitimacy or unintentional co-optation are real and require serious consideration. It should be clearly recognized, however, that the important goal of Jewish survival will not be realized in a vacuum and much can be derived from joint effort without impinging upon ideological commitment. Indeed, many of these efforts may be irrelevant to the shadings of ideological commitment. Truly, it would be a matter of tragic irony if the very tenacity and creativity that has created an Orthodox resurgence in the latter part of this century should be allowed to languish for an unnecessary and somewhat paranoid fixation with what lurks over the right shoulder.

Denominationalism and the American Experience – An Orthodox View

WALTER S. WURZBURGER

HISTORICALLY, THE AMERICAN ENVIRONMENT has been especially conducive to the development of ideologies which enabled Jews to identify as adherents of a particular religious denomination, rather than as members of an ethnic community. One need but point to the tremendous popularity of Will Herberg's thesis that Judaism represents one of the three "legitimate" versions of the American "civil religion" to realize the attractiveness of formulations which dissolve "Jewishness" into elements that could readily be fitted into a purely religious framework. The tripartite division of Judaism into three denominations (Orthodox, Conservative, Reform) made the scheme especially attractive because it seemed to reflect the pattern of the overall American civil religion which also was expressed in three different versions (Catholic, Protestant, Jew).

The flourishing of religious denominationalism was largely due to the wall of separation between Church and State that manifested itself in a policy of benign neutrality towards all religious groups. On the one hand, the anti-Establishment clause of the Constitution protected Jews from the various forms of religious discrimination to which they had been subjected in many other countries. On the other hand, the prevailing climate encouraged the practice of religion since the profession of *some* faith was deemed desirable for the proper functioning of the democratic value system. As President Eisenhower put it: "Our Government does not make sense, unless it is founded on a deeply felt religious faith, and I don't care what it is." Within such a cultural milieu, one had every reason to believe that religious commitment to Judaism was not only compatible with one's civic responsibilities, but actually enhanced one's Americanism. Many of us have time and again heard Rabbinic charges to Bar Mizvah boys, admonishing them to become better Jews and better Americans — equating the process of becoming better Jews with that of becoming better Americans!

To be sure, Jewish denominationalism is not indigenous to the American scene. Its roots go back to the Napoleonic Sanhedrin which struggled to legitimize the entry of the Jew into the modern world by pretending that being Jewish exhausts itself in the profession of a private religious faith which in no way intrudes upon the public responsibilities of a citizen

---

WALTER S. WURZBURGER *is rabbi of Congregation Shaaray Tefila, Lawrence, N.Y., president of the Synagogue Council of America and editor of* Tradition.

of a secular state to which the Jew, like all his fellow citizens of different religious persuasions, should be able to give his total loyalty. The attempt to eliminate completely all purely ethnic and nationalistic features from Jewish self-identification became even more pronounced in Germany, where one of the leading Jewish organizations deliberately shied away from using the term "Jewish." The very choice of the name *Zentral Verein Deutscher Staatsburger des Mosaischen Glaubens* (Central Organization of German Citizens of Mosaic Faith) speaks for itself. Mosaic faith sounds so analogous to Christian faith. It manages to avoid all the nationalistic and ethnic overtones associated with the term "Jew." Classical Reform's opposition to Zionism was also grounded in the belief that Judaism in the modern era must divest itself of all ethnic features and transform itself into a pure religious denomination — a process that manifested itself in the growing Protestantization of the synagogue as well as of the rabbinate.

A variety of historic realities, especially the rise of Hitler and the trauma of the Holocaust, dispelled the myth that being Jewish could be regarded merely as a matter of voluntary religious identification. After all, the Nazis were hardly interested in matters of theological belief. Insofar as they were concerned, Jewishness was defined in purely biological terms.

On the American scene, the resurgence of ethnicism in the 60s, sparked by developments in the black community, gave further impetus to the growing awareness of the ethnic components that go into the makings of Jewish identity. But this resurgence of ethnicism was in no way regarded as a challenge by the various Jewish religious denominations. As a matter of fact, they had every reason to welcome it because commitment to "religious ethnicism," as Yehezkel Kaufman defines Judaism, enabled them to endorse even purely secular expressions of Jewish self-identification as a covert religious affirmation. Kinship and solidarity with Jews everywhere represents, for religious denominations, a fundamental religious imperative. It has been suggested, therefore, that notwithstanding all irreconcilable theological differences, there is a unity amidst diversity inasmuch as each and every Jewish religious denomination subscribes to the common core belief that the survival of the Jewish people is religiously mandated.

But it is highly questionable whether, in point of fact, commitment to Jewish survival need necessarily be a function of religious impulses. Obviously, numerous secular Jews are passionately committed to the cause of Jewish survival. Although some religionists maintain that any form of identification with the Jewish people is really a covert affirmation of the religious vocation of the Jew which masquerades under secular appearances, it is highly problematic whether such "religious imperialism" is really warranted. Shouldn't non-believers be entitled to have their assertions taken seriously at face value without imputing to them "real" opinions which contradict their stated views?

Since cultivation of a sense of unity among Jews need not necessarily be a function of religious commitment, there is no need to call for an artificial ecumenism among Jewish denominations. There is hardly any theological proposition that can be shared by an Orthodox believer in supernatural Revelation and a Reconstructionist naturalist. Christians may require an ecumenical movement in order to achieve a sense of unity on the basis of shared values and beliefs. But Jews are different. Their sense of solidarity and kinship with each other transcends the sense of unity of a community of believers who share a religious vision. Since Jews form a "community of fate," they need not fall back upon a common theological denominator in order to generate a common bond. Jewish unity rests upon ethnic rather than ecumenical factors. To cite a telling example, Rabbi Chaim of Brisk, a world renowned Rabbinic leader of Lithuanian Orthodoxy, once requested that the worshipppers at a Kol Nidre service go home and return with ransom money needed to save the life of a Bundist who faced execution. Obviously, the beliefs of this radical Jew were totally incompatible with everything that Rabbi Chaim stood for, but such considerations were totally irrelevant when the life of a Jew was at stake. The sanctity of Yom Kippur had to yield to the overriding priority of saving a Jewish life — even that of an atheistic radical.

It is against this background that we can appreciate Orthodoxy's ambivalence towards non-Orthodox denominations. On the one hand, Jews are responsible for the material and spiritual welfare of their fellow Jews irrespective of their denominational affiliations. On the other hand, Orthodoxy cannot condone any deviation from *Halakhic* norms because, according to Orthodox tenets, the obligation to observe *Halakhic* norms is incumbent upon every Jew irrespective of personal preference or convictions.

To be sure, such insistence upon conformity to *Halakhic* standards clashes with prevailing notions of "religious pluralism" which go far beyond the rights of individuals to live in accordance with the dictates of their conscience. According to the tenets of religious pluralism that are currently in vogue, considerations of civility dictate that all religious denominations renounce any claim of superiority over competing belief systems. Underlying this conception of "religious tolerance" is the surrender of any notion of an objective religious truth. In this view, matters involving religious commitment of faith can possess only purely subjective validity. Since religious truth becomes totally relativized, what is "true" for one individual need not be "true" in relation to another individual.

Orthodoxy, however, cannot accept this canon of modernity. It unabashedly insists upon the communal character of Judaism and rejects the complete privatization of faith. For that matter, it cannot subscribe to the proposition that the individual human conscience serves as the final arbiter of religious truth. The preoccupation with authenticity and autonomy which is so characteristic of modernity is undoubtedly largely due to the impact of Protestant categories of thought. Parenthetically, it should be noted that exclusive reliance upon autonomy ultimately developed into *anomie*, as reflected in such modern non-cognitive approaches to ethics as emotivism and prescriptivism.

Because Orthodoxy is committed to the authority of an objectively binding *Halakhah* it has been relatively successful, at least by comparison with other denominations, in resisting the inroads of the Protestantization of Jewish religious life. Moreover, Orthodoxy's insistence that all Jews are bound by *Halakhic* norms engenders a sense of unity which derives not from a consensus with respect to shared "essential" values, but from the belief that the Covenant at Sinai obligates every single member of the Jewish people. In the self-understanding of Orthodoxy, Jewish identity is not a matter of choice but a given. What is left to the discretion of the individual is the determination whether one's Jewish identity should be merely a matter of fate or of purposeful destiny. In the terms of Rabbi Soloveitchik, the task confronting the Jew is to transform a "community of fate" into a "community of faith."

To be sure, there are "ultra-Orthodox" elements who believe that total segregation from non-observant Jews is the best strategy for insuring the attainment of important religious objectives. But it must be borne in mind that this has nothing to do with excluding non-observant Jews from the fold. Even the most dogmatic and rigid follower of the Neturei Karta will agree that Jews form one people; they are not merely members of religious denominations. *K'lal Yisrael* is not an association of religious congregations but the organic community of all Jews who are "responsible for each other" — in spite of all the attempts to drive the wedge of polarization between them.

The Conservative View of Halakhah is Non-Traditional

WALTER S. WURZBURGER

PROFESSOR ROTH'S *THE HALAKHIC PROCESS* offers a most welcome, lucid and systematic account of the basic principles governing a Conservative approach to Halakhah. Notwithstanding his adherence to the "positive-historical" school, he succeeds in avoiding the "genetic fallacy" and eschewing the kind of "historicism" which would fail to distinguish between legal and historical sources of the law. He is also correct in emphasizing that, in the final analysis, the meaning of a halakhic norm is determined by what the latest authorities declare it to be.

But, while the Halakhah proceeds from the premise that "the Halakhah follows the later authorities," Professor Roth's definition of the role, scope and methodology of contemporary Rabbinic authorities will be categoricaly rejected by traditional halakhists. One is reminded of a famous witticism attributed to a renowned philosopher, who noted: "Everybody agrees with the maxim, 'thou shalt love thy neighbor as thyself'; the only question is 'who is thy neighbor?' " Those who operate within the parameters of the traditional Halakhah as it has evolved over the centuries will be taken aback by the claim that contemporary *poskim* are authorized to set aside halakhic opinions, derived from the Tannaitic interpretations of passages of the Pentateuch, when, on the basis of the findings of modern scholarship, a different interpretation would be more plausible.

This disregard for the authority vested in the Talmudic Sages undermines the entire halakhic process, which was based upon the premise that even an Amora could not dissent from Tannaitic rulings, unless he could adduce some Tannaitic source, if only a minority opinion, in support of his position. Moreover, Maimonides, in his preface to the *Mishneh Torah*, emphasizes that, in contradistinction to the rulings promulgated by the Geonim, the opinions of the Amoraim as recorded in the Babylonian Talmud have been accepted by the entire Jewish people and are, therefore, so universally binding in matters of conduct that they can no longer be modified or revised.

To be sure, in matters of purely theoretical concern, an individual scholar has every right to offer his own independent insights. As Professor David Weiss Halivni has so succinctly put it, "tradition's realm is

WALTER S. WURZBURGER *is Rabbi of Congregation Shaaray Tefila, Lawrence, N.Y.*

behavior not intellect." As is well known, classical commentators like Rashi, Rashbam, Ibn Ezra and Bechor Shor, did not hesitate to offer, for purely exegetical purposes, interpretations of Torah passages at variance with those provided in the Talmudic literature. But this in no way prompted them to challenge the Rabbinic rulings which were based upon a completely different understanding of the Biblical texts. For that matter, Maimonides and the Gaon of Vilna at times diverged from the Gemara in their interpretations of the Mishnah. But, in all of these cases, disagreement with Tannaitic or Amoraitic opinion was limited to questions pertaining to the theoretical understanding of a text. When it came to matters involving conduct, the supremacy of the Tannaim and Amoraim was taken for granted.

The reason why rulings of the Amoraim may not be challenged by subsequent authorities has been convincingly formulated by Harav Joseph B. Soloveitchik in his essay, "Two Types of Massorah," (*Shiurim Lezecher Abba Mori, z. 1.*, pp. 320–39). In his view, the Massorah contains two distinct components: 1) transmission and analysis of the teachings of the Oral Torah and 2) generally accepted modes of conduct. Once a particular opinion has become normative for the entire Jewish community, e.g., an opinion of the Amoraim, it becomes an integral part of the "Massorah of conduct" which can no longer be changed on the basis of purely intellectual considerations. According to Rabbi Soloveitchik, this deference to rulings based upon commonly accepted usage is mandated by the Biblical verse, "Ask thy father and he will declare it to thee, thy elders and they will tell thee" (Deut.32:7).

Because so much weight is attached to the practical Massorah, those committed to the traditional Halakhah will, unlike Professor Roth, question the religious qualifications of authorities who sanction driving to the synagogue or permit turning on lights on the Sabbath. By the same token, they will reject the authority of Rabbinic scholars who are unable to accept the doctrine of *Torah min Hashomayim* as it was understood over the centuries until drastic reinterpretations of the doctrine came into vogue at the dawn of the modern era, when the intellectual climate of the age became hostile to any form of belief in the literal Revelation of the Torah.

Professor Roth maintains that the denial of the Mosaic authorship of the Pentateuch does not amount to heresy, because such denial is fully compatible with unconditional acceptance of the Halakhah as the supreme normative authority. It should be borne in mind, however, that, according to the Mishnah cited by Professor Roth, the denial of Resurrection is also regarded as sufficient ground for labeling individuals heretics, notwithstanding the fact that the rejection of this particular eschatological belief need not lead to the repudiation of the authority of the Halakhah. He also agrues that the Rabbinic dictum, "would that they had forgotten me and observed my Torah," warrants the inference that only compliance with Halakhah but not the the nature of one's religious beliefs matters with respect to the personal qualifications of a *Posek.* But it can readily be seen that this a spurious argument. The very conclusion of the statement, i.e., "for the light contained in it would lead them back to the proper standards," clearly shows that observance of halakhic norms is not the only criterion of piety. Instead, it is for purely pedagogical reasons that such a premium is placed on observance. It was believed that halakhic practice, even without proper commitment, would, in due time, engender the desirable beliefs and values. But this is a far cry from maintaining that this kind of "orthopraxis" qualifies an individual to serve as an authoritative interpreter of the Halakhah as reflecting the Will of God.

But these criticisms are by no means intended to detract from the value of Professor Roth's contribution. Traditionalists will be grateful for his candor and forthrightness. With his succinct description and bold advocacy of the Conservative version of halakhic decision-making he has rendered a real service to the entire Jewish community. He has made it abundantly clear that the Conservative approach radically diverges from what, for over a millenium, was regarded as the function of a *posek* and that the definition of the halakhic process as presented by one the most eminent representatives of the Conservative movement has little in common with the meaning of Halakhah in the traditional sense of the term.

Acknowledgements

Agus, Jacob B. "The Orthodox Stream." In Jacob Neusner, ed., *Understanding American Judaism: Toward the Description of a Modern Religion*, Volume II (New York: KTAV Publishing House, Inc., 1975): 107–30. Reprinted with the permission of Jacob Neusner. Courtesy of Jacob Neusner.

Berkovits, Eliezer. "A Contemporary Rabbinical School for Orthodox Jewry." In Jacob Neusner, ed., *Understanding American Judaism: Toward the Description of a Modern Religion*, Volume I (New York: KTAV Publishing House, Inc., 1975): 285–98. Reprinted with the permission of Jacob Neusner. Courtesy of Jacob Neusner.

Berkovits, Eliezer. "Authentic Judaism and Halakhah." *JUDAISM* 19 (1970): 66–76. Reprinted with the permission of *JUDAISM*. Courtesy of Yale University Sterling Memorial Library.

Fasman, Oscar Z. "Trends in the American Yeshiva Today." *Tradition* (1967): 48–64. Reprinted with the permission of the Rabbinical Assembly of America. Courtesy of Hebrew College, Jacob and Rose Grossman Library.

Greenberg, Blu. "Will There Be Orthodox Women Rabbis?" *JUDAISM* 33 (1984): 23–33. Reprinted with the permission of *JUDAISM*. Courtesy of Yale University Sterling Memorial Library.

Kaplan, Lawrence. "The Ambiguous Modern Orthodox Jew." *JUDAISM* 28 (1979): 439–48. Reprinted with the permission of *JUDAISM*. Courtesy of Yale University Sterling Memorial Library.

Neusner, Jacob. "The Death of Judaism and the Birth of Judaisms, Part II." In Jacob Neusner, ed., *Death and Birth of Judaism: The Impact of Christianity, Secularism, and the Holocaust on Jewish Faith* (New York: Basic Books, 1987): 73–178. Reprinted with the permission of Jacob Neusner. Courtesy of Jacob Neusner.

Rackman, Emanuel. "A Challenge to Orthodoxy." *JUDAISM* 18 (1969): 143–58. Reprinted with the permission of *JUDAISM*. Courtesy of Yale University Sterling Memorial Library.

Rackman, Emanuel. "American Orthodoxy—Retrospect and Prospect." *JUDAISM* 3 (1954): 302–09. Reprinted with the permission of *JUDAISM*. Courtesy of Yale University Sterling Memorial Library.

Rackman, Emanuel. "Truth and Wisdom: An Orthodox Approach." *JUDAISM* 10 (1961): 142–50. Reprinted with the permission of *JUDAISM*. Courtesy of Yale University Sterling Memorial Library.

Riskin, Shlomo. "Conservatism and the Orthodox Resurgence." *JUDAISM* 26 (1977): 331–33. Reprinted with the permission of *JUDAISM*. Courtesy of Yale University Sterling Memorial Library.

Schnall, David J. "Orthodoxy Resurgent." *JUDAISM* 30 (1981): 460–66. Reprinted with the permission of *JUDAISM*. Courtesy of Yale University Sterling Memorial Library.

Wurzburger, Walter S. "Denominationalism and the American Experience—An Orthodox View." *JUDAISM* 31 (1982): 299–302. Reprinted with the permission of *JUDAISM*. Courtesy of Yale University Sterling Memorial Library.

Wurzburger, Walter S. "The Conservative View of Halakhah is Non-Traditional." *JUDAISM* 38 (1989): 377–79. Reprinted with the permission of *JUDAISM*. Courtesy of Yale University Sterling Memorial Library.